The Soviet View of U.S. Strategic Doctrine

The Soviet View of U.S. Strategic Doctrine

Implications for Decision Making

Jonathan Samuel Lockwood

Foreword by Leon Gouré

Transaction Books
New Brunswick (U.S.A.) and London (U.K.)

The views and opinions expressed herein are those of the author, and do not necessarily reflect those of the Department of the Army or the Department of Defense.

Library of Congress Catalog Number: 82-14191
ISBN: 0-87855-467-X (cloth)
Printed in the United States of America

Library of Congress Cataloging in Publication Data

Lockwood, Jonathan Samuel, 1955
    The Soviet view of U.S. strategic doctrine.

    Bibliography: p.
    1. Strategy—History—20th century. 2. United States—Military policy. 3. Soviet Union—Military policy. I. Title: Soviet view of US strategic doctrine. III. Title: Soviet view of United States strategic doctrine.
U162.L63   1983   355'.0217'0973   82-14191
ISBN 0-87855-467-X

Contents

Acknowledgments

It would be beyond my abilities to list every individual who aided in one way or another with the publication of this study. Nevertheless, I must at least express my most heartfelt gratitude and appreciation to Dr. Leon Gouré and Dr. Stephen L. Speronis who have done so much to shape the direction of my career and aspirations. To the other members of my dissertation committee, Dr. Bernard Schechterman, Dr. June Dreyer, Ambassador Foy Kohler, and Dr. Michael Deane, I also express my deepest gratitude for their continuing interest.

I also thank one of my former supervisors in the Directorate of Combat Developments, LTC Richard Zeiler, for his invaluable assistance in procuring a quiet place for me to do the bulk of my research and rewriting, after duty hours and on weekends. Without it I might have never been able to block out the many distractions that are inherent in army life.

Last, but by no means least, are my family, friends, and brother officers in Officers Christian Fellowship, whose prayers and steadfast, loving support were of immeasurable help in the completion of this book. I could not have asked for more.

Foreword

It would seem self-evident that U.S. strategic and foreign policy planning and concepts should take account not only of Soviet military doctrine, but also of Soviet perceptions of U.S. strategic concepts and capabilities and of their implications for Soviet security and foreign policies. Yet this important subject has received only scant and at best, fragmentary attention on the part of Western scholars. All too often it is dealt with in the form of undocumented assertions which largely reflect their authors' personal viewpoints and biases. Many people in the West assume a priori that the logic of the nuclear era permits only one set of views on strategic power and nuclear war, essentially their own, which inevitably must be shared by the Soviet Union.

Quite aside from a lack of studies on Soviet perceptions of the United States, there has been a long-standing tendency on the part of high-ranking U.S. defense and policy planners to assume that the Soviet Union has taken, and continues to take, proclaimed U.S. strategic doctrines, declaratory deterrence pronouncements, and proposals for future U.S. strategic capabilities at face value. What has been largely ignored is the obvious fact that the Soviets assess these within the context of their own views on requirements for nuclear war for militarily and politically credible and useful strategic posture and deterrence capabilities, and in the light of past experience with U.S. defense concepts and perceptions of American objectives and intentions. Until recently, the same could also be said about the failure of U.S. strategic doctrines to take account of Soviet strategic and warfighting concepts, even though these had been extensively studied by Western scholars and intelligence analysts and found to be notably different from those entertained by the United States.

Jonathan Lockwood's study makes a significant and timely contribution to filling this major gap in our understanding of Soviet perceptions and deserves wide attention. His findings contain important implications for present and future U.S. defense programs and the development of U.S. strategic doctrine, the continuing search for an effective and credible deterrent, as well as for arms control negotiations. A great virtue of the study lies in its scope, which covers Soviet perceptions of the evolution of U.S. strategic doctrine from massive retaliation in the 1950s to the present countervailing strategy. This brings into sharper focus the elements of continuity and change in Soviet perceptions of the evolution of U.S. strategic doctrine.

Lockwood's major finding that the Soviets tend to perceive and assess U.S. strategic doctrine largely in terms of a "mirror image" of their own will undoubtedly surprise those who expected U.S. declarations to be taken by the Soviets at face value and worry those who believe it is essential for the United States to reassure the Soviets about U.S. intentions. The latter persist in seeing in the mutual assured destruction (MAD) concept and mutual vulnerability a basis for strategic stability and effective mutual deterrence as well for arms control negotiations. They not only dismiss the significance of different Soviet views on strategic questions, warfighting, and military requirements, but focus their attention primarily on opposing any significant changes in U.S. doctrine.

Lockwood's conclusion regarding the Soviet mirror image perception of U.S. strategic doctrine is an important finding with major implications for U.S. defense policies. This finding should come as no surprise, given Soviet views on the inevitability of the East/West struggle and their belief that their strategic doctrine and views on nuclear warfighting and weapons programs are entirely rational and militarily as well as politically best suited for effectively supporting Soviet security and foreign policy objectives. U.S. failures to live up to the mirror image are seen by the Soviets as temporary aberrations and potentially serious military and political vulnerabilities. Not surprisingly, the Soviets are fond of quoting Lenin to the effect that one must prepare for war seriously and that the greater the Soviet foreign policy successes, the greater also the need for such preparations. It is within the framework of these Soviet perceptions and views that the United States must seek to maintain credible and effective strategic deterrence. Lockwood provides a number of recommendations dealing with this vital problem.

The identification of Soviet perceptions and assessments of U.S. strategic doctrines and programs as distinct from Soviet propaganda, deterrence pronouncements, and attempts to reinforce and exploit what Moscow sees as desirable Western attitudes and policy proposals is fraught with considerable difficulties. These are compounded by the fact that Soviet public discussions of these questions avoid any specific comparison of U.S./Soviet strategic capabilities and Soviet arms programs. Lockwood explains how this distinction can be made and provides descriptions and analysis of both these elements in Soviet writings and pronouncements as well as of Soviet uses of declaratory deterrence in connection with changes in U.S. strategic doctrine and arms programs. The Soviets see themselves facing an even greater problem in assessing U.S. strategic doctrine, given the relative frequency of announced changes in it and the all too frequent inconsistencies between them and actual U.S. strategic capabilities. There is evidence that in light of past experience, the Soviets have learned to view announced changes in U.S. strategic doctrine with considerable skepticism, even though they expect it to increasingly mirror Soviet doctrine.

Lockwood's findings underscore that in the continuing U.S. search for credible and effective deterrence, what matters is what Soviet political and military leaders believe and how they perceive U.S. doctrines and capabilities. His study makes it clear that the answer does not lie in U.S. unilateral restraint in defense programs, nuclear freezes under conditions of significant asymmetry in U.S./Soviet strategic capabilities, or adherence to a purely retaliatory MAD doctrine. The author also makes it clear that given Soviet emphasis on war survival as an essential objective of a rational Soviet doctrine, strategy, and defense posture, the continuing self-imposed vulnerability of the United States dangerously undermines the credibility of U.S. strategic doctrines and deterrence in Soviet perceptions.

Leon Gouré

Center for Soviet Studies
Science Applications, Inc.

Introduction

Now that national defense has become one of the most intensely debated issues, studies have proliferated that address the problem from different angles. Many authors have engaged in straight numerical comparisons of U.S. and Soviet strength across the entire spectrum of nuclear and conventional capabilities. Others have examined the asymmetries in the strategic thinking of the two sides and their consequences for the respective defense programs over the period since the accession to power of the Brezhnev regime in 1964.

There has been virtually no effort to analyze the *Soviet* perspective regarding the development of U.S. strategic doctrine over the period since former secretary of state John Foster Dulles first promulgated the doctrine of "massive retaliation" in 1954.[1] The need for this kind of study had been indicated by Fritz W. Ermarth in the fall 1978 issue of *International Security*, in which he stated:

> The next five to ten years of the U.S.-Soviet strategic relationship could well be characterized by mounting U.S. anxieties about the adequacy of our deterrent forces and our strategic doctrine. There seems to be little real prospect that the SALT process, as we have been conducting it, will substantially alleviate these anxieties. Even if a more promising state of affairs emerges, however, it is hard to see us managing it with calm and confidence unless we develop a more thorough appreciation of the differences between U.S. and Soviet strategic thinking. Things have progressed beyond the point where it is useful to have the three familiar schools of thought on Soviet doctrine arguing past each other; one saying, "Whatever they say, they think as we do;" the second insisting, "Whatever they say, it does not matter;" and the third contending, "They think what they say, and are therefore out for superiority over us."[2]

A comprehensive understanding of how the Soviets perceive our strategic doctrine and the ways in which it has influenced their own development programs and employment of military power in support of their own foreign policy goals is of vital importance. Not only can it give an indication of the probable future direction of their defense programs, but a careful analysis can provide clues about what kind of strategic doctrine might best serve to deter Soviet-sponsored aggression against our vital national interests. Ermarth set forth a number of questions he believed any study of comparative strategic doctrine ought to address. Although this book proposes to deal strictly with the Soviet perception of U.S. strategic doctrine, some of the questions he raises (in modified form) provide a useful guideline:[3]

1. What are the prevailing concepts, beliefs, and assertions that appear to constitute the Soviet view of U.S. strategic doctrine in a particular period?
2. What are the hedges and qualifications introduced in Soviet pronouncements that modify the main theses of their stated thinking?
3. What propagandistic purposes, if any, are likely to motivate certain Soviet pronouncements on U.S. doctrine? Do the Soviets recognize distinctions between what ought to be true of U.S. doctrine and what actually is?
4. What perceptions have the Soviets held regarding the development of U.S. doctrine, and what effect, if any, have these perceptions had on Soviet doctrine and associated defense programs? What implications do these views have for Strategic Arms Limitations Talks (SALT)?
5. How does the Soviet perception of U.S. strategic doctrine correlate with the use of Soviet military power in support of foreign policy objectives?

Erroneous assumptions have been made before by U.S. analysts about what the Soviet view is. The first school of thought described by Ermarth could best be called the "mirror-imaging" school, which assumes that the Soviet strategic perspective is largely similar to that of the U.S. and that any observed differences or discrepancies are merely the result of a lack of intellectual "sophistication" or failure to fully understand the logic of the U.S. position. Former defense secretary Robert McNamara and former arms-control negotiator Paul Warnke are the most prominent members of this school. Yet recent studies have proven conclusively that there are indeed substantial differences in U.S. and Soviet strategic thinking and that these differences are based on a set of rational assumptions rather than mere backwardness or lack of understanding.[4]

The second school of thought contends that the sources of Soviet strategic rationale are not to be found in their writings at all. This school can best be characterized as the "historical continuity" argument. In the view of these particular analysts, Soviet strategic thinking and behavior can be explained as the natural continuation of tsarist policies. Having been invaded countless times in their history, the Russian people, and particularly the leadership, have developed a fear and even paranoia regarding the possibility of invasion from without. It is this fear of invasion that compels the current Soviet leadership to maintain large standing military forces of all types, just as the tsarist rulers felt compelled to do so. Foreign ambitions are deemed to be similar to tsarist ambitions, and the role of communist ideology is downplayed, if not disregarded altogether.

What the members of this school fail to consider is the fact that not all current national behavior can always be explained in terms of historical behavior.

There are instances in which a nation's foreign policy outlook has been ir-revocably changed by a watershed event in its history—an occurrence of such magnitude that a radical change in international outlook took place out of either necessity or a change in national values. A prime example of the former can be found in our own history. Prior to the outbreak of the Second World War, the U.S. international outlook was primarily isolationist in character. The United States had supposedly fought the "war to end all wars" back in 1917-18; the source of evil had been cleansed from the world, and America could go back to "business as usual." But the experience of the Second World War and its immediate aftermath convinced U.S. leadership that a policy of isolationism could no longer be afforded and that a change in out-look was necessary. Thus the "internationalist" school came to the forefront to dominate American foreign policy behavior.

The Russian Revolution of 1917 is an example, on the other hand, of how a nation's foreign policy outlook can be irrevocably altered as a result of a change in national values or, if you will, ideology. When the Soviet leader-ship came to power in 1917, it is true, they did have a significant threat of out-side invasion to contend with. But they brought with them something the tsars never possessed—an ideological orientation that was universal in scope and that gave the messianic strain in the Russian national character a world vision to pursue. The scope of tsarist ambitions was largely defined by the desire to unite the Slavic peoples under Russian rule (Pan-Slavism) and to acquire warm-water ports for her navy and commercial shipping; the scope of Soviet ambition, with Marxism-Leninism as the theoretical framework of perception, became unlimited. To attempt to explain the current strategic outlook of the Soviet leadership in terms of tsarist tradition, therefore, without reckoning with the historical discontinuity resulting from the Russian Revolution, is as illogical as attempting to explain the current foreign policy outlook of the United States in terms of her historical situation in 1793.

This book, then, bases its methodology on the assumption of the third school of thought described by Ermarth, which is that the Soviets mean sub-stantially what they say. The reasoning behind this position has been most co-gently stated in the monograph *Soviet Strategy for the Seventies: From Cold War to Peaceful Coexistence*:

> The members of the ruling hierarchy provide through their public utterances a substantially accurate picture of what they are up to and why, at least in a strategic sense. This is due to the requirement for uniformity that is so vital to the Soviet political system. Not only must those at the top speak with a single voice, but the entire hierarchy must echo that voice. Words are a critical factor in holding the system together. . . . The only way in which the regime can carry forward a program or effect a change in direction without creating confusion and uncertainty is to talk about it.[5]

When one is attempting to analyze Soviet writings from any source, however, it is necessary to have a means for distinguishing what the "real" Soviet perception of U.S. strategic doctrine is from propagandistic pronouncements intended to mislead unwary Western analysts into a false perception of Soviet strategic thinking. This book contends that the real Soviet view of U.S. strategic doctrine is influenced by two main factors:

1. Soviet analysts project their own strategic mindset onto U.S. strategic planners and interpret the development of U.S. strategic doctrine within the context of that mindset (i.e., Soviet analysts also fall into the error of the "mirror-imaging" fallacy.
2. Ideological interpretation of U.S. intentions as viewed through the ideological prism of Marxism-Leninism predetermines the logical course of U.S. strategic doctrine as perceived by the Soviets to a great extent.

Soviet statements that were intended for propagandistic reasons can be identified largely by their intended purpose; to discredit or otherwise reduce the credibility of U.S. strategic doctrine in terms of its deterrent value against Soviet freedom of action to employ her military power in support of her foreign policy goals. This author has termed such a Soviet practice "declaratory deterrence." By publicly denying the validity of U.S. doctrinal assumptions, the Soviets are in effect saying to the United States, "We are not going to 'play by your rules'; since we will not react in the manner in which your doctrine assumes we will react, it is therefore invalid." A variation on this theme is that the uncertainties involved in the application of any given U.S. doctrine render it "adventuristic" and therefore unreliable.

Discussion of the Soviet perceptions of NATO (North Atlantic Treaty Organization) doctrine has largely been omitted from this book, mainly because NATO doctrine falls under the category of theatre doctrine rather than strategic doctrine. Reference has been made to NATO doctrine, however, in instances where it overlaps with U.S. strategic doctrine. In any event, the implications of the Soviet view of U.S. doctrine bear great significance for NATO. This is because the Soviets perceive NATO doctrine as an extension of the aims and goals of U.S. doctrine, albeit modified to suit the needs of the individual members of the NATO alliance.[6] It is therefore more important to analyze the Soviet view of U.S. strategic doctrine and to take into account the Soviet perspective on U.S. doctrine as interpreted within the ideological framework of Marxism-Leninism.

As a further check to verify the validity of the "real" Soviet view of U.S. strategic doctrine as much as possible, Soviet foreign policy behavior during each period of U.S. doctrinal development was compared with their analyses of U.S. doctrine. This comparison aided in determining whether stated Soviet perceptions coincided with actual behavior, and to what degree U.S. doctrine had any effect on Soviet doctrine and force development. References to the actual strategic balance between the United States and the Soviet Union at a given period of time served as a further check.

Sources used in this book consisted mainly of articles from open Soviet publications. These were periodical publications for the most part, supplemented by representative books, pamphlets, and newspaper articles from each period. Translations of some of these sources into English were done either by the Soviets themselves or by translation services such as the Foreign Broadcast Information Service (FBIS), the Joint Publications Research Service (JPRS), and RAND Corporation, and the U.S. Air Force. Soviet periodicals such as *Kommunist Vooruzhennykh Sil* (*Communist of the Armed Forces*), *Mirovaia Ekonomika i Mezhdunarodnaye Otnosheniia* (*World Economy and International Relations*), *Voenno-Istoricheskii Zhurnal* (*Military-Historical Journal*), and *Voennyi Vestnik* (*Military Herald*), for which complete translations were not available, have been translated by this author. Other periodical sources used were *New Times, International Affairs* (Moscow), *SShA: Ekonomika, Politika, Ideologia* (*USA: Economics, Politics, Ideology*), and *Soviet Military Review*. In addition, there are translations from the formerly classified and highly authoritative Soviet general staff publication *Voennaia Mysl'* (*Military Thought*), the availability of which was limited to scattered issues from 1959 to 1973. (There were, however, quotations of earlier issues of *Voennaia Mysl'* cited in books by H.S. Dinerstein and R. Garthoff.) The issues used were valuable as another comparative check against open Soviet source articles, some of which were used for purposes of declaratory deterrence.

These periodicals were selected with the aim of attaining a representative sampling of the major Soviet sources of analysis of U.S. strategic doctrine. Admittedly, not all of the possible Soviet sources in book or periodical form were employed, since a few articles on U.S. strategic doctrine were found in periodicals such as *Kommunist* or *Voennie Znania* (*Military Knowledge*). However, since Soviet pronouncements on U.S. strategic doctrine for any given period were highly repetitive, using additional Soviet sources would have been superfluous and not important to the overall conclusions of the book.

These sources have been used by analysts such as Garthoff, Dinerstein, T. Wolfe, L. Gouré, R. Kolkowicz, W. Kintner, and H. Scott in assessing Soviet strategic doctrine. Some of these analysts have done research similar in nature to this book, although they all have covered a much shorter period of time. Most of the analyses were done by the RAND Corporation in the late 1950s and early 1960s, with Dinerstein, Gouré, Wolfe, and Kolkowicz providing the bulk of such studies. Later efforts by other authors include Kintner and Scott, *The Nuclear Revolution in Soviet Military Affairs*; S. Gibert, *Soviet Images of America*; L. Frank, *Soviet Nuclear Planning: A Point of View on SALT*; and Gouré, F. Kohler, and M. Harvey, *The Role of Nuclear Forces in Current Soviet Strategy*.[7]

This book is a significant departure from these other works in that it systematically evaluates Soviet pronouncements from 1954 to 1981 concerning U.S. strategic doctrine in an effort to construct the Soviet mindset and the manner in which it has evolved over the years. Although the organization of the topics in this book tends to follow a chronological order, the analysis of the statements themselves does not, since doing so would lead to tedious repetition. Also, Soviet statements regarding a particular U.S. doctrine were not merely taken from the period of the doctrine itself. For example, Soviet analyses of the "massive retaliation" doctrine were taken from articles after the period 1954-1960 as well as during it. The reason is that Soviet analysts have proved to be far more candid and less inclined to be propagandistic about a particular U.S. doctrine once it is no longer in force.

However, there are certain problems involved in using this technique, the main one being the problem of Soviet declaratory deterrence practices. In an effort to make their arguments more credible to Western readers, Soviet propagandists made frequent use of arguments found in the Western press against a particular U.S. doctrinal position. The proof of this is that these arguments were originally devised by Americans for other Americans. Prime examples of such periodicals are *New Times, International Affairs,* and *Soviet Military Review*. To a somewhat lesser extent, the same can be said of other Soviet periodicals, with the exception of *Voennaia Mysl'*. This does not mean that true Soviet perceptions cannot be obtained from these periodicals, but it does mean that not all of their pronouncements can be taken uncritically. Even so, most of these other periodicals can be regarded as authoritative on the basis of their publication by various organs of the Soviet government. For example, *Kommunist Vooruzhennykh Sil* (a military theory journal published by the Main Political Administration) can certainly be regarded as a more authoritative journal as a general rule than *New Times* (the English-language translation of the Soviet Trade Union weekly *Novoe Vremia*).

The conclusions supported by the research in this book consist of three major findings:

1. *Soviet analysts view U.S. strategic doctrine largely within the framework of their own strategic doctrine*. In other words, there has been a great deal of "mirror-imaging" done by Soviet analysts in their interpretation of U.S. strategic doctrines over the years. However, since the Soviets are projecting their concepts of nuclear warfighting onto U.S. strategic doctrine, the consequences of this are far different than has been the case when U.S. planners assumed a similar Soviet adherence to the concept of "mutual assured destruction" (MAD).

2. *Soviet analysts recognized that there was a steady progression by the United States away from nuclear warfighting concepts towards a pure deterrence doctrine and that there was a greater likelihood of limited wars being waged without escalation to strategic nuclear war.* From the Soviet perspective, this finding constituted an ideological contradiction. It was not possible, given Marxist-Leninist views regarding the "inherently aggressive" nature of imperialism as chiefly embodied by the United States, for the United States to adopt anything other than a nuclear warfighting doctrine similar to that espoused by the Soviets themselves. The Soviets saw their own strategic doctrine as "scientific" and, indeed, the only truly rational doctrine for a state to adopt in the nuclear age. And although the U.S. was seen as inherently aggressive, it was also perceived as rational (more or less). Since the United States was moving further and further away from such a doctrine towards more "limited" uses of military power, the Soviets concluded that there must have been other factors responsible for such a change that were not under U.S. control.

3. *The evolution of U.S. strategic doctrine away from a nuclear warfighting posture has been perceived by the Soviets as the natural result of a forced change in response to the continuous growth of Soviet military power, particularly Soviet strategic power.* Although Soviet analysts listed other secondary factors during various periods of U.S. strategic doctrine, this has been the reason stated most often in Soviet sources for such a momentous shift in orientation. Not only is this an entirely rational conclusion for the Soviets to have reached, but it is also a conveniently self-serving one as well, since it provides a self-sustaining motivation for the Soviet strategic buildup without any clearly definable upper limit.[8]

The remainder of this book is divided into five main parts. Part 1 is a strategic overview of U.S. and Soviet doctrinal development. It is designed to give the uninitiated reader enough familiarity with the strategic mindsets of U.S. and Soviet planners to make subsequent discussions of the Soviet perspectives on U.S. doctrinal concepts more lucid. Chapter 1 traces the development of U.S. doctrine, and chapter 2 provides a brief history of Soviet doctrinal evolution.

Parts 2 through 4 comprise the bulk of the analysis of the Soviet view of U.S. strategic doctrine; thus, the chapters all follow the same basic format. They are divided into discussions of the "propaganda line" put forth in Soviet writings, followed by discussion of the actual Soviet viewpoint. Both sections enumerate the major Soviet themes of either their declaratory deterrence statements or their actual views at the beginning of each section and then give each theme detailed documentation and analysis. Part 2 covers the massive retaliation period of U.S. strategic doctrine (1954-1960) and is made up of two chapters. Chapter 3 examines the Soviet perception of the massive retaliation concept itself, whereas chapter 4 looks at the Soviet view of the origins and development of the "limited war" concept. Part 3 also is made up of two chapters and deals with the "flexible response" period of U.S. doctrine (1961-1968). Chapter 5 analyzes the Soviet view of flexible response, and chapter 6 is devoted to the Soviet reaction to the U.S. strategic concepts of the period, such as "counterforce," "damage limitation," "assured destruction," and "escalation." Part 4 comprises three chapters, which take up the period of U.S. doctrine known as "realistic deterrence" (1969-1982). Although this is the period during which the SALT I and II negotiations were taking place, the Soviet view of SALT is not specifically covered in this book. The reasons for this are twofold. First, Soviet analysts tended to treat U.S. strategic doctrine and the SALT negotiations in a compartmentalized fashion, as if one had no effect upon the other. The Soviets rarely mentioned the two subjects in conjunction with one another, and even then only under highly unusual circumstances. Second, and more important, the Soviet perception of U.S. strategic doctrine and its development does not provide any motivation for the Soviets to treat arms-control negotiations as other than a propaganda exercise or a means for limiting any U.S. efforts at increased strategic buildup. The three chapters in part 4 highlight this point quite clearly, in addition to providing clues to what kind of strategic doctrine might best deter the Soviets. Chapter 7 analyzes the Soviet appraisal of the Nixon Doctrine, which was simply another name given to the realistic deterrence strategy. Chapter 8 concerns itself specifically with the Soviet reaction to the proposed Schlesinger doctrine featuring a strategy of "limited nuclear options" (LNO). Chapter 9 brings us up to the present with the Soviet assessment of Presidential Directive 59 (PD59) regarding the change in U.S. nuclear targeting strategy.

The final part comprises only a single chapter and is devoted to a summary and conclusion of the major themes. Chapter 10 dwells upon the implications of the evolving Soviet view for future U.S. strategic policy decision making and examines alternatives for the future.

Notes

1. An analysis of the Soviet perspective of the United States over a range of issues and areas, including a section on U.S. doctrine, can be found in Stephen Gibert's *Soviet Images of America* (New York: Crane, Russak, 1978). Its main problem as an analysis of the Soviet viewpoint concerning U.S. strategic doctrine is its contemporary perspective; the analysis does not go back farther than the period of realistic deterrence beginning in 1969. Another significant problem is its lack of depth and comprehensiveness; the author relies on government translations from FBIS and JPRS, and does not bother to go into other original Soviet sources to translate relevant articles that would strengthen his case.

2. F.W. Ermarth, "Contrasts in American and Soviet Strategic Thought," *International Security*, Vol. 3, Fall 1978, p. 140.

3. Ibid., pp. 140–41. The questions cited from the article have been slightly modified to suit the subject.

4. For a detailed analysis see Leon Gouré, *War Survival in Soviet Strategy* (Coral Gables, Fla.: Center for Advanced International Studies, 1976). See also Daniel Graham, *Shall America Be Defended? SALT II and Beyond* (New Rochelle, N.Y.: Arlington House, 1979).

5. F.D. Kohler et al., *Soviet Strategy for the Seventies: From Cold War to Peaceful Coexistence* (Coral Gables, Fla.: Center for Advanced International Studies, 1973), p. 5.

6. V.D. Sokolovskii, *Soviet Military Strategy*, trans. and annotated H.S. Dinerstein, L. Gouré, and T. Wolfe (Santa Monica, Calif.: The RAND Corporation, R-416-PR, April 1963), p. 205. Essentially the same statement is made in the 2nd and 3rd editions of Sokolovskii's work, the latter edition having been translated and analyzed by Harriet Fast Scott. See V.D. Sokolovskii, *Soviet Military Strategy*, trans. and ed. H.F. Scott (New York: Crane, Russak, 1975).

7. The works of these authors dealt with the Soviet perspective of U.S. strategic doctrine from a contemporary point of view rather than an evolutionary one. The research done from an evolutionary perspective addressed the evolution of Soviet strategic thought itself. A recent work that provides an overview of Soviet strategic thought is W. Scott and H.F. Scott, *The Armed Forces of the USSR* (Boulder, Colo.: Westview, 1979).

8. Corresponding viewpoints can be found in Kohler et al., *Soviet Strategy*; Gibert, *Soviet Images*; and Scott and Scott, *Armed Forces*.

Part I

DOCTRINAL OVERVIEW

1.
The Development of U.S. Strategic Doctrine

The term "massive retaliation" first came into vogue as a result of a speech made by then secretary of state John Foster Dulles on January 12, 1954, in which he stated that "local defenses must be reinforced by the further deterrent of massive retaliatory power." This marked the first official enunciation of a U.S. strategic doctrine by an American administration. Dulles's statement, harmless enough by itself, gained greater importance from other statements within the context of his speech, which implied that primary reliance would be placed on strategic power for deterring local aggression.[1]

Actually, the idea of massive retaliation as a strategic doctrine did not originate with the 1954 statement of Dulles. Prior to his speech, the Eisenhower administration had in 1953 inaugurated the so-called New Look, which was a strategic program based largely on economic considerations. Not wishing to spend enormous sums of money for defense for fear of damaging the national economy in the long run, the Eisenhower administration decided that severe budget constraints should be placed on the military in general. In addition, the main effort was to be made in the development of strategic air power in hopes of maximizing deterrence at minimum cost.[2]

The strategic rationale behind massive retaliation was also fairly straightforward. Its deterrent value rested "upon a great capacity to retaliate, instantly, by means and at places of our own choosing."[3] This stressed the importance of seizing and retaining the strategic initiative, a distinctively military consideration. Deterrence would be achieved by forcing the Soviet Union to consider the possibility that any local aggression they initiated might provoke a nuclear response by U.S. strategic air power on cities in the Soviet heartland.

The major difficulties of the massive retaliation doctrine as a credible strategic doctrine were twofold. The first lay in the reasoning behind the doctrine itself. A doctrine of massive retaliation served to deter a direct attack against the United States itself, and in retrospect apparently served to deter a

Soviet invasion of Western Europe. However, for conflicts short of such magnitude, it was clear that the Soviets were not completely convinced of the credibility of the American threat. The outstanding example of this was the Korean War. Well before the formal declaration of massive retaliation, the Korean conflict was a precedent that rejected the tenets of that doctrine. Not only had the United States not seized the strategic initiative in that conflict, it was the United States that sought to keep the conflict "limited" by deliberately not attempting to carry the war beyond the bounds of the Korean peninsula to the Soviet Union, or even to the People's Republic of China (PRC). Given such a precedent, the declaration of massive retaliation in 1954 made little sense other than as a repudiation of the intent to engage again in Korean-style intervention in response to local aggression. Nevertheless, the threat was not considered credible enough by the Soviets to have prevented them from intervening in Hungary in 1956 or from indulging in "saber-rattling" exercises in the Suez and Berlin crises.[4]

It must also be noted that the credibility of massive retaliation depended heavily on the belief that the United States would remain relatively invulnerable to retaliatory strikes by the Soviet Union. While the United States possessed an atomic monopoly from 1945 to 1949, this belief was well founded. However, once the Soviet Union had begun to develop and stockpile atomic and hydrogen bombs, it possessed the makings of a strategic deterrent, no matter how few and unreliable the early means of delivery might be. Even though Soviet bombers of the mid-to-late 1950s could only have reached the continental United States on one-way missions, this by itself nullified the basic assumption of massive retaliation—the assumption that the United States could launch a major nuclear attack on the Soviet Union and emerge totally unscathed.[5] Once this was realized in the United States, there was a gradual move toward the advocacy of the "tactical" use of lower-yield nuclear weapons as a more "believable" response to local aggression.[6]

The other major problem with the massive retaliation strategy was the fact that the United States did not actually have the capacity to inflict a decisive degree of absolute damage on the Soviet Union. Until the acquisition of the B-52 bomber in 1955, the workhorse of U.S. strategic air power was the B-29, followed by the B-36 and B-47 medium-range bombers, all of which had to be based overseas in Great Britain and Western Europe in order to be within range of the Soviet heartland. The preponderance of U.S. strategic air power in relative terms would not have been enough by itself to prevent the Red Army from occupying Western Europe, thus depriving the United States of most of its bases.[7] And there is little doubt that the Soviet Union would have been able to occupy Western Europe if war occurred, since NATO forces were insufficient in number to be much more than a "trip-wire" to verify the fact of invasion.

The predominant attitude that permeated the doctrine of massive retaliation was one that saw the atomic weapon as an *absolute* weapon, capable of deciding the outcome of a war by itself. As will be seen in a subsequent chapter, the Soviets did not agree with this view, asserting instead that the nuclear weapon was merely a *decisive* weapon within the context of a nuclear war-fighting doctrine. In order for U.S. strategic doctrine to have any credibility, it was necessary to have a means for dealing with forms of Soviet-sponsored aggression that could not be adequately deterred by strategic air power alone. It was thus that the doctrine of limited war evolved.

The U.S. Rationale for Limited War

In the October 1957 issue of *Foreign Affairs*, then secretary of state Dulles announced a modification in the strategic doctrine of the United States. Instead of a doctrine of pure massive retaliation, the new concept was later to be known as "graduated deterrence." [8] Subsumed under this concept was the use of limited war as an instrument of the policy of "containment." [9] Dulles characterized the need for greater flexibility in U.S. doctrine in his article:

> However, the United States has not been content to rely upon a peace which could be preserved only by a capacity to destroy vast segments of the human race. Such a concept is acceptable only as a last alternative . . . .
>
> In the future it may thus be feasible to place less reliance upon deterrence of vast retaliatory power. It may be possible to defend countries by nuclear weapons so mobile, or so placed, as to make military invasion with conventional forces a hazardous attempt. Thus . . . the nations which are around the Sino-Soviet perimeter can possess an effective defense against full-scale conventional attack and thus confront any aggressor with the choice between failing or himself initiating nuclear war against the defending country. . . .[10]

There were several important considerations that justified the development of a doctrine of limited war. Henry Kissinger, in his book *Nuclear Weapons and Foreign Policy*, published in 1958, listed the following three reasons:

1. Limited war represents the only means for preventing the Soviet bloc, at an acceptable cost, from overrunning the peripheral areas of Eurasia.
2. A wide range of military capabilities may spell the difference between defeat and victory in an all-out war.
3. Intermediate applications of U.S. power offer the best chance to bring about strategic changes favorable to the United States.[11]

The employment of limited wars, as explained by Kissinger, provided a means for the United States to enforce its policy of containment at an acceptable cost. Although the massive retaliation doctrine had done an acceptable job of deterring a Soviet attack on the United States or Western Europe, it was becoming less and less effective against lesser forms of aggression because of the growing Soviet capability to retaliate against the United States.[12] Under the massive retaliation doctrine, the United States could respond to limited acts of aggression only with either inaction or all-out war.[13] Massive retaliation relied primarily on the credibility of the U.S. threat to strike the Soviet homeland in order to reduce the chance of local aggression ever occurring, which would permit the United States to spend minimal amounts of her resources on the strengthening of conventional forces.[14] Once the Soviets had developed an intercontinental ballistic missile (ICBM) capability, this threat was less believable because of increased U.S. vulnerability to retaliation. An alternative to either waging all-out war or simply doing nothing was therefore needed in order to strengthen U.S. deterrent power.

A limited war strategy required a wider range of military capabilities than under the massive retaliation doctrine, capabilities that Kissinger argued could provide victory even in the event of an all-out war. Since it was possible that a nuclear exchange might result in the exhaustion of the strategic stockpiles of both sides, a premium would than be placed on other elements of military power in order to decide the victor.[15] A capacity to wage limited war would therefore be valuable in the event of escalation to general war as well as in fighting limited wars. This reasoning would subsequently provide the basis for the even broader requirements of the later doctrine of flexible response.

Limited war was not supposed to replace the threat of massive retaliation. Instead, the idea was to shift the risk of initiating an all-out war to the Soviet Union by using the U.S. capability for massive retaliation as a "shield" against Soviet initiation of nuclear war. This would enable the U.S. to fight local actions on its own terms, inflicting local reverses against attempted Soviet gains.[16]

Such a strategy was not without its weaknesses, however; although it reduced the chances of escalation to general nuclear war, it increased the likelihood of local aggression. This was because the Soviets, since they did not have to fear the threat of massive retaliation if they initiated a local war, would therefore be less discouraged from engaging in less risky forms of conflict. On the other hand, though the massive retaliation strategy theoretically minimized the chance that a local act of aggression would ever occur (assuming, of course, that the Soviets believed the threat to be completely credible), it also maximized the probability of escalation to general nuclear war. Given the fact that the massive retaliation strategy was becoming less effective, the necessity of engaging in local conflicts in order to enforce containment was a more palatable choice.[17]

Limited war, then, involved the imposition of oneself of limited means in order to attain correspondingly limited goals. This strategy became readily accepted in the United States, mainly because the thought of actually having to employ nuclear weapons in an all-out conflict had become an unthinkable prospect, according to analysts such as Bernard Brodie.[18] The concept of limited war was the first step taken by the United States in the direction of more limited uses of military power in order to support a foreign policy of containment. It would remain the centerpiece of the subsequently declared doctrine of flexible response during the Kennedy administration.

The U.S. Doctrine of Flexible Response

The principles of flexible response were formally declared by Defense Secretary Robert S. McNamara in a speech before the American Bar Association on February 17, 1962.[19] The real foundation of flexible response, however, can be said to have been laid by General Maxwell D. Taylor in the January 1961 issue of *Foreign Affairs*. Addressing the problem of an outmoded strategic doctrine because of an unfavorably altered military balance, Taylor said:

> What are the principles which need to be asserted and accepted as the platform for a new military balance? The most obvious one, perhaps, is that world conditions have changed drastically since the adoption of the New Look in 1953 and its supporting strategy of massive retaliation, and that a new program is needed which will take the changes into account. Such a program needs to be based on a flexible military strategy designed to deter war, large or small, and to assist the West in winning the cold war.[20]

In his book *The Uncertain Trumpet*, Taylor postulated a U.S. need to have the capability ''to react across the entire spectrum of possible challenge.'' The ostensible reasoning behind Taylor's assertion was that ''it is just as necessary to deter or win quickly a limited war as to deter general war. Otherwise, the limited war which we cannot win quickly may result in our piecemeal attrition or involvement in an expanding conflict.''[21] In reality, Taylor's motivation was also a more self-serving effort on behalf of the heretofore neglected U.S. Army. By formulating a strategic doctrine that basically said that ''it is better to have more of everything,'' he could cause more attention to be given to building up conventional forces as well, and the U.S. Army would be the chief beneficiary. Indeed, in order to support the requirements of ''flexible response,'' the quantity of both general purpose as well as strategic nuclear forces would have to be increased considerably.[22] It was McNamara who further defined the need for ''balanced forces'':

> As we develop a balanced, modern non-nuclear force, ready to move rapidly against aggression in any part of the world, we continue to inhibit the opportunities for the successful conduct of Khrushchev's ''local wars'' [i.e., ''wars of

national liberation"]. It is tempting to conclude that our conventional forces will leave us free to compete with communism in the peaceful sphere of economic and social development, where we can compete most effectively.[23]

McNamara then described the threat from Communist "insurgency" movements in Third World countries and outlined the proposed strategy of "counterinsurgency."[24] It is obvious that the doctrine of flexible response, in trying to respond to the complete spectrum of conceivable threats, required far larger military expenditures across the board than the massive retaliation strategy under the Eisenhower administration.

At the same time that flexible response was officially adopted as doctrine, however, there was a movement sponsored by the newly ascendant "systems analysis" school in the Defense Department. These analysts were looking for a more "organized" approach to planning military force level requirements, particularly for strategic forces. Their goal was to devise a theory that would provide a quantitative answer to the question "How much is enough?" This produced a clash between the flexible response doctrine, which tended to push the requirements for strategic forces upwards, and the cost-effectiveness calculations of the systems analysts, which pushed such requirements downwards.[25]

However, the chief test of flexible response was to be the war in Indochina, which initially proved frustrating for the advocates of flexible response and ultimately proved a serious setback. The major change in U.S. strategic doctrine after this period, though still emphasizing the desirability of a wide range of options as a response and deterrent to Soviet aggression, would deemphasize the requirement for the participation of U.S. combat forces. Instead, it would be the nations under attack that would bear the main burden of providing the manpower.[26]

The McNamara Concepts

During the period of flexible response, McNamara devised several strategic nuclear concepts that were to influence U.S. strategic doctrine long after the demise of the flexible response doctrine itself. These concepts—called counterforce, damage limitation, and assured destruction—therefore deserve special attention. The first concept was enunciated by McNamara in an address at Ann Arbor, Michigan, on June 16, 1962.[27] The concepts of damage limitation and assured destruction were explained by McNamara in statements before the Committee on Armed Services and the Subcommittee on Department of Defense of the Committee on Appropriations, U.S. Senate, 89th Congress, 1st Session, February 24, 1962.[28]

Another concept gained prominence during this period, although it was not officially a part of U.S. strategic doctrine. This was the concept of escalation, an idea given its theoretical birth by Herman Kahn in his book *On Escalation*.[29] The principal feature of this work was the 44-step "escalation ladder," which ran the gamut of levels of conflict from "precrisis manuevering" to the ultimate paroxysm of violence, called "spasm war." Although this concept was quite influential, it had been intended only as a descriptive model rather than a prescriptive guideline for policy. It is mentioned here because the Soviets mistakenly perceived it as an actual tenet of U.S. strategic doctrine. The nature and consequences of this error will be discussed in a later chapter.

In outlining the counterforce strategy, McNamara was assuming that the United States, along with NATO, had "overall nuclear strength adequate to any challenge confronting it," and that "this strength not only minimizes the likelihood of major nuclear war but makes possible a strategy designed to preserve the fabric of our societies if war should occur."[30] McNamara stated the essence of the counterforce strategy in the following passage:

> The United States has come to the conclusion that, to the extent feasible, basic military strategy in a possible general nuclear war should be approached in much the same way that more conventional military operations have been regarded in the past. This is to say, principal military objectives, in the event of a nuclear war stemming from a major attack on the alliance, should be the destruction of the enemy's military forces, not of his civilian population.[31]

There were two important implications of the counterforce strategy as outlined by McNamara above. The more significant was the implication that the United States would initiate a "preemptive strike" on Soviet nuclear forces in response to a "major attack on the alliance" and not merely as a response to a surprise attack on the United States. Any references to a first strike, however, were subsequently downplayed in favor of a retaliatory posture. Nevertheless, given this kind of statement, it is not surprising that Soviet analysts would see their own idea of the "preemptive blow" in the counterforce strategy, since counterforce lent itself easily to the idea of a first strike (after all, a counterforce attack would be more effective before the enemy launched his missiles). Also implicit in McNamara's statement was the idea of "city avoidance," that is, not targeting civilian population centers as ends in themselves.

Counterforce remained the dominant concept in U.S. nuclear strategy for only a short while, however, because it began to lose prominence after 1964 with the rise of the damage limitation and assured destruction strategies.[32] McNamara outlined these new ideas in his speech before the Senate Committee on Armed Services in February of 1965:

> The first of these capabilities required to deter potential aggressors we call "assured destruction," i.e., the capability to destroy the aggressor as a viable society even after a well-planned and executed surprise attack on our forces. The second capability we call "damage limitation," i.e., the capability to reduce the weight of the enemy attack by both offensive and defensive measures and to

provide a degree of protection for the population against the effects of nuclear detonations.[33]

However, there was a serious contradiction between these two ideas. A damage limitation approach, when taken in conjunction with a strategy of counterforce, most resembled a nuclear warfighting doctrine based on having an ability to survive a nuclear war. On the other hand, assured destruction led in the opposite direction to a "war avoidance" strategy that relied on the threat of being able to inflict "unacceptable damage" on the Soviet Union. Since an assured destruction strategy was obviously cheaper to implement than a nuclear warfighting strategy, it was deemed a more cost-effective solution by McNamara. This line of thinking was the major strategic consequence that the systems analysis school of thought was to have for U.S. strategic doctrine. Indeed, McNamara later defined unacceptable damage as "the capability to destroy one-quarter to one-third of [the enemy's] population and about two-thirds of [the enemy's] industrial capacity." This was obviously a retreat from the initial definition of assured destruction, which was the ability "to destroy the enemy as a viable society."[34]

The assured destruction strategy, which was later to evolve into the doctrine of mutual assured destruction, was also as much an arms-control concept as it was a strategy. As it became more dominant, coupled with the growth of Soviet strategic forces to near parity by 1969, counterforce and damage limitation were discarded.[35] Since assured destruction later called for only a "minimum" capacity to inflict unacceptable damage, force level requirements were correspondingly lowered. This was the reasoning behind the decision to freeze ICBM deployment at 1,054 and submarine-launched ballistic missiles (SLBMs) at 656 after 1965.[36]

Also implied in the strategy of mutual assured destruction was McNamara's assumption that "both sides have the same general strategic objectives." From this followed the reasoning that "our assured destruction problem is the other side's damage limiting problem, and our damage limiting problem is their assured destruction problem."[37] As will be seen in the following chapter on Soviet doctrinal development, however, this assumption was incorrect.

The general course of U.S. nuclear strategy during the 1960s, therefore, was marked by a gradual transition from the warfighting-oriented strategies of counterforce and damage limitation to the war avoidance strategy of mutual assured destruction by the late 1960s and early 1970s. This strategy was to influence heavily subsequent developments in U.S. strategic doctrine.

The U.S. Doctrine of Realistic Deterrence

On February 17, 1972, Secretary of Defense Melvin R. Laird formally outlined in detail the tenets of the new strategic doctrine that had, in effect, been adopted shortly after the accession of President Nixon to office in January of 1969. The new doctrine, although given the name realistic deterrence by Laird in his 1972 statement, had earlier been known as the "Nixon Doctrine."[38] Secretary Laird stated the necessity for a "new" approach to national security strategy:

> Successful implementation of the strategy of realistic deterrence is, I believe, the most difficult and challenging national security effort this country has ever undertaken. This is so because we must move forward in an environment of virtual balance in the strategic nuclear field, and in a period of vigorous Soviet military expansion at sea, on the land, in the air, and in space. In addition, we must pursue our goal with due regard for the influences of today's other constraining realities—realities which I will discuss at some length.[39]

According to Secretary Laird, the defense strategy of the United States was to be based on the following three main aspects of the Nixon Doctrine:

1. The United States would keep all of its treaty commitments.
2. The United States would "provide a shield" if any nuclear power threatened the freedom of a nation allied with the United States or of a nation whose survival the United States considered vital to its security.
3. In cases involving "other types of aggression" the United States would furnish military and economic assistance when requested and as appropriate. The United States, however, would "look to the nation directly threatened to assume the primary responsibility of providing the manpower for its defense."[40]

In other words, realistic deterrence would place primary emphasis on U.S. strategic power only for deterring strategic nuclear war between the United States and the Soviet Union. For theatre nuclear and other conventional conflicts, the United States would share the burden of deterrence with its allies. Deterrence of communist insurgency wars was to be the main responsibility of the country being threatened, with the United States providing only logistical support except in those cases where the United States believed a vital interest was at stake.[41]

For the purpose of this book, it is best to concentrate on the portion of realistic deterrence that was concerned with deterrence of strategic nuclear war between the superpowers. From the standpoint of how much offensive strength was needed for a believable deterrent, the requirement had been steadily declining. From a requirement for "superiority" during the 1950s and early 1960s this had changed to "parity" in 1964, and again to "sufficiency" by 1969.[42] In addition to the concept of MAD, the term "crisis stability" was now added. This simply meant the maintenance of "an adequate second-strike capability to deter an all-out surprise attack'' on U.S. strategic forces with the objective of ''providing no incentive for the Soviet Union to strike the United States first in a crisis.''[43]

Another part of the requirement for sufficiency was the retention of the ability to inflict roughly equal amounts of damage vis-à-vis the Soviet Union. The idea was to prevent the Soviets ''from gaining the ability to cause considerably greater urban/industrial destruction than the United States would inflict on the Soviets in a nuclear war.'' Although the stress was still on targeting cities, counterforce gradually began to receive greater attention as a way of dealing with lesser challenges short of an all-out exchange.[44] However, these efforts were impaired (and still are today) by the U.S. lack of a significant ability to destroy Soviet missile silos. And while the possible effectiveness of the Soviet civil defense program might be open to question, there is little doubt that it would have been more effective than the comparatively nonexistent U.S. civil defense capability. This raised significant doubts about the ability of the United States to achieve assured destruction against Soviet cities.[45]

The other side of the sufficiency coin was the ability to defend ''against damage from small attacks or accidental launches.''[46] This need was supposedly taken care of by the installation of the safeguard antiballistic missile system (ABM), which, however, was abandoned after the construction of only the early-warning sites.[47]

Thus, the doctrine of realistic deterrence neither served to foster the kind of strategic flexibility deemed necessary by President Nixon,[48] nor appreciably affected the U.S. force posture and defense programs. The criteria of parity, sufficiency, and eventually ''essential equivalence'' were all attempts to apply rigid rules emphasizing statistical strengths as opposed to comparative capabilities. Using these criteria, arms-control efforts became vital to the defense posture, and not merely convenient or desirable.[49] Although some half hearted attempts had been made to move away from the pure retaliatory posture of MAD, no important proposed changes were to be declared until the announcement of the Schlesinger Doctrine in January 1974.

The Schlesinger Doctrine and Limited Nuclear Options

In his annual Defense Department report to the Congress for fiscal year 1975, Defense Secretary James Schlesinger set forth principles for a new U.S. strategic doctrine. Schlesinger outlined the main features of the proposed new strategic posture as follows:

1. A capability sufficiently large, diversified, and survivable so as to provide us at all times with high confidence of riding out even a massive surprise

attack and of penetrating enemy defenses, and with the ability to withhold an assured destruction reserve for an extended period of time.
2. Sufficient warning to insure the survival of our heavy bombers together with the bomb alarm systems and command-control capabilities required by our National Command Authorities to direct the employment of the strategic forces in a controlled, selective, and restrained fashion.
3. The forces to execute a wide range of options in response to potential actions by an enemy, including a capability for precise attacks on both soft and hard targets, while at the same time minimizing unintended collateral damage.
4. The avoidance of any combination of forces that could be taken as an effort to acquire the ability to execute a first-strike disarming attack against the Soviet Union.
5. An offensive capability of such size and composition that all will perceive it as in overall balance with the strategic forces of any potential opponent.
6. Offensive and defensive capabilities and programs that conform with the provisions of current arms-control agreements and at the same time facilitate the conclusion of more permanent treaties to control and, if possible, reduce the nuclear arsenals.[50]

It was the second and third features of the proposed posture that were to cause the greatest interest and consternation among Soviet analysts. These particular tenets were calling for increased nuclear targeting flexibility so as to create a greater number of options for a U.S. president to choose from in the event of a confrontation. In arguing for such flexible options, Schlesinger pointed out that credible deterrence must rest on the possession of a wide range of options with matching capabilities:

> Threats against allied forces, to the extent that they could be deterred by the prospect of nuclear retaliation, demand both more limited responses than destroying cities and advanced planning tailored to such lesser responses. Nuclear threats to our strategic forces, whether limited or large-scale, might well call for an option to respond in kind against the attacker's military forces. In other words, to be credible and hence effective over the range of possibility contingencies, deterrence must rest on many options and on a spectrum of capabilities to support these options.[51]

Schlesinger further argued that "flexibility of response is also essential because, despite our best efforts, we cannot guarantee that deterrence will never fail; nor can we forecast the situations that would cause it to fail." His rationale for limited nuclear options under these circumstances was based on his assertion that "if deterrence fails, we may be able to bring all but the largest nuclear conflicts to a rapid conclusion before cities are struck. Damage may thus be limited and further escalation avoided."[52]

It is interesting that Schlesinger referred to the formerly discarded concept of damage limitation, particularly within the context of a warfighting scenario if deterrence failed. Although the assured destruction strategy was still in use, it was no longer an arbitrary measure of population fatalities. Instead, it was to be a gauge in terms of postwar political objectives that were relevant to a nuclear war. Deterrence was now also a function of postwar political objectives; mainly, a reduction of the enemy's ability to recover quickly from the effects of a nuclear war and to attain a superior political-military position. The Schlesinger doctrine would therefore seem to lend itself more to a nuclear warfighting doctrine than the deterrence-oriented strategy of MAD.[53]

Ironically enough, the concepts then being resurrected by Schlesinger had previously been abandoned in order to exercise a self-restraint that, it had been hoped, the Soviets would imitate, only to be reconsidered later precisely because of the lack of any such restraint on their part. Indeed, the Soviet buildup rendered the U.S. assured destruction capability highly questionable except as a deterrent to the threat of a massive Soviet attack on U.S. cities as well as on U.S. strategic forces. The continuous growth of the Soviets' strategic power coupled with their steadfast rejection of the notion of mutual assured destruction eventually forced the U.S. to reconsider its strategic doctrine.[54]

The logic behind the strategy of limited nuclear options (LNO) was twofold. First, it was designed to introduce more flexibility into the available range of options for the use of strategic nuclear weapons so that, in a crisis, the president could theoretically order the *selective* use of nuclear weapons on military targets in the Soviet Union. The idea was to create the greatest uncertainty possible in the minds of Soviet leaders about what action the United States would be likely to take in response to a Soviet move that threatened an American vital interest. Ideally, this uncertainty would be so great that the Soviet leadership would be inhibited from making any aggressive moves. Second, the purpose was to strengthen the overall credibility of the U.S. deterrence strategy, which was correctly believed to have been eroded by continued reliance on an all-out nuclear response as embodied in the concept of MAD.

However, once Schlesinger was fired by President Ford in 1976, the issue of whether to modify U.S. strategic doctrine in the direction of a nuclear warfighting strategy was temporarily sidetracked. After the demise of LNO, there was essentially a hiatus in U.S. doctrinal development until President Carter announced a change in U.S. strategy in August 1980.

Presidential Directive 59

In a speech to the Naval War College on August 20, 1980, Defense Secretary Harold Brown explained the Carter administration's new concept of nuclear strategy:

> The overriding objective of United States strategic nuclear forces is to deter nuclear war, for which three requirements must be met. First, we must have strategic nuclear forces that can absorb a Soviet first strike and still retaliate with devastating effect. Second, we must meet our security requirements and maintain an overall strategic balance at the lowest and most stable levels. Third, we must have a doctrine and plans for the use of our forces (if they are needed) that make clear to the Soviets the hard reality that, by any course leading to nuclear war, they could never gain an advantage that would outweigh the unacceptable price they would have to pay. The ability of our forces to survive a surprise attack is the essence of deterrence.[55]

PD 59 was not, in fact, anything new or innovative when compared with previous strategic doctrine, and Secretary Brown conceded as much. "It was a refinement, Brown said, "a codification of previous statements of strategic policy. PD 59 took the same essential strategic doctrine and restated it more clearly, more cogently in the light of current conditions and current capabilities."[56]

The state of U.S. strategic doctrine, therefore, is currently at an impasse. Although the inherent weaknesses of a doctrine based merely on the threat to punish the enemy if he initiates a nuclear war have been duly recognized, if reluctantly, the U.S. leadership is still unable to bring itself to the point of wholehearted adherence to a nuclear warfighting doctrine. Perhaps this is out of fear of the political or strategic consequences, or both; it is a moot point. Unless the Reagan administration is able to formulate a strategic doctrine attuned to the realities of the nuclear age, the massive resources it proposes to spend on national defense will only help to implement the shopworn doctrine of the past.

Notes

1. B. Brodie, *Strategy in the Missile Age* (Princeton, N.J.: Princeton University Press, 1959), p. 248.
2. Ibid., p. 250. See also R. Bonds, *The US War Machine* (New York: Crown, 1978), p. 58. For a defense of the massive retaliation doctrine, see P. Peeters, *Massive Retaliation: The Policy and its Critics* (Chicago: Foundation for Foreign Affairs, 1959).
3. Brodie, *Strategy*, p. 250.
4. Ibid., pp. 251-253. See also R. Garthoff, *Soviet Military Policy: A Historical Analysis* (London: Faber & Faber, 1966), pp. 112-114.
5. R. Bonds, ed., *The Soviet War Machine* (New York: Chartwell, 1976), p. 202.
6. Brodie, *Strategy*, pp. 261-263.
7. E. Bottome, *The Missile Gap* (Cranbury, N.J.: Associated University Presses,

1971), pp. 221-224. For a discussion of the U.S. contingency plan for a projected war with the Soviet Union in 1957, see A. Brown, ed., *Dropshot: The United States Plan for War with the Soviet Union in 1957* (New York: Dial Press, 1978).

8. Dulles stated the broad outlines of the new policy in J.F. Dulles, "Challenge and Response in U.S. Policy," *Foreign Affairs*, Vol. 36, No. 1, October 1957, pp. 30-33.

9. For the details of the overall policy of "containment" and its rationale, see X (George Kennan), "The Sources of Soviet Conduct," *Foreign Affairs*, Vol. 25, No. 4, July 1947, pp. 566-582.

10. Dulles, "Challenge and Response in U.S. Policy," p. 31.

11. H. Kissinger, *Nuclear Weapons and Foreign Policy* (Garden City, N.Y.: Doubleday, 1958), p. 125.

12. A.W. Buzzard, "Massive Retaliation and Graduated Deterrence," *World Politics*, Vol. 8, No. 2, January 1956, p. 232.

13. Kissinger, *Nuclear Weapons*, p. 23.

14. M.W. Hoag, *On Local War Doctrine* (Santa Monica, Calif.: The RAND Corporation, P-2433, August 1961), p. 6.

15. Kissinger, *Nuclear Weapons*, p. 125.

16. Ibid., p. 127.

17. Hoag, *Local War*, pp. 6-8.

18. Brodie, *Strategy*, pp. 312-314.

19. Excerpts from McNamara's speech are in J.E. Endicott and R.W. Stafford, Jr., eds., *American Defense Policy* (New York: Johns Hopkins University Press, 1977), pp. 71-73.

20. General M.D. Taylor, "Security Will Not Wait," *Foreign Affairs*, Vol. 39, No. 2, January 1961, p. 175.

21. General M.D. Taylor, *The Uncertain Trumpet* (New York: Harper, 1959), pp. 5-7. Quoted in J.M. Collins, *American and Soviet Military Trends since the Cuban Missile Crisis* (Washington, D.C.: Center for Strategic and International Studies, 1978), p. 158.

22. Bonds, *US War Machine*, p. 61.

23. Quoted in Endicott and Stafford, *American Defense*, p. 73.

24. Ibid.

25. Bonds, *US War Machine*, p. 61.

26. Collins, *Military Trends*, pp. 159-166.

27. Endicott and Stafford, *American Defense*, p. 77. Excerpts from McNamara's speech on pp. 74-75.

28. Ibid., pp. 76-77.

29. See H. Kahn, *On Escalation: Metaphors and Scenarios* (New York: Praeger, 1965), pp. 37-195, for a detailed description of the rungs of the escalation ladder.

30. Quoted in Endicott and Stafford, *American Defense*, p. 74.

31. Ibid., pp. 74-75, passim.

32. Bonds, *US War Machine*, pp. 61-62.

33. Endicott and Stafford, *American Defense*, p. 75.

34. Ibid.

35. Bonds, *US War Machine*, pp. 61-62. See also Collins, *Military Trends*, pp. 77-80.

36. Bonds, *US War Machine*, pp. 61-62. See also Collins, *Military Trends*, pp. 84, 94.

37. Endicott and Stafford, *American Defense*, p. 75.

38. Ibid., p. 78.

39. Ibid.
40. Ibid., p. 79. Although the Nixon Doctrine included the strategy of realistic deterrence, it was intended as a general statement of degrees of defense or security commitments that the realistic deterrence strategy itself did not cover.
41. Ibid.
42. Collins, *Military Trends*, p. 83.
43. Endicott and Stafford, *American defense*, p. 80. See also Bonds, *US War Machine*, p. 65.
44. Collins, *Military Trends*, p. 80.
45. Ibid., pp. 85-88. See also Gouré, *War Survival In Soviet Strategy* (Coral Gables, Fla.: Center for Advanced International Studies, 1976), p. 7.
46. Endicott and Stafford, *American Defense*, p. 80.
47. Collins, *Military Trends*, p. 130.
48. Endicott and Stafford, *American Defense*, p. 80.
49. Collins, *Military Trends*, pp. 80-84.
50. Endicott and Stafford, *American Defense*, pp. 87-88. See also Bonds, *US War Machine*, pp. 65-66.
51. Endicott and Stafford, *American Defense*, p. 85.
52. Ibid. See also Collins, *Military Trends*, pp. 80-81.
53. Bonds, *US War Machine*, p. 66.
54. Ibid.
55. Stewart Menaul, "Changing Concepts of Nuclear War," *Conflict Studies*, No. 125, December 1980, p. 4.
56. Ibid.

2.
The Evolution of Soviet Strategic Doctrine

The period from the end of World War II to the death of Stalin in 1953 was characterized by stagnation in Soviet military thinking. Most of the commentary in Soviet publications dealt with a reiteration of the lessons of the past war and a continuous exposition of what came to be known as Stalin's "permanently operating factors" of war. According to Stalin's view, which was promulgated in 1942 after it had become apparent that the Germans had not achieved victory in their initial campaign, war was a massive social phenomenon in which the strengths of two or more societies were pitted against each other. Since war was a social phenomenon, it followed that it was subject to the laws that governed the development of the society itself. Within such a context, the permanently operating factors would decide the outcome of the war, and not such "transitory factors" as surprise. These permanently operating factors were "the stability of the rear, the morale of the army, the quantity and quality of divisions, the armament of the army, the organizational ability of the army commanders."[1] Whichever side was superior in the permanently operating factors would be victorious.

Such a concept, of course, was completely truistic. Its applicability pertained primarily to the world wars. In a nuclear war, it would certainly be important to have superiority in the permanently operating factors, but the question of the potential influence of the nuclear weapon on a future war was never discussed. In this sense, Stalin's ideas served to prohibit any discussion of foreign military thought on a serious basis until 1954.[2]

Of course, one has to consider the immediate postwar strategic situation that confronted Stalin. The basic need Stalin perceived was how to restrain the United States from reacting strongly to Soviet political moves and from attempting to exploit East European unrest. In the longer run, the problem he faced was how to get the Soviet Union safely through a period in which it would be vulnerable to U.S. strategic nuclear power. The solution Stalin chose was to downplay publicly the significance of the nuclear weapon, emphasizing instead the elements of military power in which the Soviets had the biggest advantage, namely, land power as embodied in mass armies.[3] Furthermore, by deploying large numbers of Soviet ground forces in Eastern Europe, thus giving the impression that the Soviets were preparing to invade Western Europe if war with the United States occurred, Stalin made Soviet land power an effective "counterweight" to U.S. strategic air power. By holding Western Europe hostage, so to speak, the Soviet Union had a credible deterrent against U.S. initiation of war.[4]

Discussion of foreign military thought was quite limited and superficial during this period, confined for the most part to propagandistic rhetoric accusing the United States of preparing a "nuclear blitzkrieg" against the Soviet Union. Not unexpectedly, this alleged reliance on a so-called atomic blitzkrieg was decried for ignoring the permanently operating factors governing the outcome of war, and thus was doomed to failure.[5] Soviet commentary did not depart from this basic line until after the death of Stalin.

Emergence of Soviet Nuclear Strategy

After the death of Stalin, Soviet military theorists were able to express disagreement with the concept of the permanently operating factors governing the outcome of war, virtually unchallenged up to that time. The first step taken in this direction was in the form of an article in *Voennaia Mysl'* by its editor, Major General N.A. Talensky, in September 1953. Although not completely breaking with Stalin's concepts, Talensky did speak of the possibility of the "decisive defeat in a limited time of one or another opponent."[6] This opened up the discussion concerning the question of the validity of the permanently operating factors, which culminated in the rejection of the concept as "old-fashioned" three years later.[7]

This transition period was also marked by a recognition of the potential decisiveness of nuclear weapons in helping to determine the outcome of a war. This is not to say that the Soviets at any time adopted anything resembling the American notion that the nuclear weapon was an *absolute* weapon able to decide the outcome of a war by itself. Indeed, the Soviets clearly rejected such an idea, asserting that they could aid in achieving decisive results, but not attributing all-powerful qualities to them.[8]

There also seems to have been some early debate during this period of the early to mid-1950s among Soviet military analysts over how much emphasis should be placed on the use of nuclear weapons. There were those who argued, on the one hand, that heavy reliance should be placed on nuclear weapons as a means of achieving decisive results on the battlefield. On the other hand, there were those, such as Lieutenant General Krasilnikov of the Soviet General Staff, who claimed that "weapons of mass destruction not only require mass armed forces, but require their inevitable increase."[9] However, once Khrushchev was firmly in power in 1955, the emphasis was to be in favor of preparation for a nuclear war, with a corresponding deemphasis on land forces.[10]

The greatest change, however, was in the Soviet estimation of the value of strategic surprise. The initial contentions were somewhat inconsistent, simultaneously claiming the primacy of the permanently operating factors while also suggesting that a surprise attack with nuclear weapons might determine the course, and possibly the outcome, of the entire war.[11] This debate was not entirely resolved until the May 1955 issue of *Voennaia Mysl'* , in which it was editorially stated that ''the task is to work out seriously all sides of this question [of surprise] and above all to elaborate ways and means of warning of surprise attack by the enemy and of dealing to the enemy preemptive blows on all levels—strategic, operational, and tactical.''[12] In other words, the Soviets had settled on the adoption of a preemptive strike strategy to be used in the event that an attack by the United States appeared imminent.[13] Although the Soviets still did not regard surprise as a sufficient prerequisite for victory by itself, it was nevertheless considered potentially decisive enough by the Soviets for them to want to deny the advantages of surprise to the United States.

However, Soviet delivery capabilities in 1955 were so poor that one wonders why the Soviets even bothered with a preemptive strategy. The answer to this is that the Soviets did not have, from their standpoint at least, any more desirable alternatives. One alternative was the avoidance of war at any cost, no matter what concessions had to be made. The problem with such a course of action is that it had failed miserably in 1941 in attempting to ward off a German invasion of the Soviet Union. Besides, the Soviets were now in a much stronger relative position vis-à-vis her major adversaries, in addition to the fact that the Eisenhower administration posed no threat comparable to Hitler's. The other alternative, initiating a preventive war with the United States, was even more undesirable. Given the much weaker Soviet delivery capabilities at the time, there was little chance of the Soviet Union's being able to inflict sufficient damage on American bases to prevent major retaliation. The requirements for a successful preemptive strategy, chief among them being reliable advance warning of an enemy attack, were at least unequivocal, and possibly attainable. Seen in this light, a preemptive strategy was undoubtedly the best of a bad set of choices.[14] Once the Soviet Union attained an ICBM capability in 1957, however, the preemptive strategy became much more feasible, now that the means of surprise attack had become nearly invulnerable and unstoppable.

Soviet Doctrinal Development in the 1960s

The development of Soviet military doctrine during the 1960s can be divided into two main periods: (1) the period leading up to Khrushchev's ouster in 1964 from the initial enunciation of his strategic doctrine in January 1960, and (2) the Brezhnev-Kosygin period of doctrinal development to 1970.[15] The first period differed significantly in doctrine and force requirements from the latter period, as will be seen.

The declaration of Soviet strategic doctrine by Khrushchev on January 14, 1960, in addition to those made by then defense minister Malinovskiy on January 14 and 19 of the same year, placed its main emphasis on the decisiveness of nuclear weapons in a future war. Referred to mistakenly by one Western analyst as Khrushchev's version of "massive retaliation,"[16] its implication was that any U.S. attempts at limiting armed conflict would not succeed, and that all wars between the capitalist and socialist camps would quickly escalate to all-out war.[17] Defense Minister Malinovskiy concisely stated the nature of a future world war:

> A future would war, if the imperialists succeed in unleashing it, will be a decisive armed clash of the opposed social systems: . . . it inevitably will be thermonuclear, a war in which the main means of its delivery to the target will be the rockets. . . . Now war might arise without the traditional clearly threatening period, by surprise, as a result of the mass use of long-range rockets armed with powerful nuclear warheads.[18]

Merely because the above passage stressed the "single-option" strategy of immediate escalation to strategic nuclear war is not to say that the Soviets categorically denied the possibility of limited wars ever taking place. Certain statements made during Khrushchev's tenure give one reason to conclude that Soviet willingness to escalate to all-out conflict was declaratory rather than real; an exercise in declaratory deterrence, if you will. One Soviet military analyst conceded that "limited wars have occurred in the past; they may also occur in the future." The chance of a protracted war was also not ignored, because strategic capabilities of both sides were still relatively small in 1960.[19]

There has been some disagreement by Western analysts over the nature of Soviet doctrinal development during the Khrushchev period. Some claimed that there was a "debate" occuring between two schools of thought said to exist within the Soviet military. One school was referred to as the "traditionalist" school, which supposedly affirmed the necessity for the maintenance of multimillion-man armies for the purpose of replacing the enormous losses inherent in nuclear warfare. The other alleged school of thought was called the "modernist" viewpoint, which was ostensibly pressing for a radical adaptation of modern technology to military affairs to the extent of placing the main emphasis on nuclear weapons. It was further contended by such analysts as Wolfe that the "debate" resulted in the emergence of a "centrist" viewpoint, which was a compromise between the two schools.[20]

The idea of a doctrinal "debate" between factions of the Soviet military has not been without its critics, however. William F. Scott, a former military attaché to the Soviet Union, recently argued in *Strategic Review* that the basic trust of Soviet military doctrine throughout the 1960s to the present has always been and continues to be oriented around the notion of the primacy of nuclear weapons. Since the declaration of a particular doctrine can precede the deployment of forces for carrying it out by as much as 10 years (mainly because of the long lead times involved in the development of modern weapons systems), the large Soviet nuclear forces of today are actually the result of decisions made at the beginning of the 1960s.[21]

In truth, there was no contradiction between the idea that the nuclear weapon was to be the decisive weapon and the claim that multimillion-man armies were required in order to sustain the anticipated losses of a nuclear war; both concepts could easily coexist within the same doctrine without conflict. It should be noted that, even with Khrushchev's actual as well as planned reductions in manpower taken into account, the fact that manpower levels were being reduced did not mean a rejection of the notion that multimillion-man armies should be maintained. The lowest figure for Soviet manpower levels projected by Khrushchev was 2.4 million men, which still constituted a fairly large army, and was hardly an outright rejection of the so-called traditionalist school. The *actual* reductions, furthermore, resulted in an overall decrease of 2.7 million men from 5.7 million men in 1955 to approximately 3 million men by Khrushchev's ouster in 1964.[22] The main point that should be emphasized is that there was no debate in the sense of an actual conflict over *doctrine* during the period from 1960 to 1964. What argument that existed was not over whether one was to have multimillion-man armies or not, but over how large those armies were to be. In other words, the disagreements were over matters of implementation of doctrine as opposed to doctrine itself. The primacy of nuclear weapons was to remain the predominant theme in Soviet strategy. It is important to remember that any evidence of "debates" in Soviet military journals is not a sign that the Soviet military is challenging the political authority of the CPSU, since these debates take place within carefully prescribed and authorized limits defined by the party.[23] In Khrushchev's opinion, 2.4 million men was the level of manpower he deemed adequate for the purpose of maintaining a multimillion-man army. He also claimed that any reduction in manpower would be made up by the increase in firepower from nuclear weapons:

> A reduction of the numerical strength of our armed forces will not prevent us from maintaining the country's defensive power at the proper level. We shall have all the means required for the defense of our country, and our enemy will know it very well. In case he does not, we are warning him and telling him outright: by reducing the numerical strength of our armed forces, we shall not be diminishing their firepower. On the contrary, their firepower will increase many times over in terms of quality.[24]

With the ouster of Khrushchev in 1964, however, there were some modifications in doctrine, although the nuclear emphasis remained unaltered. Soviet doctrine began moving away from the assertion that war between the capitalist and socialist states must inevitably escalate to general nuclear war. Indeed, there were increasing indications in public Soviet journals, as well as in the following passage from the Soviet General Staff publication *Voennaia Mysl'* , that the Soviets were recognizing the need to be prepared for conflicts which were less than all-out war:

> Consequently, according to the means of conducting warfare, consideration is given both to nuclear and non-nuclear, and according to its scales—world and local.[25]

Public recognition of the necessity to be prepared for nonnuclear conflict was made by then minister of defense Marshal A.A. Grechko in a speech to the All-Army Conference of Young Officers in November 1969:

> Much attention is being devoted to the reasonable combination of nuclear rocket weapons with perfected conventional classic armaments, to the capability of units and subunits to conduct combat actions under nuclear as well as nonnuclear conditions. Such an approach ensures the high combat capabilities of the troops and their constant readiness for action under conditions of variously shaped circumstances.[26]

A theme that remained constant throughout the 1960s, and was in fact a carryover from the resolution of the debate over the role of surprise in *Voennaia Mysl'* in 1955,[27] was the Soviet emphasis on a preemptive strike strategy in the event of war. Although the idea of a preemptive strike was not directly stated in public pronouncements, the implication was nonetheless clear that the Soviets intended to launch the first strike in the event of total war. They perceived this strategy as the best for achieving survival and, therefore, also achieving victory. However, Soviet capabilities were still not up to the requirements of doctrine. The best example of this kind of statement was in the third edition of Sokolovskiy's *Soviet Military Strategy* (hereafter referred to as *Military Strategy*):

> However, possibilities of averting a surprise attack are constantly growing. Present means of reconnaissance, detection, and surveillance can opportunely disclose a significant portion of the measures of direct preparation of a nuclear attack by the enemy and in the very first minutes locate the mass launch of missiles and the take-off of aircraft belonging to the aggressor and, at the right time, warn the political leadership of the country about the impending danger. Thus, possibilities exist not to allow a surprise attack by an aggressor, to deliver nuclear strikes on him at the right time.[28]

The strategy of a preemptive strike was to be one of the main components of the Soviet emphasis on a nuclear warfighting strategy during the 1960s and into the 1970s. The essence of Soviet thinking regarding its warfighting strategy was expressed in an article in a September 1965 issue of *Kommunist Vooruzhennykh Sil* by Lieutenant Colonel E. Rybkin, then a candidate of philosophical science. At the time, Rybkin's article was regarded by Western analysts such as Roman Kolkowicz and William Zimmerman as an aberration on the side of militancy, rather than as evidence of a consensus within the Soviet military. Instead, they interpreted Rybkin's article as indicating the existence of a hawkish fringe element within the Soviet military as opposed to the more moderate views expressed by Major General N. Talensky in the May 1965 issue of *International Affairs*. Talensky claimed that "there is no more dangerous illusion than the idea that thermonuclear war can still serve as an instrument of politics" and appeared to oppose the notion "that it is possible to find acceptable forms of nuclear war."[29] However, these analysts were unfamiliar with Soviet declaratory deterrence techniques and overlooked the fact that Talensky was a retired major general at the time and was writing his article for *International Affairs*, a publication not directed toward a Soviet military audience. On the other hand, Rybkin was writing for *Kommunist Vooruzhennykh Sil*, a military theory journal published by the Main Political Administration, thus indicating that Rybkin's views had the prior approval of the CPSU. Rather than being representative of a hawkish element in the Soviet military therefore, Rybkin's article demonstrated that the Soviets were pursuing a line of strategic thinking much different from the one that would lead the United States into a strategy relying on mutual assured destruction.[30]

In his assessment of "imperialist" military theory, Rybkin asserted that "until recently, militarist ideologues have altered the interpretation of this formula in order to relate and unite the concepts of war and politics and have even 'overturned' Clausewitz's formula to mean that 'politics is war.'"[31] Rybkin disagreed, claiming that "it is clear that it is definitely incorrect to identify the concept of 'a continuation of politics' with that of 'an instrument of politics.' War is always the continuation of politics, but it cannot always serve as the latter's instrument."[32] Rybkin eschewed the position taken by Talensky concerning the nonutility of nuclear war as an instrument of state policy on the grounds that "an a priori rejection of the possibility of victory is harmful because it leads to moral disarmament, to a disbelief in victory, and to fatalism and passivity."[33] For Rybkin to have said otherwise would have been going in opposition to the ideological assertions of many Soviet analysts that a future nuclear war would result in the final destruction of capitalism, thus implying the survival of the Soviet Union and the triumph of socialism. From Rybkin's standpoint, then, Talensky's statements were both militarily and politically unpalatable. (One must also take into account, however, the likelihood that the Soviets were setting up a false debate as part of their declaratory deterrence strategy to mislead Western analysts.)

Rybkin, though, was not a "superhawk" (as erroneously contended by Kolkowicz and Zimmerman) in the sense of being more willing to wage a nuclear war than his supposedly more moderate colleagues. In the following passage, Rybkin qualified his disagreement with Talensky:

> Thus, nuclear war because of its consequences transcends the framework of previous ideas regarding the correlation of politics and war. Though nuclear war still represents a continuation of politics *it is now circumscribed as an instrument of politics because of the effects of atomic weapons.* This fact does not negate either the possibility of the aggressors unleashing a war *or the possibility of our victory in the war.* The chief conclusion derived from the analysis of this problem is that it is necessary to do everything in order to avert a world nuclear war . . . . Moreover, the CPSU Program and the decisions of the party and the government *obligate our Armed Forces to be constantly in the state of complete readiness and by their decisive actions to bring to naught the schemes of the aggressors and to inflict upon them a retaliatory, all-crushing blow.* [34] [Emphasis added]

It is clear, therefore, that Rybkin was not only arguing that it was possible for the Soviet Union to fight and win a nuclear war, but that he was also advocating a preemptive strike strategy as part of a nuclear warfighting doctrine should war occur.

The objective of victory in a nuclear war was confirmed in the third edition of Sokolovskiy's *Military Strategy.* Although the editors of the third edition had altered their statement regarding war between the Soviet Union and the imperialists to read that "such a war *might* take the nature of a world war with the majority of the countries in the world participating in it," [35] they still emphasized the possibility of attaining victory via a nuclear warfighting strategy should war occur:

> The ability of a nation's economy to engage in mass production of military equipment, especially nuclear rocket weapons, to create a superiority over the enemy in modern means of armed combat determines the material prerequisites of victory. *A decisive factor for the outcome of a future war will be the ability of the economy to assure the maximum strength of the Armed Forces, in order to inflict a devastating strike upon the aggressor during the initial period of the war.* [36] [Emphasis in original]

The main points of Soviet thinking regarding a nuclear warfighting doctrine can be summarized as follows:

1. Nuclear war is possible.
2. If nuclear war is possible, it should be fought to achieve victory.
3. Correct capabilities and strategies make it possible to attain victory.
4. Adherence to mutual assured destruction deprives Soviet strategic forces of their political and military utility and gives the United States a free hand in the conduct of limited wars.

The development of Soviet strategic doctrine during the 1960s thus contained elements of continuity from the 1950s, mainly the continuing emphasis on the importance of surprise and a preemptive strategy with the objective of victory in the event of general nuclear war. The decade of the 1960s was further characterized by a shift in emphasis following the ouster of Khrushchev from a single-option strategy relying on a "minimum deterrence" posture to a doctrine that recognized the need for greater flexibility in military capability across the spectrum of conflict, and therefore called for a greater buildup in conventional as well as nuclear capability.[37] The decade was especially marked by the rapid growth of Soviet strategic forces to the point where they began to exceed those of the United States; the Soviets would perceive this development as decisive in terms of its effect on the evolution of U.S. strategic doctrine.[38]

Soviet Doctrinal Developments in the 1970s

The orientation of Soviet strategic doctrine throughout the 1970s and up to the present time has remained that of a nuclear warfighting/war survival doctrine. The assumption underlying this doctrine is that the better prepared the Soviet armed forces are to fight and win a nuclear war, the more effective they will be as a deterrent to an attack on the Soviet Union as well as an "umbrella" under which the Soviets can pursue a more aggressive foreign policy. Deterrence, therefore, is an implied goal of Soviet strategic doctrine, and is not treated separately from a warfighting doctrine. Rather, it remains an inseparable part of Soviet doctrine.[39]

Implicit in the Soviet warfighting strategy is the notion of war "survival," with civil defense being one of the main means of achieving it.[40] The Soviet reasoning is that no country can rationally threaten another with nuclear war if both know that such a war would be suicidal for the country that initiated it. Furthermore, a Soviet war survival capability increases the credibility of Soviet deterrence by undermining the (until very recently) fundamental tenet of U.S. strategic doctrine; that of being able to threaten the Soviet Union with assured destruction. This also provides the Soviets with greater opportunity to exploit their military power for the pursuit of foreign policy goals, since it increases the likelihood that the United States would make concessions in the face of Soviet-supported advances rather than run the risk of confrontation or war.[41]

Still another aspect of Soviet doctrine that has remained unchanged since 1955 has been the role of the preemptive strike as the best means of maximizing the chances of survival in a nuclear war, and thus attaining victory.[42] This intention was again expressed in an August 1972 issue of *Kommunist Vooruzhennykh Sil*:

In the current phase, the Armed Forces should be capable of stopping a surprise attack by the aggressor in any situation and use rapid, crushing blows to destroy his main nuclear missile weapons and troop formations, thus securing favorable conditions for further conduct of and victorious conclusion to the war.[43]

This assumption was also reflected in the fifth edition of *Marxism-Leninism on War and Army*, published that same year:

Soviet military doctrine proceeds from the assumption that the imperialists are preparing a surprise nuclear attack against the USSR and other socialist countries. At the same time they consider the possibility of waging military operations escalating into military actions involving the use of nuclear missile weapons. Therefore, the chief and main task of the Armed Forces consists in being constantly ready to repel a sudden attack of the enemy in any form, to foil his criminal intentions, no matter what means he might use.[44]

The rationale behind the preemptive strike strategy has also remained substantially unaltered, contending that "the first massive nuclear strikes are able largely to predetermine the subsequent course of the war and to inflict such heavy losses in the rear and among the troops that they may place the people and the country in an extraordinarily difficult position." Even so, the Soviets still do not believe that nuclear weapons can determine the outcome of a war by themselves. Instead, they argue that "final victory over the aggressor can be achieved only as a result of the joint actions of all the arms of the services, which must utilize in full measure the results of the nuclear strikes at the enemy and fulfill their specific tasks."[45]

During the 1970s, however, the Soviets had begun emphasizing an even more ambitious requirement for Soviet doctrine, the capability for projecting Soviet military power into distant areas of the globe.[46] Although Brezhnev had cautiously hinted at this new change in his address to the Twenty-fourth Party Congress in March 1971,[47] it was more directly stated in a book published by the Institute for World Economy and International Relations in 1972:

Greater importance is being attached to Soviet military presence in various regions throughout the world, reinforced by an adequate level of strategic mobility of its armed forces.

In connection with the task of preventing local wars and also in those cases wherein military support must be furnished to those nations fighting for their freedom and independence against the forces of international reaction and imperialist interventions, the Soviet Union may require mobile and well-trained and well-equipped forces....

Expanding the scale of Soviet military presence and military assistance furnished by other socialist states is being viewed today as a very important factor in international relations.[48]

This theme was reaffirmed as an official addition to Soviet military doctrine by Marshal A.A. Grechko in 1974. Writing in a leading party theoretical journal, he said:

> At the present state the historic function of the Soviet Armed Forces is not restricted to their function in defending our Motherland and the other socialist countries. In its foreign policy activity the Soviet state purposefully opposes the export of counterrevolution and the policy of oppression, supports the national liberation struggle, and resolutely resists imperialists' aggression in whatever distant region of the planet it may appear.[49]

Although Soviet strategic doctrine has undergone these new modifications during the 1970s, the essence of Soviet strategic doctrine has remained basically unchanged since 1960. The stress is still on the decisiveness of the nuclear weapon in determining the course and outcome of a future world war. This emphasis, with its concomitant principles of war fighting and war survival, remains the foundation of Soviet strategic doctrine to the present day.[50] Such a doctrine is a clear rejection of the concept of mutual assured destruction, since the Soviets contend that they ''are not for peace at any price and . . . are not, of course, for any freezing of social-political processes taking place inside the countries'':[51]

> War can and must be banned as a means for resolving international disputes. But we must not ''ban'' civil or national liberation wars, we must not ''ban'' uprisings and we by no means ''ban'' revolutionary mass movements aimed at changing the political and social status quo.[52]

It is evident from the two preceding chapters that the evolution of U.S. and Soviet strategic doctrine has proceeded along two entirely different paths over the period of time since the end of World War II. The United States, operating under the assumption that nuclear war was unthinkable and unwinnable, evolved toward a war-avoidance strategy. The Soviet Union, however, still adhering to the idea that nuclear war could serve as a continuation of state policy (albeit in a somewhat circumscribed fashion) eventually developed a nuclear warfighting doctrine based upon the concepts of war survival and the preemptive strike. Both sides perceived the other's strategic doctrine within the context of their own strategic mindset; the consequences of this, however, would be quite different for Soviet than for U.S. planning, as will be seen in the following chapters.

Notes

1. H.S. Dinerstein, *War and the Soviet Union* (New York: Praeger, 1959), pp. 6-7.

2. R. Garthoff, *Soviet Strategy in the Nuclear Age* (New York: Praeger, 1958), p. 70.
3. R. Bonds, ed., *The Soviet War Machine* (New York: Chartwell, 1976), p. 202. See also H. Kissinger, *Nuclear Weapons and Foreign Policy* (Garden City, N.Y.: Doubleday, 1958), pp. 93-96.
4. T. Wolfe, *Soviet Power and Europe, 1945-1970* (Baltimore: Johns Hopkins Press, 1970), pp. 32-35.
5. A. Dallin, *Red Star on Military Affairs, 1945-1952* (Santa Monica, Calif.: RAND, RM-1637, February 10, 1956.), p. 21.
6. Dinerstein, *War and the Soviet Union*, p. 41.
7. Ibid., pp. 53-54.
8. Garthoff, *Soviet Strategy*, pp. 76-78.
9. Ibid., p. 79.
10. Bonds, *Soviet War Machine*, p. 204.
11. Dinerstein, *War and the Soviet Union*, p. 183.
12. Garthoff, *Soviet Strategy*, p. 85.
13. Bonds, *Soviet War Machine*, p. 204.
14. Dinerstein, *War and the Soviet Union*, pp. 200-202.
15. Bonds, *Soviet War Machine*, 207-208.
16. H.S. Dinerstein, *Soviet Strategic Ideas: January 1960* (Santa Monica, Calif.: RAND, RM-2532, February 19, 1960), p. 25.
17. Bonds, *Soviet War Machine*, p. 208. See also H.F. Scott and W.F. Scott, *The Armed Forces of the USSR* (Boulder, Colo.: Westview, 1978), p. 45. See also Dinerstein, *Soviet Strategic Ideas*, pp. 28-29.
18. R. Malinovskiy, *Bditel' no Stoyat Na Strazhe Mira (Vigilantly Stand Guard over the Peace) (Moscow: Voyenizdat, 1962), pp. 24-27. Quoted in Scott and Scott, Armed Forces*, p. 45.
19. Quoted in L. Gouré, *Soviet Limited War Doctrine* (Santa Monica, Calif.: RAND, P-2744, May 1963), p. 3. For other pronouncements regarding protracted war, see D. Palevich and I. Poznyak, "The Peculiarities and Nature of a World Nuclear-Rocket War," *KVS*, No. 20, October 1964, pp. 78-79. See also V.D. Sokolovskiy, *Soviet Military Strategy*, ed. and trans. H.F. Scott (New York: Crane, Russak, 1975), pp. 64-69, for discussion in detail of the limited war concept.
20. T. Wolfe, *Soviet Power*, pp. 161-162.
21. W.F. Scott, "Soviet Military Doctrine and Strategy: Realities and Misunderstandings," *Strategic Review*, Vol. 3, No. 3, Summer 1975, pp. 60-62.
22. Wolfe, *Soviet Power*, pp. 164-166.
23. H.F. Scott, *Soviet Military Doctrine: Its Continuity, 1960-1970* (Menlo Park, Calif.: Stanford Research Institute, SSC-TN-8974-28, 17 June 1971), pp. 65-69. See also Scott and Scott, *Armed Forces*, pp. 41-56. The role of the Main Political Administration in Soviet party-military relations has been comprehensively examined in M.J. Deane, *Political Control of the Soviet Armed Forces* (New York: Crane, Russak, 1977). For a more recent exposition, see also J.J. Dziak, *Soviet perceptions of Military Power: The Interaction of Theory and Practice* (New York: National Strategy Information Center, 1981).
24. H.F. Scott, *Soviet Military Doctrine: Its Continuity, 1960-1970*, p. 78.
25. S. Ivanov, "Soviet Military Doctrine and Strategy," *Voennaia Mysl'*, No. 5, May 1969, trans. FBIS, FPD, No. 0116/69, 18 December 1969, p. 49.
26. A.A. Grechko, "The Growing Role, Tasks, and Obligations of Young Officers at

the Contemporary State of the Development of the Soviet Armed Forces,'' *Krasnaya Zvezda*, 27 November 1969. Quoted in Scott and Scott, *Armed Forces*, p. 55. See also G. Semenov and V. Prokhorov, ''Scientific-Technical Progress and Some Questions of Strategy,'' *Voennaia Mysl'*, No. 2, February 1969, trans. FBIS, FPD, No. 0060/69, 18 June 1969, p. 29; N. Vasendin and N. Kuznetsov, ''Modern Warfare and Surprise Attack,'' *Voennaia Mysl'*, No. 6, June 1968, trans. FBIS, FPD, No. 0005/69, 16 January 1969, p. 45.

27. See the discussion of this in Garthoff, *Soviet Strategy*, pp. 82-87.

28. Sokolovskiy, *Soviet Military Strategy*, p. 280. See also N. Krylov, ''The Nuclear-Missile Shield of the Soviet State,'' *Voennaia Mysl'*, No. 11, November 1967, Trans. FBIS, FPD. No, 0157/68, 18 November 1968, pp. 18-19, passim.

29. N. Talensky, ''The Late War: Some Reflections,'' *International Affairs*, No. 5, May 1965, p. 15.

30. R. Kolkowicz, *The Red "Hawks" on the Rationality of Nuclear War* (Santa Monica, Calif.: RAND, RM-4899-PR, March 1966). See also W. Zimmerman, *Soviet Perspectives on International Relations, 1956-1967* (Princeton, N.J.: Princeton University Press, 1969), p. 233.

31. E. Rybkin, ''On the Essence of a World Nuclear-Rocket War,'' *KVS*, No. 17, September 1965, p. 51.

32. Ibid., pp. 52-53.

33. Ibid., p. 55.

34. Ibid., p. 56.

35. Sokolovskiy, *Soviet Military Strategy*, p. 208.

36. Ibid., p. 209.

37. Bonds, *Soviet War Machine*, p. 208.

38. Ibid., p. 210. See also Wolfe, *Soviet Power*, pp. 451-457.

39. L. Gouré, F. Kohler, and M. Harvey, *The Role of Nuclear Forces in Current Soviet Strategy* (Coral Gables, Fla.: Center for Advanced International Studies, 1975), p. 47. See also B. Lambeth, *The Political Potential of Equivalence: The View from Moscow and Europe* (Santa Monica, Calif.: RAND, P-6167, August 1978.

40. L. Gouré, *War Survival in Soviet Strategy* (Coral Gables, Fla.: Center for Advanced International Studies, 1976), pp. 6-8.

41. Ibid., pp. 23-24.

42. Garthoff, *Soviet Strategy*, pp. 84-87. See also Gouré, Kohler, and Harvey, *Nuclear Forces*, pp. 102-112. The Soviet ''preemptive strike'' strategy was reaffirmed during the late 1960s and early 1970s in the following articles from the classified Soviet General Staff journal *Voennaia Mysl' (Military Thought)*: S. Lukonin and A. Migolat'yev, ''The 24th CPSU Congress on Current Problems in the Building of Communism and the Strengthening of the Defensive Might of the USSR,'' *Voennaia Mysl'*, No. 5, May 1971, trans. in FBIS, FPD No. 0016/74, March 18, 1974, p. 13; Editorial, ''The Tasks of Soviet Military Science in Light of the Decisions of the 24th CPSU Congress,'' *Voennaia Mysl'*, No. 8, August 1971, trans. FBIS, FPD No. 0011/74, February 28, 1974, p. 6; Editorial, ''On Guard for Peace and the Building of Socialism,'' *Voennaia Mysl'*, No. 12, December 1971, trans. FBIS, FPD No. 0003/74, January 17, 1974, p. 8.

43. I. Forofonov, ''The 24th CPSU Congress on Missions of the Soviet Armed Forces in the Current Phase,'' *KVS*, No. 15, August 1971, p. 77. Quoted in F. Kohler et al., *Soviet Strategy for the Seventies: From Cold War to Peaceful Coexistence* (Coral Gables, Fla.: Center for Advanced International Studies, 1973), p. 87.

44. *Marxism-Leninism on War and Army* (Moscow: Progress Publishers, 1972), trans. under the auspices of the U.S. Air Force (Washington, D.C.: U.S. Government Printing Office, 1972), p. 305.
45. Ibid., p. 304.
46. Bonds, *Soviet War Machine*, p. 208.
47. Quoted in Scott and Scott, *Armed Forces*, p. 56. See also Kohler et al., *Soviet Strategy for the Seventies*, pp. 93-95.
48. V.M. Kulish, *Voennaia Sila i Mezhdunarodnie Otnosheniia (Military Force and International Relations)* (Moscow: International Relations Publishing House, 1972), p. 137, quoted in Scott and Scott, *Armed Forces*, p. 57.
49. A.A. Grechko, "The Leading Role of the CPSU in Building the Army of a Developed Socialist Society," *Problems of History of CPSU*, May 1974. Quoted in Scott and Scott, *Armed Forces*, p. 57. See also Editorial, "The Party of Lenin: The Fighting Vanguard," *Voennaia Mysl'*, No. 3, March 1971, trans. FBIS, FPD No. 0020/74, March 29, 1974, pp. 6-7, passim.
50. Ibid., p. 58. See also Gouré, Kohler, and Harvey, *Nuclear Forces*, pp. 46-62. See also Gouré, *War Survival*, pp. 1-9.
51. *Pravda*, January 30, 1974. Quoted in Gouré, Kohler, and Harvey, *Nuclear Forces*, pp. 62-63.
52. Izvestia, September 11, 1973. Quoted in Gouré, Kohler, and Harvey, *Nuclear Forces*, p. 63.

PART II

MASSIVE RETALIATION PERIOD
(1954-1960)

3.
The Soviet View of Massive Retaliation

How may one best determine what the actual Soviet perception of the massive retaliation doctrine was during the period when it was actually in force? In answering such a question, Soviet declarations must be considered in conjunction with Soviet foreign policy behavior and their military programs. In addition, one must look carefully at statements that are not in consonance with Soviet strategic doctrine, since these are part of the soviet declaratory deterrence strategy to mislead Western analysts.

The actual Soviet interpretations as determined in this chapter reveal a preoccupation with the problem of deterring the "worst possible case", a preemptive nuclear strike by the United States. This was largely a mirror-imaging by the Soviets of their own estimation of the value of surprise as a decisive factor in determining the outcome of a war, as well as a reflection of the fact that the Soviets had little corresponding capability to so threaten the United States until the development of the Soviet ICBM. The key to undermining the massive retaliation doctrine, from the Soviet perspective, lay in negating the U.S. perception of its own invulnerability by using propagandistic rhetoric as well as by striving to attain an intercontinental capability as soon as possible.

This goal was confirmed in the military programs of the Khrushchev regime. Roughly 2,000 of the Tu-16 bombers were produced in all after their entry into service in 1954. Although the range of this bomber made an intercontinental capability possible only with one-way missions or in-flight refuelling, it was sufficient to give the Soviets *some* intercontinental capability, however unreliable.[1] It is interesting that only approximately 300 of the longer-range Tu-20 bombers were produced after its entry into service in 1957, since Khrushchev may have decided to devote more attention to the nascent Soviet ICBM program.[2]

Because the Soviets placed such a high value on the potential decisiveness of surprise in determining the outcome of a war, it is logical that they would do everything in their power, whether through propaganda or through their military programs, to undermine the credibility of a U.S. strategic doctrine they perceived as depending on surprise attack. The tactics of bluff and deception practiced by the Soviets regarding their own ICBM capability were intended to discourage such an attack as well as to reap possible political gains. Yet the Soviets realized that their ''superiority'' was an illusion, and so they did not attempt to press their advantage when it appeared that their bluff might be called.

However the Soviets might have *publicly* questioned the credibility of the massive retaliation doctrine, the fact remains that there was no instance during the period when it was officially in force (1954-1960), with the exception of the Soviet intervention in Hungary in 1956 (where the Soviets obviously believed they were forced to take risks), in which they actually *committed* an act of local aggression that might have called for the carrying out of the threat implied by massive retaliation. To be sure, there were several instances during this period in which the Soviets made both implied and direct threats to use their strategic capability.[3] For example, during the 1956 Suez crisis, the Soviets threatened both Great Britain and France with nuclear weapons. In 1958, *after* the Quemoy-Matsu crisis, Khrushchev threatened to retaliate against the United States if she attacked China. And of course, the period from 1957 to 1962 was characterized by exaggerated claims and veiled threats regarding Soviet ICBM capability and possible employment. The Soviets also used military manuevers frequently during this period, as typified by the Soviet announcement in 1958 of military manuevers in the Transcaucasus and Bulgaria in response to the U.S. intervention in Lebanon (see Appendix B). Common to all of these responses though, is that they were not *direct* uses of military power against the West, and therefore the Soviets were deterred in large measure from local aggression during this period. As will be seen in this chapter, this was a combination of Soviet strategic weakness and respect for the relatively massive U.S. capability, rather than a genuine belief in the credibility of the massive retaliation doctrine itself. The lack of a strong U.S. response to the Soviet intervention in Hungary undoubtedly contributed to this impression.[4]

All of this ought to be considered within the context of the ''peaceful coexistence'' policy as espoused by Khrushchev. The main points of this policy were as follows:

1. War is no longer ''fatalistically'' inevitable.
2. Neither general nor local war is desirable.
3. A peaceful way is possible and preferable for the attainment of socialism.
4. War among capitalist states is no longer a likely ''midwife of revolution.''
5. In any event, the Soviet Union and the socialist camp do not require war of any kind to win on a world scale.
6. Already the correlation of forces is moving relentlessly in favor of the Soviet Union.

7. The Soviet Union can expect the shift in the correlation of world forces to accelerate because of changing attitudes and new opportunities for Moscow in the Third World.[5]

According to Khrushchev, the focus of the competition between the United States and the Soviet Union was now the economic rather than the military sphere. He appeared to have little doubt at the time that the Soviet Union would be the ultimate victor in such a competition, provided it was allowed to proceed without the occurrence of a nuclear war in which, he contended, there would be no possibility of triumph for either side (this contention seems quite questionable, given the tenets of Soviet nuclear strategy as held even at this time).[6] As will be demonstrated in this chapter, the Soviet perception of the massive retaliation doctrine was quite rational when considered within the framework of Soviet nuclear strategy and the foreign policy of peaceful coexistence. First to be considered, however, are the Soviet efforts to discredit the massive retaliation doctrine with their declaratory deterrence strategy.

The Soviet Propaganda Line

It should always be kept in mind that the primary objective of Soviet declaratory deterrence statements during this period was to confuse U.S. observers about Soviet intentions and strategic capabilities. The major points of this propaganda line were seldom, if ever, repeated in later Soviet analyses of massive retaliation, since the Soviets probably believed that it was safer to comment candidly on a particular U.S. doctrine if it was no longer in force. The four major themes of Soviet declaratory deterrence, with appropriate explanation and documentation of each, are summarized below:

1. *The Soviets denied that the United States could achieve decisive results in a nuclear war with the Soviet Union (i.e., attain victory) by relying on the use of surprise in its doctrine of massive retaliation.*

The claim that the U.S. could not achieve decisive victory in a nuclear war with the Soviet Union was advanced more often during the early part of the massive retaliation period. For example, it was argued in *New Times* that if the United States "embarked on atomic aggression," the only result would be to "bring down incalculable misery on their own country." The launching of a so-called preventive war, it was claimed, "can earn its initiators nothing but tremendous loss of moral and political prestige."[7] The implication, of course, was that the United States could not win.

It is important to note that the above did not mean that the United States would actually lose such a conflict, but rather that the cost would be so excessive that any victory would be meaningless. Obviously, the purpose here was to discourage the United States from trying to enforce massive retaliation with its nuclear arsenal. The assumption was also apparently made by the Soviets that victory in a nuclear war, rather than pure deterrence, was the United States' objective.

From the ideological standpoint, it was only natural for the Soviets to say that the massive retaliation doctrine indicated a U.S. desire to initiate a nuclear war with the Soviet Union and that the United States was therefore engaging in deception regarding its allegedly defensive intentions. Since massive retaliation suggested a defensive posture within the context of a "grand strategy" of containment,[8] this ran counter to the Soviet claim that U.S. "imperialism" was "inherently aggressive" and was the "source of all wars." Assuming that the Soviets were not inclined to fly in the face of ideological principle, they had no real alternative as far as their public declarations were concerned. Either they had to claim that the United States was lying about its defensive intentions, or they would have to concede that "United States imperialism" was not inherently aggressive. This would then have raised the ideologically nettlesome question why an inherently "aggressive" state was adopting a defensive posture vis-à-vis an inherently "peace-loving" state.

The Soviets' public denial of the decisiveness of the factor of surprise had another motivation as well. As noted previously, the Soviets placed a great deal of emphasis themselves on surprise, going so far as to have approved the adoption of a preemptive strike strategy in the May 1955 issue of *Voennaia Mysl'*.[9] Considering the high value the Soviets therefore placed on surprise, their public efforts to discredit a preemptive strike strategy had two likely reasons:

1. The Soviets intended the denial as a deterrence statement of sorts in an attempt to dissuade the United States from reliance on what they perceived as a strategy of surprise attack.
2. The Soviets lacked confidence in their own capabilities for mounting an effective preemptive strike and therefore were not anxious to see the United States adopt such a strategy.

2. U.S. discussions of a preemptive strike strategy meant that the United States was planning a preventive war against the Soviet Union.

The predominant Soviet propaganda line was that the United States was actually planning to undertake a preventive war against the Soviet Union. This was a distortion of the admittedly fine line between the two concepts of a preemptive strike and preventive war. A preemptive strike involves attacking an enemy who is about to mount an attack himself. The preemptive strike is thus designed to wrest the strategic initiative from an opponent with whom one is about to be at war in any case. A preventive war, on the other hand, is based more upon longer-range political considerations as opposed to the imminent threat of attack involved in a decision regarding a preemptive strike. A preventive war may be undertaken in order to more easily defeat a perceived long-term enemy while the military balance is still regarded to be preponderantly in one's own favor, thus insuring a less costly victory.

The ideological problem posed for the Soviets by U.S. discussion of a preemptive strike was a significant motivating factor in the public Soviet attribution to the United States of an intent to undertake a preventive war. As explained above, a preemptive strike is made against an enemy who is about to attack, in order to wrest the strategic initiative from him. Such a strategy presumes that the opponent has already made a political decision in favor of declaring war, thus making a preemptive strike a defensive measure forced upon one out of sheer necessity. For the Soviets to have publicly conceded any necessity for the United States to adopt such a strategy would have been tantamount to admitting the possibility of their initiating war. The Soviets denied this possibility, since it was contradictory to the allegedly peace-loving nature of their social system and, consequently, contradictory to their foreign policy and strategic doctrine. Moreover, if the United States were only planning to employ a preemptive strike strategy—and not for the sake of preventive war—and the Soviets *were* basically peaceful, then there was actually no threat of U.S. aggression, since the Soviets alone controlled the trigger cause for war. For ideological reasons, then, it was necessary for the Soviets to equate *publicly* the alleged U.S. concepts of preemptive strike and preventive war as no different from each other to all intents and purposes. As shown below, however, the Soviets well understood the difference between the two concepts, even while using them interchangeably in describing U.S. intentions.

In the following excerpt from an article from an April 1958 issue of *Krasnaya Zvezda (Red Star)*, the terms "preemptive blow" and "preventive war" were used in such a manner as to blur the distinction between them. Yet it can be seen from the passages below that the author himself knew the difference:

> The ideas of preventive war, *and the dealing of a pre-emptive blow as a means of attack and of unleashing war,* are incompatible with socialist ideology. These ideas do not correspond to the interests of the Soviet people who are building communism.

> ....But the Soviet Union has never threatened anyone with *an attack, "preventive war," or dealing a pre-emptive blow.* Always, beginning with the first days of the existence of the Soviet Union, the leaders of the Communist Party and of our state have said that, in the event of an attack upon us, an immediate retaliatory blow will be dealt to the aggressor.

> Naturally, the idea of dealing a retaliatory blow *does not mean conducting only defensive actions.* If any aggressor tried to make an attack upon us, *the Soviet armed forces would conduct the most resolute aggressive action upon him.*[10]
> (Emphasis added.)

The last paragraph is especially significant, since the Soviets publicly denied that a preemptive strike was part of their doctrine in the event of war. The wording of the last paragraph was such that it implied that the Soviets would not wait for an attack to be accomplished but would instead "conduct the most resolute aggressive action." This, of course, was the very essence of the so-called preemptive blow the Soviets denied they planned to use.

The most noteworthy example of Soviet distortion of the distinction between preemptive blow and preventive war appeared in the December 1960 issue of *International Affairs* (Moscow). The authors used Bernard Brodie's book *Strategy in the Missile Age* as the documentation for their arguments:

> It goes without saying that the advocates of a "preventive" war, or, *what is in effect the same thing, a "pre-emptive" nuclear attack on the Soviet Union,* do not, as a rule, venture to make public their cannibalistic views. Brodie writes that "those in favour have had grounds for considering it impolitic to express their views too publicly, especially if they happened to be in the public service."[11] [Emphasis added.]

In the footnote of their citation of Brodie, the authors also explained that "the advocates of a 'preventive' war *often try to disguise it as a 'pre-emptive' one,* i.e., a war in which the aggressor strikes the first blow *when he 'becomes convinced' that the other side is preparing to attack.*"[12] (Emphasis added.) It is clear, therefore, that the Soviets recognized the difference between a preemptive strike and a preventive war.

3. *The development of the Soviet ICBM negated U.S. strategic superiority. The implication was that the Soviet Union now had at least parity, and that the United States would be unable to avoid significant destruction in a nuclear war with the Soviet Union.*

The record of Soviet ICBM claims has already been well documented elsewhere; therefore, an extensive reiteration of Soviet claims is not altogether necessary.[13] The purpose of the claims was to cast doubt in the minds of U.S. readers about the strategic superiority of the United States over the Soviet Union. The Soviets argued that because of the arrival of the ICBM, neither participant in a future war "can now avoid the destructive force of an adversary possessing these weapons."[14] This argument was used as part of a declaratory deterrence effort against the U.S. strategy of using Western European bases as launchpoints for its medium-range bombers, contending the U.S. strategy "is obviously premised on the assumption that the main retaliatory blow will be delivered against the bases in Europe, not against U.S. territory."[15]

Soviet propagandists also capitalized on the debate in the U.S. over the merits and disadvantages of the massive retaliation doctrine. One of the reasons the Soviets cited for the debate was the alleged shift in technological superiority in favor of the Soviet Union:

> In recent years the American press has given increasing space to the views of those who claim that the strategic conception of so-called "massive retaliation" . . . and related building of military bases abroad no longer conform to the new political and strategic situation. Moreover, they have pointed out that the main factor which brought about this changed situation was the collapse of the myth of the technical superiority of the United States over the Soviet Union. Now the question is no longer whether the United States has fallen behind the Soviet Union in technical achievement, but how big the lag is.[16]

The Soviet strategic bluff reached its zenith by the beginning of the 1960s, typified by such claims as the one in an issue of *International Affairs* (Moscow), which asserted that "the Soviet Armed Forces possesses all modern weapons, including a whole range of ballistic missiles; intercontinental and intermediate range, short range and large number of tactical missiles." Of course, these were claimed to have the capability "for striking a crushing retaliatory blow at the aggressor."[17]

Not only were Soviet ICBM claims intended to mislead the U.S. about the actual level of strategic forces in the Soviet Union, but also the Soviets were attempting to undermine the credibility of the U.S. deterrent by asserting that the ICBM had rendered U.S. bombers obsolete. Since the United States "had now lost any superiority with regard to means of delivery," the problem thus posed for the United States to regain its superiority or invulnerability was not going to be solved by simply catching up with the Soviet Union in numbers of missiles. Therefore, argued one analyst, "the assurances of many American authors that the 'problem' will be solved when the United States overtakes the Soviet Union in rocketry and matches it in strategic striking power, are meaningless."[18] This was an attempt to dissuade the United States from undertaking any attempt to gain strategic superiority in missiles by publicly downgrading the value of such superiority.

4. *The Soviets claimed that they had sufficient forces to inflict a "crippling blow" on the United States, regardless of which side struck first.*

The Soviet claim that a kind of "mutual deterrence" existed between the United States and the Soviet Union grew out of their ICBM claims. Their line of argument was that since the Soviet Union possessed a capability for inflicting a crippling retaliatory strike regardless of whether the United States struck first, war was no longer a viable option for the United States, at least in the sense of an all-out nuclear war. According to one Soviet analyst, this was so because the United States no longer possesed the clear supremacy said by such U.S. analysts as Henry Kissinger to be required for victory in a nuclear war:[19]

> Henry Kissinger, the notorious American theoretician of nuclear war, supposes that the concept of "total retaliation," which is the main element of the entire "atomic age strategy," can be considered "reasonable" only while the United States possesses clear supremacy in the event of unlimited war. But if the United States does not have that clear supremacy, then is it possible to talk of any "equalization" or "balance"? After all, the basic consequence of the radical change in the world strategic situation which followed the advent of the rocket age lies in the tilting of the scales—and not to the advantage of the United States.[20]

The implication of this was that *any* change in the perceived strategic balance against the United States negated the kind of superiority required to make a massive retaliation strategy credible. This led to the argument that U.S. strategic doctrine had been based on an incorrect estimation of the so-called correlation of forces between the United States and the "socialist camp," but especially the Soviet Union. It will be shown in this chapter, however, that the Soviets had been stressing relative military factors such as the Soviet development of an ICBM capability as having played a leading role in "forcing" the United States to consider modifying its doctrinal stance. Thus, while there were certainly other factors that the Soviets considered in the calculus of the correlation of forces, it will become evident that the Soviets assigned (and continue to assign) a leading role to military power in such a calculation, particularly strategic nuclear power.[21] Also, as pointed out earlier, the Soviets were significantly more restrained in the use of their military power during this period than the United States was, which indicates that the Soviet leadership certainly did not believe their own propaganda about the alleged "nonutility" of nuclear superiority.

Soviet propagandists frequently made use of the writings of their own prominent military men in an effort to give their declaratory deterrence statements more credibility. Major General N. Talensky wrote an article in the July 1960 issue of *International Affairs* that combined elements of the "real" Soviet view with deterrence propaganda:

> . . . . Rocket and nuclear weapons, or rather Soviet superiority in this field, strategically deflates one of the keystones of American military policy—the system of aggressive military blocs and military bases associated with it. United States territory has ceased to be invulnerable. America's military economic and political centers are no longer beyond reach. Moreover, the strategy of modern and total nuclear and rocket war would make them the first and principal objectives in the event of hostilities. Should the U.S.A. start another war, no amount of blocs or bases would be able to save it. *Neither would preventive war or sudden attack. The stocks of rocket missiles, their distribution and method of use are now such that the side subjected to a surprise attack would always be left with sufficient means of dealing the aggressor a mortal blow.*[22] [Emphasis added.]

It is highly questionable, however, in view of the number of ICBMs estimated to have been deployed by the Soviet Union at that time (35 ICBMs as compared to 18 for the United States),[23] that the author seriously believed his own claim of mutual deterrence, especially considering the relative preponderance of U.S. strategic air power. Rather, the statement was designed to take advantage of apparent U.S. uncertainty over Soviet ICBM strength.[24] It is still more questionable when one remembers that Soviet strategic doctrine was and is based on the execution of a preemptive nuclear strike and not, as was publicly claimed, on a retaliatory second strike.

The effect of the Soviet declaratory deterrence strategy was twofold and mutually reinforcing. The first effect was to help undermine the credibility of U.S. deterrence by creating an inflated picture of Soviet strategic capabilities vis-à-vis the United States. Conversely, the other effect of Soviet declaratory deterrence was to enhance the deterrence capability of Soviet strategic power by publicly discrediting the massive retaliation doctrine.

The Actual Soviet View of Massive Retaliation

The actual Soviet view of massive retaliation can be derived from a combination of Soviet hindsight analyses from later periods and Soviet mirror-imaging of their own strategic concepts onto U.S. strategic doctrine, as well as from a comparison of Soviet evaluations against declared U.S. doctrine to determine their degree of accuracy. The Soviet perception consisted of four main themes, as detailed below.

1. *Massive retaliation envisaged preparation for only one type of war against the Soviet Union: a total nuclear war. As part of this preparation, the United States was relying chiefly on strategic air power while its European and Asian allies were supplying the troops.*

This first theme of Soviet perception was essentially accurate.[25] Given the U.S. desire during this period to achieve maximum deterrence at minimum cost, and that the New Look policy of the Eisenhower administration did not give the U.S. military establishment the kind of power projection capability that would have been required with a more flexible doctrine, it is difficult to dispute the validity of this Soviet perception. Although one could argue that the later statements by Dulles were moves away from a pure massive retaliation doctrine,[26] the emphasis of U.S. military programs proved that the original concept of massive retaliation was the one that dominated U.S. defense policy.[27]

The Soviets were also accurate in observing that the U.S. was placing its chief reliance on strategic air power while relying on its allies to provide the bulk of the troops. In the August 1956 issue of *International Affairs* (Moscow), there appeared a professional assessment of massive retaliation by Colonel A. Konenenko, author of several analyses of U.S. military strategy. He described U.S. strategy as patterned after the theories of Douhet, an Italian military theorist who argued that air power would be the all-decisive arm in a future major war. Konenenko asserted that future U.S. strategy would concentrate on the civilian population centers, with particular importance being attached to "suddenness of action by the strategic air force."[28]

Quoting then SAC commander General Curtis LeMay from *US News & World Report*, Konenenko cited the main tasks of the strategic air force as: (1) to win the battle in the air in the initial stage of war by destroying the enemy's vitally important centers, air bases, atomic plants, and air and ground striking forces; (2) total and systematic destruction of the enemy's industry and the sources of his economic strength through coordinated attacks on targets chosen in advance; (3) readiness to support the ground forces in the theater of operations.[29]

Konenenko also took note of the controversy of the "doctrinal differences" between the U.S. Army and the Air Force in their approach to future strategy:

> They [American military leaders] publish proposals for cutting down the ground forces considerably, on the assumption that the future war will be short and that it will be fought by the United States chiefly with aircraft and atomic weapons. According to this view, the tactical use of atomic weapons should enable relatively small forces to cope with tasks which formerly had to be assigned only to big land armies. The proponents of this view hold that it is sufficient for the United States to have small mobile ground forces chiefly for exercising police functions in occupied enemy territories.[30]

On the other hand, Konenenko perceived two arguments being used by the Army in defense of maintaining large ground forces. For the military aspect of the argument, he cited General Ridgway's opinion that "armies are an essential element in our ability to conduct global war successfully, regardless of whether or not atomic and hydrogen bombs are used. The importance of the Army's role in geographically limited wars is equally clear."[31]

However, according to Konenenko, the U.S. Army was also considering the political value of keeping American ground forces stationed in Europe and Asia:

> Ridgway and other American generals are against reduction of land armies also for political reasons, in view of the situation in European and Asian countries where the people are resolutely opposing war. Ridgway emphasizes the police functions of American troops in allied countries. . . . Morale of the U.S. allies in Europe, for example, is said to depend largely on the presence of American divisions, as concrete evidence that the U.S.A. is firmly committed to defense of that area. In Asian countries . . . it is . . . still more important to keep big American ground forces in constant combat preparedness for fighting the national-liberation movement.[32]

Konenenko concluded that the Air Force view had won out, since the emphasis of the military programs of the Eisenhower administration "is paying attention principally to aviation," particularly to strategic air power. This argument, incidentally, was corroborated in various earlier issues of *Voennaia Mysl'* as well as other Soviet sources. The idea of the United States "fighting with other people's hands" has been a long-held Soviet view; hence, Konenenko's reiteration of it was not surprising. The Soviet leadership must privately have thought that the United States had a good idea, considering the extent to which the Soviets make use of Cuban and East European "proxy troops" at the present time, now that the strategic balance is much more in the Soviets' favor. The emphasis on air power was seen by Konenenko as "the cardinal objective and is based on the wide use of atomic and thermonuclear weapons, which is fully in line with the demands of Dulles' 'new policy.' "[33]

2. *Massive retaliation assumed that the United States would be relatively invulnerable to any sort of retaliatory strike by the Soviet Union and that the United States possessed superior delivery capability.*

At least before the development of the Soviet ICBM in 1957, it appears, the Soviets had tacitly conceded this sort of relative invulnerability. For example, one Soviet general, on the pretext of attacking U.S. overseas bases as "offensive springboards," implied such U.S. invulnerability in a March 1955 issue of *New Times*:

> The aggressive elements in the United States calculated—and largely do now—on being able to deliver a massive atomic attack on the vital centres of the Soviet Union and other peaceable countries. They believed, moveover, that the United States would be relatively invulnerable to retaliation. The imperialist strategists are not in the least perturbed by the generally recognized vulnerability of their satellites in Western Europe and other areas where the United States has military bases.[34]

Since the author did not attempt to refute U.S. invulnerability by claiming a Soviet retaliatory capability against the United States but instead implied Soviet retaliation against Western European bases, it is apparent that the Soviets were admitting their own inability at that time to retaliate effectively against U.S. territory. (The mainstay of the Soviet bomber force in 1955 was the TU-4, which possessed a range of no more than 2,000 miles and thus could not have reached most of the continental United States.)[35]

Even the later Soviet claims about the effects of ICBM development on U.S. doctrine admitted that the United States had been invulnerable from their point of view. It was stated in the November 1965 issue of *Soviet Military Review* that "the Soviet Union's achievements in creating powerful nuclear weapons and intercontinental and other missiles reduced to naught America's quondam 'invulnerability,' bringing about the utter collapse . . . of the 'strategy of massive retaliation.' ''[36] The same admission was also made by Soko-lovskiy in *Voennaia Strategia*, conceding that "previously the United States could, with almost complete immunity, threaten the unrestrained use of nuclear weapons in any incident, even in local military conflicts which might possibly arise." In retrospect as well as at the time, therefore, the Soviets clearly recognized U.S. immunity prior to their development of the ICBM.[37]

Much the same sort of validity can be attributed to the Soviet contention regarding the U.S. assumption of superior delivery capability. Soviet analysts had argued that the development of the Soviet ICBM meant that the United States "had now lost any superiority with regard to means of delivery," which of course implied that the United States had been superior prior to that time.[38] The authors of *Voennaia Strategia* also stated as much in their argument that the United States "was assuming that the countries of the socialist camp would not dare to take this step [i.e., initiate a nuclear war] because of their unfavorable position with respect to offensive nuclear forces."[39]

3. *The strategy of massive retaliation placed a significant emphasis on surprise, particularly in light of U.S. discussions of a preemptive strike strategy.*

In chapter 3 it was demonstrated that the Soviets themselves had significantly upgraded their own estimation of the value of surprise, proof of which was their endorsement of a preemptive strategy in the May 1955 issue of *Voennaia Mysl'* :

> Modern wars begin as a rule by surprise. The role of surprise in war as a whole, in the strategic and operational dimensions, has grown especially with the appearance of weapons of mass destruction. This obligates the armed forces to many things. The matter is not only to understand the significance of the factor of surprise in its entirety, to study the facts and examples of the use of surprise in the past wars. The task consists in a serious study of all sides of this question and above all in working out the ways and means of preventing surprise attack by the enemy and inflicting on the opponent pre-emptive blows in all dimensions—strategic, operational, and tactical.[40]

The same article concluded that "the duty of the Soviet armed forces is not to permit an enemy surprise attack on our country" by the use against him of a surprise "pre-emptive blow."[41] This suggests that the Soviets believed U.S. doctrine to be based on a surprise first strike. Indeed, the massive retaliation doctrine was apparently alluded to in the following passage:

> The military figures of the United States and Britain openly declare that they intend to open war against us by means of surprise strategic blows with atomic and hydrogen weapons on the vitally important targets deep in the rear of the countries of the camp of peace and democracy, calculating in a few days to knock out the basic industrial targets, to paralyze transport, to demoralize the

population. The American-British strategists suppose that, utilizing these weapons, they can defeat the enemy as a result of an initial strike, and seize the initiative in the war.[42]

It was further contended that ''surprise attack is a favorite means of the aggressor for unleashing war and proceeds from the very nature of the imperialist states.''[43] But ''surprise attack'' as embodied in the concept of the preemptive blow had become an accepted part of *Soviet* military strategy. One can only conclude that the Soviets were projecting their own strategic thinking onto the United States.

Furthermore, since the discussion and acceptance of a preemptive strategy took place in *Voennaia Mysl'*, a restricted journal not intended for foreign dissemination, it is clear that the Soviets did not want to admit publicly that they had adopted such a strategy. The most obvious reason was that since the Soviets believed U.S. doctrine to have been founded on surprise attack they may have feared that admitting such a strategy on their part might have provoked the United States into a first strike. One should also consider that the Soviets probably had little confidence in their ability to execute a preemptive strike because of their unreliable intercontinental capability at the time.

Although the Soviets did not publicly admit to a preemptive strategy except in the most oblique terms, they did publicly express their view that U.S. doctrine was in fact based on similar considerations. An example of this is found in the March 1957 issue of *Mirovaia Ekonomika i Mezhdunarodnaye Otnosheniia* (hereafter referred to as *MEMO*):

> A future war, in their opinion, appears to be of short duration, yet exceptionally destructive. The outcome of it will be decided with the aid of aviation and guided jet missiles, and yet even so, large scale land forces will be brought into action. The land forces and military-naval fleets should only consolidate successes attained as a result of the activities of strategic aviation.
>
> Proceeding from this, American propagandists of the air war theory draw the following conclusion: the military-air forces, particularly strategic aviation and atomic weapons, will play the decisive role at the outbreak of war; *for in order to win in contemporary war, it is necessary to deal a first surprise attack and to take the initiative in one's own hands.*[44] [Emphasis added]

A further indication of the value placed by the Soviets on surprise was an article in the August 1958 issue of *International Affairs* by Major General N. Talensky. In it he stated that ''surprise attack as a factor giving great advantage to those who employ it, making it possible in many cases to compensate in some degree for an unfavourable correlation of other factors determining the outcome of war, will always be very tempting to the aggressors.''[45] The implication was that considerable advantage is entailed in the use of a surprise attack, no matter which side decides to use it. If great advantages could be had by the side judged to be inferior in the overall correlation of forces, how much more advantageous might such an attack be for the side in whose favor the correlation of forces was allegedly shifting? Thus it is evident, both from Soviet pronouncements in their own doctrine as well as from their assessments of the alleged emphasis on surprise in U.S. strategic doctrine, that the Soviets were mirror-imaging their own concepts of surprise and the preemptive strike onto U.S. doctrine. As will be shown in subsequent chapters, this mirror-imaging tendency has significant implications for U.S. doctrinal planning.

4. *The development of the Soviet ICBM undermined the basis of the massive retaliation doctrine by rendering the United States vulnerable to a Soviet retaliatory strike. Once the United States realized that it was no longer invulnerable to a Soviet retaliatory strike, it was forced to adopt a different doctrine.*

The Soviets could find support for this contention among U.S. analysts, since U.S. vulnerability was being admitted by Bernard Brodie and Henry Kissinger in their respective analyses of massive retaliation at this time.[46] Not only did Soviet analysts regard Soviet ICBM deployment as a decisive factor at the time, but they still regarded it as such later on, claiming that "the achievement of superiority by the Soviet Union over the imperialist aggressors in the might of nuclear ammunition and the possibility of the inexorable and accurate delivery of them to the designated target forced the military and political leadership of the imperialist states to openly recognize the need to 'reassess values.'"[47]

The Soviets were quick to exploit their launching of an ICBM in August 1957. Indeed, for the next four years, the Soviets would engage in a very successful exercise in "strategic bluffing," convincing most U.S. observers that they were proceeding with ICBM production and deployment at a rate far greater than was actually the case. Khrushchev, in his public statements, found it useful to suggest two apparently contradictory theses: that the Soviets were rapidly acquiring a force capable of destroying the United States, and that they would take steps to acquire such a force if U.S. behavior did not become less hostile.[48] Ultimately however, the Soviet leaders must have regretted their reliance on such a bluff for so long, since it resulted only in a redoubled U.S. ICBM effort in the early 1960s, which produced a larger, if temporary, margin of U.S. strategic superiority than before.

Typical of Soviet statements contending that the Soviet ICBM capability was forcing the United States to reconsider its strategic doctrine was an article in the January 1960 issue of *International Affairs* that correctly observed that the United States had lost the near-absolute invulnerability to nuclear attack upon which the massive retaliation doctrine had been based:

The program and aims of the United States remained unchanged even after it had lost its nuclear monopoly. The American rulers thought that, having the bombs and also the "near-absolute power of delivery," the United States would for a long time retain decisive predominance in this field, as well as a *monopoly of invulnerability* and hence "freedom of action" in time and space. This was an illusion. American military authorities now have to acknowledge that the "atomic age strategy" is in a state of deep crisis.[49] [Emphasis in original]

The implication of this Soviet perception is quite critical since it represented a means by which the Soviets could exert influence on U.S. strategic doctrine without having to rely on anything not under Soviet control. In later Soviet analyses, this was to be regarded as a major qualitative shift in the overall "correlation of forces" between the United States and the Soviet Union.

Conclusions

The main thing that ought to be remembered concerning this period of the Soviet perception of U.S. strategic doctrine is that the Soviet views of the utility of strategic power were formulated during this period and eventually became the basis for later Soviet versions of a nuclear warfighting doctrine. The Soviets perceived themselves as restrained by U.S. nuclear superiority during this period, although they only admitted this publicly in retrospect. They also saw a great deal of similarity between U.S. strategic doctrine and their own, which also contributed significantly to the inhibition of the use of Soviet military power. With the exception of the Soviet suppression of the Hungarian revolution in 1956, the Soviet use of military power during the period of the massive retaliation doctrine was confined to threats and military manuevers (see Appendix B).

At this particular stage of U.S. strategic doctrine, it is difficult to see the significant effect that U.S. doctrine and strategic power was eventually to have on Soviet military programs. This will become increasingly evident, however, in later chapters. Once the United States began to formulate strategic concepts advocating more "limited" uses of military power, however, Soviet analysts were confronted with a new problem, as will be seen.

Notes

1. R. Bonds, ed., *The Soviet War Machine* (New York: Chartwell, 1976), pp. 86, 105.
2. Ibid., pp. 86, 106. This opinion is shared by Wolfe in *Soviet Power and Europe, 1945-1970*, pp. 178-184.

3. Examples of such behavior are given in Garthoff, *Soviet Military Policy: A Historical Analysis*, pp. 110-130. Also Horelick and Rush, *Strategic Power and Soviet Foreign Policy*, pp. 105-156.

4. See Horelick and Rush, *Strategic Power*, pp. 30-31.

5. F.D. Kohler et al., *Soviet Strategy for the Seventies: From Cold War to Peaceful Coexistence* (Coral Gables, Fla.: Center for Advanced International Studies, 1973), pp. 32-38.

6. Ibid., p. 39.

7. F. Isayev, "Fallacies of the Policy of Strength," *New Times*, No. 10, March 1955, p. 9.

8. X(G. Kennan), "The Sources of Soviet Conduct," *Foreign Affairs*, Vol. 25, No. 4, July 1947, pp. 566-582.

9. Garthoff, *Soviet Strategy in the Nuclear Age*, p. 85.

10. V. Kurasov, "On the Question of the Preemptive Blow," *Krasnaia Zvezda*, April 27, 1958, trans. H.S. Dinerstein (Santa Monica, Calif.: RAND, T-87, May 12, 1958).

11. L. Gromov and V. Strigachov, "The Arms Race: Dangers and Consequences," *International Affairs*, No. 12, December 1960, p. 15. Brodie did not help matters by referring to "preemptive strike" as merely a variation of "preventive war," which is incorrect. As pointed out in the text, the motivational emphasis for the two strategies is different. See Brodie, *Strategy in the Missile Age*, pp. 241-242.

12. Gromov and Strigachov, "The Arms Race," p. 15.

13. Horelick and Rush, *Strategic Power*, pp. 35-102.

14. N. Talensky, "Military Strategy and Foreign Policy," *International Affairs*, No. 3, March 1958, p. 27.

15. M. Mil'shtein, "Bases and Security," *New Times*, No. 6, February 1958, p. 6.

16. B. Teplinksy, "Military Bases and American Strategic Doctrine," *International Affairs*, No. 9, September 1959, p. 84.

17. Ibid., p. 85.

18. I. Yermashov, "The Crisis of American 'Atomic Age Strategy,'" *International Affairs*, No. 1, January 1960, p. 54.

19. H. Kissinger, *Nuclear Weapons and Foreign Policy*, pp. 106-07.

20. Yermashov, "The Crisis of American 'Atomic Age Strategy,'" p. 53.

21. See M. Harvey, L. Gouré, and V. Prokofieff, *Science and Technology as an Instrument of Soviet Policy* (Coral Gables, Fla.: Center for Advanced International Studies, 1972), pp. 4-5. See also M. Deane, *The Soviet Concept of the "Correlation of Forces"* (Arlington, Va.: Stanford Research Institute, Strategic Studies Center, 1976).

22. N. Talensky, "The Military Aspect of Co-existence," *International Affairs*, No. 7, July 1960, pp. 65-66.

23. Bonds, *Soviet War Machine*, p. 210. For examples of the widely varying public estimates of the strategic balance at the time, see E. Bottome, *The Missile Gap*, pp. 227-228.

24. This was the opinion of Horelick and Rush about another article of a similar nature by Talensky. See *Strategic Power*, p. 80.

25. The following sources contained virtually identical analyses: R. Simonyan, "Doctrine of the American Aggressors," *Soviet Military Review*, No. 1, January 1969, p. 50; V.V. Glazov, "The Evolution of U.S. Military Doctrine," *Soviet Military Review*, No. 11, November 1965, p. 56; I. Potapov, "The Evolution of

the Strategic Concepts of Imperialism in the Postwar Priod," *Voenno-Istoricheskii Zhurnal*, No. 5, May 1971, p. 57; S. Konstantinov, "The Military Doctrine of American Imperialism," V.D. Sokolovskiy, *Soviet Military Strategy*, trans. and ed. H.F. Scott (New York: Crane, Russak, 1975), p. 54.

26. Bottome, *Missile Gap*, p. 25.
27. Brodie, *Strategy in the Missile Age*, p. 249.
28. A. Konenenko, "U.S. Military Doctrines," *International Affairs*, No. 9, September 1956, p. 63.
29. Ibid.
30. Ibid., pp. 64-65.
31. Ibid., p. 65.
32. Ibid.
33. Ibid., p. 66. Konenenko reiterated these same views in more detail in his later book entitled *Atomnoe Oruzhie v Voennykh Planakh SShA (Atomic Weapons in the Military Plans of the USA)* (Moscow: Voennoe Izdatelstvo, 1957), pp. 18-70.
34. F. Isayev, "Fallacies of the Policies of Strength," *New Times*, No. 10, March 1955, p. 4.
35. Sokolovskiy, *Soviet Military Strategy*, pp. 56-57.
36. Bottome, *Missile Gap*, p. 222.
37. Glazov, "U.S. Military Doctrine," p. 56.
38. Yermashov, "Atomic Age Strategy," p. 54.
39. Sokolovskiy, *Soviet Military Strategy*, p. 54.
40. "World-wide Historic Victory of the Soviet People," *Voennaia Mysl'*, No. 5, May 1955, pp. 12-13. Trans. J.R. Thomas (Santa Monica, Calif.: RAND, T-110, 1959), p. 25. Khrushchev, in retrospect, admitted early Soviet weakness in the mid-1950s in Pravda, August 12, 1961. Quoted in Horelick and Rush, *Strategic Power*, p. 30.
41. P. Rotmistrov, "On the Role of Surprise in Contemporary War," *Voennaia Mysl'*, No. 2, February 1955, p. 14. Quoted in Dinerstein, *War and the Soviet Union*, p. 187.
42. Ibid., p. 19. Quoted in Garthoff, *Soviet Strategy*, p. 120.
43. Ibid.
44. M. Mil'shtein and A. Slobodenko, "The Aggressive and Adventuristic Character of US Strategic Concepts," *MEMO*, No. 3, March 1957, p. 80. Translation by L. Gouré, *Some Soviet Views on Air Strategy* (Santa Monica, Calif.: RAND, T-84, April 3, 1958). See also A. Horelick, *Some Soviet Views on the Nature of a Future War and the Factors Determining Its Course and Outcome* (Santa Monica, Calif.: RAND, T-97, September 15, 1958).
45. N. Talensky, "Prevention of a Surprise Attack," *International Affairs*, No. 8, August 1958, p. 54.
46. Kissinger, *Nuclear Weapons*, pp. 41-42. Also Brodie, *Strategy in the Missile Age*, pp. 261-263.
47. N.A. Lomov, ed., *Scientific-Technical Progress and the Revolution in Military Affairs*, trans. U.S. Air Force (Washington, D.C.: U.S. Government Printing Office, 1973), p. 253. See also Sokolovskiy, *Soviet Military Strategy*, pp. 56-57; V. Larionov, "The Development of Armed Means and Strategic Concepts of the USA," *MEMO*, No. 6, June 1966, p. 75.
48. See Horelick and Rush, *Strategic Power*, pp. 42-81, for a chronological account of Soviet ICBM claims and the corresponding U.S. reaction to them.
49. Yermashov, "Atomic Age Strategy," p. 48.

4.
Limited War: Can "U.S. Imperialism" Restrain Itself?

As suggested in the title for this chapter, Soviet analysts initially had difficulty with the implications of the U.S. concept of "limited war" enunciated in 1957 by then secretary of state Dulles. The image of an inherently aggressive capitalist state publicly announcing its intentions to limit its own uses of military power in support of foreign policy objectives must have seemed contradictory to the Soviet leadership, not to mention highly suspicious. As will be seen, however, Soviet commentators resolved the apparent contradiction in a way that was entirely compatible with the Soviet strategic mindset.

The lessons to be drawn from the Soviet interpretation of limited war are several. The first is that the Soviets perceived limited war as a necessary concession to the qualitative and quantitative growth of Soviet strategic power. Once U.S. "invulnerability" to nuclear attack had been clearly compromised by the development of the Soviet ICBM, the idea of "limiting" conflict was seen by the Soviets as a necessary adjustment for the United States in order to improve the credibility of U.S. deterrence. Khrushchev was so convinced of the decisiveness of the shift in relative strategic power that he felt confident enough to rely principally on a "minimum deterrence" posture based mainly on Soviet nuclear retaliatory capability as the foundation for an aggressive political strategy against the West.

Another relevant lesson was that the Soviets, Khrushchev in particular, saw little possibility of an actual U.S. initiation of a total war with the Soviet Union, as well as a corresponding U.S. reluctance to escalate to dangerous levels in a crisis situation. The main reason behind such an appraisal was the consistent U.S. failure to react with the degree of military force implied in its doctrines of massive retaliation and limited war to Soviet provocations (in addition to the major instance of Soviet local intervention in Hungary) before the Cuban missile crisis in October 1962. This failure probably contributed as much to the weakening of the credibility of U.S. deterrence against acts of aggression as the actual strengthening of the Soviet strategic deterrent did. In fact, this perception was undoubtedly the predominant influence on Khrushchev's decision to emplace intermediate-range missiles in Cuba in 1962. This explains in large measure the Soviet evaluation of limited war as a lower-risk alternative for the United States.

This was confirmed by the military policy of the Khrushchev regime. With their primarily nuclear emphasis (and correspondingly low flexibility), Soviet military programs reflected a belief in the decisiveness of the nuclear weapon both as a warfighting instrument and as a restraint upon U.S. escalation. As a result of this belief, conventional forces were given a much lower priority. This was demonstrated in Khrushchev's speech to the Supreme Soviet in January 1960, which asserted the primacy of the nuclear weapon over other types of armament in addition to the contention that a future nuclear war would be of short duration. This was used as the rationale for an announced reduction by Khrushchev of the Soviet armed forces from 3.6 to 2.4 million men.[1] The "nuclearization" of Soviet theatre forces in Europe was both a reflection of Khrushchev's new strategic stance and a carry-over from the Stalinist strategy of holding Western Europe "hostage" as a guarantee of U.S. good behavior. In the event of war, Soviet theatre nuclear weapons would have been used in massive retaliation against NATO Europe. In fact, there is no indication, despite the claims of some Western analysts to the contrary, that the nuclear emphasis of Soviet theatre doctrine has been altered.[2]

It should be stressed that the tendency of Soviet analysts to fall into the mirror-imaging fallacy of projecting their own strategic culture and mindset onto the United States was a source of considerable difficulty for them. For example, they placed a great amount of weight on the pronouncements of such academics as Kissinger, Brodie, et al., as well as on statements by U.S. military and political figures, in an attempt to determine true U.S. strategic intentions. These analysts assumed that there was a degree of government control over the U.S. press similar to that in the Soviet Union. Therefore, under this assumption, no opinion or pronouncement on U.S. doctrine would have been published unless it had the backing of some U.S. political figure or government agency. This assumption led to trouble for Soviet analysts then and later, because they were often confronted with a bewildering array of contradictory pronouncements. This being the case, these analysts apparently selected those U.S. pronouncements or analyses that most readily conformed to their own preconceived notions concerning the nature of U.S. strategic doctrine.

From the ideological standpoint, the U.S. limited war concept must have seemed peculiar. From the standpoint of a revolutionary state bent upon permanent alteration of the international status quo in its favor, it was difficult to comprehend that its principal adversary actually intended to limit itself regarding the use of force in a future war. Most Soviet analysts would probably have expected the United States to take its struggle with the Soviet Union with all the seriousness it deserved and therefore to see things in the same "rational" manner as they did. Their projection onto U.S. doctrine of their own strategic concepts such as the value of surprise in a nuclear war was illustrative of such an attitude.[3] Given this kind of thinking, the logical conclusion for Soviet analysts to draw without contradicting their own ideology was that the limited war strategy was a forced development brought about by the growth of Soviet strategic power perceived by the U.S. leadership.

The Soviet Propaganda Line

As in the case of the massive retaliation doctrine, Soviet declaratory deterrence efforts were aimed at discrediting the U.S. limited war strategy by casting doubt in the minds of the U.S. leadership about the likely Soviet reaction to a limited use of military power by the United States, particularly if the United States contemplated using tactical nuclear weapons in a "limited" nuclear war in Europe.

1. *It is impossible to use nuclear weapons on a limited tactical scale because of their highly destructive nature.*

Major General N. Talensky, writing in January 1955 against NATO's then recently announced "trip-wire" strategy involving the use of tactical nuclear weapons, argued that the very nature of nuclear weapons militated against the likelihood of their being used on a tactical scale. He claimed this even though the Soviets were pushing early for their own tactical nuclear weapons,[4] thus causing one to doubt the general's sincerity:

> Atomic weapons, on the other hand, by the very nature of their combat properties, are designed, above all, for action against big economic and political centres, against big cities, against the civilian population. An atomic bomb, an atomic rocket or an atomic shell can be of little efficacy against troops, operating in present-day, highly dispersed battle order, which are able to take cover in specially equipped trenches and shelters built by modern engineering methods in a relatively short time. In any case, such weapons are much less effective when used against troops in the field than against cities and economic centres, that is, ultimately against the civilian population.[5]

The statement that nuclear weapons are designed only for use against "economic and political centers" was aimed not only at the United States. Although Talensky was correct at the time because of the high yield and poor accuracy of then so-called tactical weapons, it is likely that he was also directing his criticism at those in the Soviet Union who emphasized the role of nuclear weapons on the battlefield and tended to view a future war in terms of a nuclear exchange. Since his article was written in January 1955, well before the Soviet enunciation of its preemptive strike strategy in the May 1955 issue of

Voennaia Mysl', and years before Khrushchev's endorsement of the decisive role of the nuclear weapon in his January 1960 speech to the Supreme Soviet, there was still apparently room for criticism. It was Khrushchev who was to come around to the views of those being criticized by Talensky in his subsequent efforts to "nuclearize" Soviet European theatre forces while cutting back sharply on manpower.[6] Even so, for purposes of declaratory deterrence the Soviets made statements designed to dissuade the United States from relying on tactical nuclear weapons. An example of this is an article by Major General Isayev in the March 1955 issue of *New Times*:

> That tactical atomic weapons—or "small atomic weapons," as the NATO politicians and strategists also call them—would be used on a small scale is hardly likely because *that would be inexpedient from the purely military and tactical standpoint. Small-scale tactical tasks can be achieved no less successfully with conventional weapons*. Hence, what the Pentagon strategists have in mind is the employment of "tactical" atomic weapons on a *massive* scale, and in that case, no matter what name they are given, remain weapons of mass destruction.[7] [Emphasis added]

The above statement is interesting because it represented a counterpoint of sorts to the statement made by Talensky. The idea of massive use of theatre nuclear weapons was later to become a central theme in Soviet theatre doctrinal writings, particularly Colonel Sidorenko's 1972 work, *The Offensive*. As the Soviets acquired their own tactical nuclear weapons, however, this theme of Soviet declaratory deterrence receded in prominence.

2. *The use of nuclear weapons in a limited war may escalate into their use on a strategic scale.*

This theme of Soviet declaratory deterrence has been stated ever since NATO introduced tactical nuclear weapons into its arsenal in the mid-1950s and is still a prominent theme of Soviet propaganda, as evidenced by the recent Soviet reaction to President Reagan's remarks concerning the feasibility of a "limited nuclear war" in Europe.[8] One of the earliest statements of this type was Major General Talensky's implication of escalation to a "total" war in the event of the use of tactical nuclear weapons in Europe:

> The present development of the means of atomic attack makes it possible to strike powerful blows across oceans as well. Consequently, the American atom-maniacs have no grounds for considering that if they precipitate atomic war, the territory of the United States will remain invulnerable. In a war against a strong adversary, it is impossible in our days to count on striking blows at the enemy without being subjected to his counter-blows, which might be even of greater impact.[9]

Thus the Soviets claimed that the United States could not escape some form of retaliatory blow against its territory in the event of U.S. first use of nuclear weapons, *whether on a strategic scale or on a tactical scale*. The likelihood was greater, however, given the comparatively poor Soviet delivery capabilities in 1955 vis-à-vis the United States, that the Soviets were more wary of the latter possibility's being chosen by the United States in the event of a war in Europe and so were hoping to create as much uncertainty in the minds of U.S. decision makers as possible.[10]

Soviet declaratory deterrence statements concerning the possible U.S. initiation of limited nuclear wars were often ambiguous, and deliberately so. For example, one military analyst contended that "there can be no guarantee that the use of 'tactical' atomic weapons will not lead to the use of 'strategic' nuclear weapons. On the contrary, use of 'tactical' nuclear weapons would *greatly increase* the likelihood of the use of 'strategic' nuclear weapons."[11] (Emphasis added.) It is interesting to note that while the author quite correctly claimed that one cannot guarantee that escalation from the "tactical" level use of nuclear weapons to the "strategic" level would not occur, he by no means was saying that such escalation was inevitable. Aside from the deterrence of U.S. limited nuclear wars against the "socialist camp," the Soviets would not have wanted the United States to know with any degree of certainty that it had a limited nuclear war option to exercise in the event of local Soviet aggression.[12]

The Soviet claims about the dangers of escalation to strategic nuclear war were also an attempt to dissuade the United States either from initiating limited wars for the suppression of so-called wars of national liberation or from preparing to defend against Soviet-initiated local wars.[13] By introducing such uncertainty into U.S. calculations about the possibility that a limited war might escalate to unacceptably dangerous levels, the Soviets were undoubtedly hoping to prevent the United States from engaging in such wars at all. On the other hand, the Soviets would not have wanted to state that such escalation to total war was absolutely inevitable. For if the Soviets closed off the option of limitations, the United States would be faced with the choice of either taking no action or immediately resorting to general war. Given U.S. discussions at the time about the merits of a preemptive strike and the known level of U.S. strategic capabilities,[14] the Soviets were probably willing to leave well enough alone. It is a direct reflection of the profoundly altered strategic balance in favor of the Soviet Union that Soviet pronouncements using the threat of escalation to strategic nuclear war are far less ambiguous now than they were during the mid-to-late 1950s.[15]

A variation on this theme was the assertion that the "coalitional" nature of local wars made their escalation into total war all the more likely. The reasoning was that since there existed several military blocs with binding treaty obligations, if any member of such a bloc should initiate a war then it was possible to bring in the entire bloc to participate. Thus, it was claimed that "in this way an armed conflict can rapidly expand to dangerous size."[16] The falsity of this argument is in its assumption that Western alliances were designed for an offensive war rather than as collective defense organizations. This was a case of distortion for the sake of propaganda, since the Soviets could not publicly attribute defensive intentions to any U.S.-supported military alliance without admitting the possibility that a "peace-loving" socialist state might be the initiator of a war against such organizations.

The most prominent example of Soviet declaratory deterrence using the threat of uncontrolled escalation was Khrushchev's speech to the Supreme Soviet on January 14, 1960. By dismissing limited wars as "nonsense," but not "wars of national liberation," Khrushchev sought to create the impression that any military involvement against the communist countries or their clients would develop into a world war:[17]

> If a war were to start now, hostilities would take a different course since the nations would have means of delivering their weapons to points thousands of kilometers away. It is first of all deep in the belligerent's territory that a war would start. Furthermore, there would not be a single capital, no large industrial or administrative center, and no strategic area left unattacked in the very first minutes let alone days, of the war. In other words, the war would start in a different manner, if at all, and would proceed in a different manner.[18]

Khrushchev seemed to have been placing primary emphasis on a posture of minimum deterrence, relying heavily upon the image, if not the reality, of Soviet retaliatory power as the basis for an aggressive political strategy. Khrushchev assumed that the U.S. reluctance to escalate was great enough that he could pursue an aggressive diplomatic strategy without worrying about his bluff's being called. If it ever was, he apparently had confidence in his ability to control the ensuing risk of war. Khrushchev's error was in thinking that the Western "threshold of concession" was low enough that it could be overcome without producing situations that carried an unacceptable risk of escalation to all-out war.[19]

3. *The United States is using limited conventional wars as a preparation for unleashing a total nuclear war against the Soviet Union.*

This assertion was included along with otherwise quite valid observations such as U.S. use of limited wars against the "national liberation movement," contending that "the theory of 'local' war is a mask designed to conceal the preparations for total war and to justify the use of nuclear weapons in the struggle against the peoples who have unfurled the banner of national liberation."[20] In other words, the Soviets claimed that the concept of a limited war was camouflage designed to conceal preparation for a total nuclear war and that any so-called limited war that occurred was merely a potential pretext for escalation to all-out war. Although the Soviets realized that the lack of credibility of massive retaliation made limited war a safer means of enforcing the containment strategy for the United States, ideological constraints prevented the Soviets from making public speculation on this point. Indeed, given their assertion that the United States represented a social system that was immutably and inherently hostile and aggressive towards socialism, they could do little publicly other than assert that the U.S. limited war doctrine was really designed to conceal preparations for an all-out war.

It is noteworthy that Soviet analysts tended to qualify their statements regarding this theme with the phrase "should [or "if"] the aggressors succeed in unleashing war." This implied that there were restraining factors at work at the time that prevented the United States from following its "natural" inclination to initiate an all-out conflict against the socialist states. The development of the Soviet ICBM capability was pointed to as being one of the main constraints on U.S. freedom of action, since contemporary war could now "bring fearful destruction to both sides." It was further asserted that "a thermonuclear blow can shatter the faith of a people in the economy, government, and national aim."[21] It is difficult to believe, however, that the Soviets actually trusted their own statements of this type, given the fact that Soviet strategic capabilities were exceedingly limited with respect to the United States, even in 1958, when the Soviet ICBM was being deployed. For comparison, the U.S. strategic force at that time possessed over an estimated 2,150 strategic bombers capable of delivering megaton-range weapons to the Soviet Union. Of these, 250 were B-52s, with the remainder being 1,800 B-47s and less than 100 B-58s. The Soviets, on the other hand, had a force of slightly over 1,000 Bisons and Badgers with a capability of reaching the periphery of the United States only by one-way missions. Even by 1960, the United States had at least a 3-to-1 advantage in long-range bombers. The first Soviet operational ICBM was deployed in numbers that were virtually negligible (only 10 operational SS-6s by late 1959).[22] Nevertheless, it was argued by such Soviet analysts as Talensky that the United States and its allies could not easily resort to all-out war, despite their alleged wishes to do so:

> Such statements are fully justified, for Kissinger admits that thermo-nuclear war will lead to the collapse of the social system of Western Europe. This circumstance, plus the desire to conceal from the public, which is working for peace, the preparations for an all-out struggle for world dominion, explain the advocacy of the "local war" theory.
>
> But this cannot deceive anyone, because the strategy of "local war" serves also foreign policy aims connected with the struggle for world dominion. A head-on attack in this case is replaced by a system of manoeuvring [sic] with "local" wars, behind which looms the shadow of nuclear war.[23]

It is revealing of the Soviets' real lack of confidence in their intercontinental capability that Talensky claimed that a thermonuclear war would be disastrous for Western Europe but omitted mentioning the United States.

A similar argument was that the United States, restrained by "the forces of peace," had been successfully restricted to the use of limited wars. At the same time, because of the allegedly aggressive nature of imperialism, the United States was nevertheless continuing to make preparations for war, whether limited or total. This usually accompanied the accurate recognition of the United States attempting to find a more realistic approach to its strategic deterrence/warfighting doctrine. The resulting line was that the supposedly aggressive nature of imperialism carried with it the perpetual threat of war. This line has persisted to the present day.[24]

Aside from the propaganda value of this third theme, there was some strategic value in it as well. The only circumstances under which a limited war could not be possible were if (1) either the Soviets themselves launched an all-out thermonuclear attack (in which case the Soviets would already have decided against limitation of the conflict) or (2) the United States itself launched such an attack (in which case the United States would not have been serious about the idea of limitations anyway).[25] By contending that the United States was using limited war as a smokescreen to conceal preparations for a general war, the Soviets could thus argue that such limitations could not reasonably be expected to hold up in actual practice.

Even in such propagandistic statements, however, there were indications that the Soviets were hedging in their public statements concerning U.S. use of limited war as a prelude to total war. An example of this is given below:

> The "limited" war concept has attracted the Pentagon directors because, in their view, it enables them to prepare for total war through a series of small wars, with *ample time for logistical preparation of a "major blow"*.[26] [Emphasis added]

These authors were clearly assuming a U.S. policy of *deliberate and controlled escalation*, rather than a surprise attack to initiate a total war. The passage further implied that the necessary logistical preparation would not be fully prepared in advance of the conflict. This indicates that the Soviets were well aware that the U.S. would not be initiating local "aggression" in most cases, but rather it would be the Soviet Union sponsoring its clients in "wars of national liberation."

The most important point is that the Soviets publicly claimed that the United States would be controlled and deliberate in its preparations for unleashing a total war by means of limited wars, even though (as shown in the preceding chapter) the Soviets ascribed to U.S. strategic doctrine a similar appraisal of the value of surprise. Such being the case, if Soviet analysts assumed a U.S. policy of deliberate and controlled escalation as inherent in limited war strategy, *thus reducing the degree of surprise*, it would not have made sense to Soviet analysts for the United States to so negate surprise unless there were no U.S. intent to start a total war in the first place. This proves that this third theme of Soviet declaratory deterrence was pure propaganda, since it did not agree with their mirror-imaged view of U.S. strategic doctrine.

The Soviets obliquely admitted as much in the following passage from the August 1958 issue of *MEMO*. The author camouflaged his recognition that the United States had no intention to start a nuclear war by claiming that the United States had admitted the "impossibility" of destroying the Soviet Union in such a war:

> Thus, the doctrine of "limited war" originates from the calculations on the possibility of the successful conduct of "local wars" against the nations of the socialist camp. *It is interesting that the starting point of this concept appears to be the realistic recognition of the impossibility of destroying the camp of socialism with the aid of a total nuclear war.* Yet is in this case the doctrine of "limited war" realistic, which also has its own prerequisite suppositions about the "superiority" of the western nations over the USSR in military-technological relations? Today such calculations appear to be incorrect even among influential circles in the west.[27] [Emphasis added]

However, Soviet commentators still had to deal with the fact that Korea had not escalated as they had claimed it should have; indeed, the United States had taken pains to keep the war from going beyond the Korean peninsula by not attacking the Chinese mainland with U.S. airpower. Nor did the United States ever introduce tactical nuclear weapons into the battle, although Truman had, it is said, briefly toyed with the idea. The Indochinese conflict was still at a comparatively low level of U.S. involvement, the French only recently having exited the scene following their debacle at Dien Bien Phu in 1954. In order to explain such conflicts, the standard Soviet line was that it had been "the forces of peace" that restrained the United States from escalating these wars into a total war. This claim was clearly false, since if the Soviets had really believed that these conflicts could have led to an all-out war with the United States, they would never have encouraged them:

> But aggressive tendencies are organically inherent in imperialism. Recent history has repeatedly borne out this Leninist precept. However, the objective possibilities of putting their aggressive plans into effect are slipping away from the imperialists owing to the new balance of forces. In 1950, for example, the imperialists were still able to keep up the aggression in Korea, but already unable to turn it into a world war in spite of the fact that America's atomic monopoly was then only just breached. Three or four years later the forces of peace were strong enough to compel the imperialists to accept a cease-fire in Korea and Indochina, and to give up their plan of involving new states and peoples in armed conflicts.[28]

Despite the especially great amount of propagandistic rhetoric and "disinformation" that accompanied Soviet analyses and commentaries on the U.S. limited war concept, it is still possible to discern the actual Soviet perception of the limited war strategy by a variety of means, which will now be discussed.

The Actual Soviet View

One of the best means of checking the actual Soviet evaluation of limited war was the course of Soviet foreign policy during the years of the Khrushchev regime. The failure of the United States to make the Hungarian Revolution of 1956 a *casus belli* may have contributed heavily to Khrushchev's belief that the likelihood of U.S. initiation of nuclear war against the Soviet Union had greatly declined. There were also subsequent situations in which the Soviets "baited" the United States with missile threats. Examples were the Turkish-Syrian tensions in October 1957, the Quemoy Straits crisis from August to September 1958, the Soviet exertion of diplomatic pressure against Berlin from 1958 to 1961, and, of course, the Cuban missile crisis of October 1962.[29] After each of these provocations, with the exception of the Cuban missile crisis, the lack of an especially strong U.S. response undoubtedly helped to convince Khrushchev that he was operating within safe limits and that Soviet deterrence was effective against the possibility of threatening U.S. escalation. On the other hand, it should be noted that with the aforementioned exception of Indochina there were no overtly Soviet-sponsored "wars of national liberation," which would have put U.S. limited war doctrine to a decisive test.[30] In any event, Khrushchev was apparently not deterred from provocative actions, even if he was deterred from actual aggression, by either the massive retaliation or limited war strategies of the United States.

During the entire span of Soviet analysis of the limited war concept, two predominant themes have emerged as the most consistent. These are discussed below.

1. *The U.S. doctrine of limited war represents a U.S. search for a more credible strategic doctrine as a forced result of the qualitative shift in the strategic balance in favor of the Soviet Union. The United States hopes to avoid Soviet nuclear retaliation through the use of limited wars.*

One of the first Soviet analysts to discuss the U.S. rationale behind its limited war doctrine on a serious level was N. Inozemtsev, a political analyst for *MEMO* who was later to become the head of the Institute of World Economics and International Relations (IMEMO) in July 1966.[31] In his March 1958 article in *MEMO*, he described the massive retaliation doctrine as essentially a "subjective idea; a relative conception of force based upon US interpretation of its own superiority in the area of thermonuclear weapons.'' According to Inozemtsev, the growth of Soviet nuclear potential in combination with the improved capability of the Soviet Union to deliver such weapons had caused U.S. "ruling circles" not to dare "to unleash atomic war."[32] Given these circumstances, he described how U.S. leadership resolved the impasse:

> What was the way out? A rejection of the policy "from positions of strength" and "atomic diplomacy," of plans which had gone bankrupt, bound together by the groundless calculations of the "atomic superiority" of the USA? Nothing of the sort happened! The solution was merely a few variations and additions to the "massive retaliation" doctrine. This was done by means of setting forth in the years 1956-1957 the concepts of so-called "graduated restraint" ("graduated deterrence") and "local," "limited," wars.[33]

Inozemtsev did not claim that graduated deterrence was a fundamentally new departure in U.S. doctrine, arguing instead that it was simply a derivation of massive retaliation:

> The concept of "graduated restraint" is no less aggressive than all previous atomic concepts. It has the same basis as that of "massive retaliation": the rejection of the prohibition of thermonuclear weapons, the orientation towards atomic war. Kissinger admits this, declaring that "limited war" and the "gradual application of force" present themselves "not as an alternative, but a supplement to massive retaliation."[34]

In other words, the U.S. was attempting to increase its options by the expedient of changing its strategic doctrine to meet the needs of an altered power balance, or correlation of forces. It was natural, therefore, for the Soviets to have recognized this attempt and make use of declaratory deterrence statements in an effort to discredit the new concept.

One of the most controversial defense issues during the late 1950s was the publication of the Rockefeller and Gaither reports (or at least, in the case of the classified Gaither report, the accepted version of the report that was leaked to the public). The Gaither and Rockefeller reports were the results of classified and unclassified studies, respectively, that were made in late 1957 concerning virtually every aspect of U.S. defense policy. Although initially appointed by Eisenhower for the purpose of investigating the future role of civil defense in U.S. defense policy, the Gaither committee (which was to receive far more publicity than the unclassified and less pessimistic Rockefeller Report) carried its investigation further than had been originally envisioned. Although the report remained classified, leaks of the contents of the report from various persons led to the emergence of a widely accepted version of its findings over a period of several months.

The greatest single impact of the Gaither Report was on the missile debate.

The committee claimed that the Strategic Air Command (SAC) would be vulnerable to a major attack from a large projected Soviet ICBM force by the early 1960s. It called for additional military spending on missile sites once the U.S. developed an operational ICBM.[35]

The Rockefeller and Gaither reports were regarded as especially significant by the Soviets. One analyst, in the July 1958 issue of *MEMO*, claimed that the United States was moving toward a more flexible strategic doctrine, because "inasmuch as the risk, connected with the delivery of an aggressive nuclear blow on the USSR has become too dangerous, the Rockefeller group is recommending using a more flexible strategy." Ergo, this meant that U.S. doctrine had actually changed under the primary impetus of the growth of Soviet strategic power.[36] This view was more explicitly stated by Colonel A. Konenenko in the July 1958 issue of *International Affairs*:

> It is not for nothing that American publications of all kinds are paying more attention to the idea of "limited," "local" and "little" wars, trying even to create the impression that a major world war can be replaced by a series of "little" wars, thus preventing military operations from touching American soil. . . . The fear that the capitalist system would collapse as a result of a total nuclear war is the main reason for the interest in "little" wars. Henry A. Kissinger, the American military writer, writes in his *Nuclear Weapons and Foreign Policy* that "the fear that an all-out thermonuclear war might lead to the disintegration of the social structure offers an opportunity to set limits to both war and diplomacy."[37]

Konenenko reiterated this theme in the October 1958 issue of *MEMO*, claiming that "at the present time, political, military-economic and strategic centers on U.S. territory can come under retaliatory strikes of nuclear and rocket weapons of those nations which they are attacking in the event of American aggression."[38] This opinion was similar to one expressed in an earlier issue of *MEMO*, in which the authors asserted that "bourgeois ideologists" did not want to take into account the "new correlation of forces between the two systems" and therefore were making use of "limited" wars.[39] Both articles stressed the emergence of changes in the military balance which had *forced* the United States to consider changes in its strategic doctrine. The earlier article recognized, however, that the United States did not accept Soviet claims implying changes in the correlation of forces.

This theme was repeated during the 1960s as well.[40] The most authoritative source for this theme, however, was found in an article in the July 1969 issue of *Voennaia Mysl'*, in which the characteristics of limited wars were analyzed:

> The imperialists count mainly in these wars on the use of conventional means of destruction. True, in certain conditions they also permit the use of tactical nuclear weapons. However, before utilizing them, they must think a great deal

about the possible consequences. In any case, the idea of achieving the goals in local wars by such means and methods which would not engender retaliatory nuclear strikes against the territory of the aggressor himself constitutes the most attractive idea for the monopolists.[41]

It is clear, therefore, that the Soviets were quite genuine in their perception of "limited" war as a forced accommodation by the United States to increased relative Soviet strategic power in addition to its being a "lower-risk" approach.

2. *The United States is employing limited war as a means of suppressing the "national-liberation movement," thereby attempting to enforce its overall strategy of containment.*

The accuracy of this Soviet theme of perception is based on the fact that it was merely a recognition of the defensively oriented "grand strategy" of the United States, given the name "containment" by George Kennan, former U.S. ambassador to the Soviet Union, in his well-known article outlining the containment strategy and its rationale in the July 1947 issue of *Foreign Affairs*.[42] One of the initial statements of this line was made in an October 1958 issue of *New Times*, in which the authors tacitly recognized limited war as an instrument of the overall strategy of containment:

> Believers in "limited" war suggest concentration on the achievement of partial aims, such as suppression of the national-liberation movement and bolstering of reactionary regimes, as a prelude to total war.[43]

Further corroboration was found in an October 1958 issue of *MEMO*. The author asserted that the U.S. espousal of a limited war doctrine meant that "they are attempting to galvanize the adventuristic policy 'from positions of strength,' consolidate the loosened system of colonialism, and to prolong the world support for the old discredited path of 'cold war.'"[44]

Soviet observers, therefore, did not perceive any U.S. willingness to restrain its own behavior, or even to remain so once such constraints had been placed upon it. Once U.S. invulnerability had been lost with the development of Soviet intercontinental capability, it seemed logical to the Soviets that the United States would do everything it could to restore the credibility of U.S. strategic doctrine. Such was the view of one Soviet political analyst, who observed that the advocates of local war believed that "it restores the geographical factor—that it guarantees the United States invulnerability from without while keeping intact the possibility of waging war abroad, in Europe, Asia, and Africa."[45]

As with the other theme of Soviet perceptions on limited war this notion of limited war as an instrument of the containment strategy was echoed in more authoritative Soviet journals in later years. And again, the premier example can be found in the July 1969 issue of the classified Soviet general staff publication *Voennaia Mysl'* :

> They [local wars] are usually unleashed and conducted by the imperialist states for the purpose of suppressing the national-liberation movement of the peoples or overthrowing the governments in a particular country liberated from colonial oppression which are unsuitable to the main imperialist powers, as well as seizing the important economic and strategic territories.[46]

Public Soviet statements were fully in consonance with that expressed above, charging that limited war was designed "as a means of gradually 'shattering' socialism, suppressing the national-liberation movement, and thereby shoring up the positions of capitalism."[47] Thus, it is clear that Soviet pronouncements were consistent and accurate in their recognition of the defensive objectives of the limited war concept, even though such recognition was camouflaged by a great amount of propagandistic rhetoric as part of the Soviet declaratory deterrence strategy.

Conclusions

What effect did U.S. strategic doctrine have upon Soviet doctrine and policy development during the massive retaliation period (1954-1960)? When one looks at the content of Khrushchev's speech in January 1960 and the military programs that preceded and followed that speech, one would have to say that Khrushchev, at least, was impressed enough by the potential decisiveness of nuclear weapons as a deterrent to have placed significant reliance on his own version of massive retaliation.

The demise of Khrushchev's minimum deterrence posture came with the denouement of the Cuban missile crisis in October 1962. The lesson of that publicly humiliating confrontation was forcefully driven home to the subsequent Soviet leadership under Brezhnev: In a confrontation situation, perceived strategic superiority in favor of one of the protagonists exerts a decisive influence on the outcome and enhances the use of other forms of military power to achieve political objectives. This explains the rapid strategic buildup following the accession of the Brezhnev regime to power in October 1964, in addition to an across-the-board increase in conventional forces, especially naval forces. Khrushchev's version of the Soviet nuclear warfighting doctrine had been discredited by the Cuban missile crisis; as will be seen in subsequent chapters the U.S. doctrine of flexible response was to play its role in influencing Soviet doctrine and programs. It is the Soviet perspective concerning flexible response that we will examine next.

Notes

1. T. Wolfe, *Soviet Power and Europe, 1945-1970* (Baltimore: John Hopkins, 1970), pp. 144-145.
2. See Joseph D. Douglass, Jr., *The Soviet Theater Nuclear Offensive* (Washington, D.C.: U.S. Air Force, 1975), pp. 101-107.
3. See ch. 3.
4. Wolfe, *Soviet Power*, p. 195.
5. N. Talensky, "Atomic and Conventional Arms," *International Affairs*, No. 1, January 1955, p. 26.
6. Wolfe, *Soviet Power*, pp. 160-184. See also F. Isayev, "The Small Atomic Weapons Myth," *New Times*, No. 13, March 1955, p. 7.
7. Ibid.
8. The reader is referred to issues of the *New York Times* in late November 1981 for documentation on the official Soviet reaction to President Reagan's remarks on the feasibility of limited nuclear war in Europe.
9. Talensky, "Atomic and Conventional Arms," p. 29.
10. Garthoff, *Soviet Strategy in the Nuclear Age*, p. 110.
11. Isayev, "Weapons Myth," p. 8.
12. Garthoff, *Soviet Strategy*, p. 110.
13. M. Mil'shtein and A. Slobodenko, "The Aggressive and Adventuristic Character of US Strategic Concepts," *MEMO*, No. 3, March 1957, p. 77. See also the book wirtten by these same authors at the end of the "massive retaliation" period, *O Burzhuaznoi Voennoi Nauke (Concerning Bourgeois Military Science)* (Moscow: Voennoe Izdatelstvo, 1961), pp. 303-320. See also Garthoff, *Soviet Strategy*, p. 111.
14. See ch. 2.
15. See n. 8.
16. V. Mochalov and V. Dashichev, "The Smoke Screen of the American Imperialists," *Krasnaia Zvezda*, December 17, 1957. Trans. L. Gouré, *Soviet Commentary on the Doctrine of Limited Nuclear Wars* (Santa Monica, Calif.: RAND, T-82, 5 March 1958), p. 8.
17. See the analysis of Khrushchev's speech by H.S. Dinerstein in *Soviet Strategic Ideas: January 1960* (Santa Monica, Calif.: RAND, RM-2532, February 19, 1960), pp. 27-28.
18. See H.F. Scott, *Soviet Military Doctrine: Its Continuity, 1960-1970* (Menlo Park, Calif.: Stanford Research Institute, SSC-TN-8974-28, 17 June 1971), p. 78, for a translation of Khrushchev's speech.
19. Bonds, *Soviet War Machine*, p. 206. See also Wolfe, *Soviet Power*, p. 89; Horelick and Rush, *Strategic Power and Soviet Foreign Policy* (Chicago: University of Chicago Press, 1966), p. 115.
20. N. Talensky, "Military Strategy and Foreign Policy," *International Affairs*, No. 3, March 1958, p. 28.
21. Ibid., p. 29.
22. Bottome, *Missile Gap*, pp. 223-224. See also Bonds, *Soviet War Machine*, pp. 207, 212; Bonds, ed., *The US War Machine* (New York: Crown, 1978), p. 60, for the estimated number of operational B-58s; O. Penkovskiy, *The Penkovskiy Papers*, trans. P. Deriabin (New York: Doubleday, 1965), pp. 320-335; Wolfe, *Soviet Power*, p. 180.
23. Talensky, "Military Strategy," p. 29.

24. L. Dikin, "problems of US Military Policy and Strategy in the Reports of the Rockefeller and Gaither Committees," *MEMO*, No. 7, July 1958, pp. 100-101, passim.
25. Garthoff, *Soviet Strategy*, p. 111.
26. M. Mil'shtein and A. Slobodenko, " 'Limited War': Weapon of Unlimited Aggression," *New Times*, No. 40, October 1958, p. 14.
27. O. Bogdanov, "Nuclear Weapons and the Problem of World Security," *MEMO*, No. 8, August 1958, p. 9.
28. L. Fyodorov, "International Relations and the Battle of Ideologies," *International Affairs*, No. 3, March 1960, pp. 9-10.

29. Wolfe, *Soviet Power*, pp. 88-89. See also Horelick and Rush, *Strategic Power*, pp. 105-141.
30. Wolfe, *Soviet Power*, pp. 88-89.
31. *Directory of Soviet Officials, Volume I: National Organizations* (Washington, D.C.: National Foreign Assessment Center, CR 78-14025, 1978), p. 381.
32. N. Inozemtsev, "US 'Atomic Diplomacy': Plans and Activities," *MEMO*, No. 3, March 1958, p. 38. See also V. Korzun, "Strategy of Aggression," *KVS*, No. 3, February 1967, p. 91, for a later corroboration.
33. Inozemtsev, "Atomic Diplomacy," p. 38.
34. Ibid., p. 39.
35. See Bottome, *Missile Gap* (Cranbury, N.J.: Associated University Presses, 1971), pp. 44-48.
36. Dikin, "Problems of US Military Policy and Strategy in the Reports of the Rockefeller and Gaither Committees," *MEMO*, No. 7, July 1958, p. 97.

37. A. Konenenko, "Present U.S. Military Thinking and the Arms Drive," *International Affairs*, No. 7, July 1958, p. 35.
38. A. Konenenko, " 'Local Wars' in the Policy and Strategy of the USA," *MEMO*, No. 10, October 1958, pp. 17-18.
39. M. Mil'shtein and A. Slobodenko, "The Problem of the Correlation of Policy and War in Contemporary Imperialist Ideology," *MEMO*, No. 9, September 1958, p. 73.
40. The following references all contain the same corroboration of this theme: Y. Oleshchuk, "Small Wars and the Aggression in Vietnam," *International Affairs*, No. 5, May 1966, pp. 35-36; V. Matsulenko, "The Small War Theory at the Service of the Imperialists," *Soviet Military Review*, No. 4, April 1966, p. 53; P. Zhilin *International Affairs*, No. 10, October 1973, p. 27; T. Kondratkov, "Limited War—Instrument of Imperialist Aggression," *KVS*, No. 8, April 1967, p. 25; B. Teplinsky, "U.S. Military Programme," *International Affairs*, No. 8, August 1967, p. 47; V.D. Sokolovskiy, *Soviet Military Strategy*, trans. and ed. H.F. Scott (New York: Crane, Russak, 1975), p. 64.
41. V. Zemskov, "Characteristic Features of Modern Wars and Possible Methods of Conducting Them," *Voennaia Mysl'*, No. 7, July 1969, trans. Foreign Broadcast Information Service (hereafter FBIS) No. 0022/70, 6 April 1970, p. 25.

42. See X (George Kennan), "The Sources of Soviet Conduct," *Foreign Affairs*, Vol. 25, No. 4, July 1947, pp. 566-582. See also Dikin, "Problems of US Military Policy and Strategy in the Reports of the Rockefeller and Gaither Committees," p. 97.
43. Mil'shtein and Slobodenko, " 'Limited War'—Weapon of Unlimited Aggression," p. 14.

44. A. Konenenko, "Local Wars," pp. 17-18. See also N. Talensky, "On the Character of Modern Warfare," *International Affairs*, No. 10, October 1960, p. 26; Bogdanov, "Nuclear Weapons," p. 10.
45. I. Yermashov, "The Doctrine of 'Acceptable War': Illusions and Reality," *International Affairs*, No. 11, November 1960, p. 17.
46. Zemskov, "Modern Wars," p. 25. See also S. Malyanchilov, "On the nature of Armed Struggle in Local Wars," *Voennaia Mysl'*, No. 11, November 1965, trans. FBIS, No. 953, 8 March 1966, pp. 12.-24.
47. V. Mochalov, "What Lies Behind the Theory of 'Limited Wars'?" *Soviet Military Review*, No. 8, August 1969, p. 54. See also note 40 above.

PART III

FLEXIBLE RESPONSE PERIOD
(1961-1968)

5.
Flexible Response and Soviet Reaction

Did U.S. strategic doctrine ever exert an influence on Soviet military behavior and programs? Up until the fall of Khrushchev in 1964, one could not really answer in the affirmative with any solid evidence. Once the Brezhnev-Kosygin regime was firmly entrenched, however, Soviet military programs were sharply increased across the spectrum of nuclear and conventional capability. As will be shown in this chapter, the Soviet perception of flexible response had much to do with these decisions, as well as with the gradual increase in scale of the Soviet use of military power in support of her foreign policy objectives during the latter half of the 1960s.

There are three main conclusions that can be drawn about the Soviet perception and reaction to the new U.S. strategic doctrine of flexible response. These conclusions were reflected in Soviet foreign policy behavior as well as in Soviet military programs during this period. First of all, the Soviets continued to project their own strategic concepts onto U.S. doctrine during this period. This was a carry-over from massive retaliation, and was primarily manifested in Soviet analyses claiming that the United States was emphasizing surprise and the possibility of delivering a successful preemptive strike on the Soviet Union at the outset of a future war. (This Soviet mirror-imaging tendency became more pronounced, as the following chapter shows.)

Second, the Soviets continued to perceive the evolution of U.S. strategic doctrine as the result of a forced response to the growth of Soviet strategic power. Following the development of the Soviet ICBM, the United States was compelled to come up with a doctrine that would restore the credibility of U.S. deterrence to its former predominance, without having to rely principally on its massive nuclear capability. Moreover, the U.S. abandonment of the flexible response doctrine in 1969 (when the realistic deterrence doctrine was outlined by President Nixon), although due in part to the U.S. failure in Vietnam, was also seen as having been caused by the Soviet attainment of strategic parity with the United States in 1969. This meant, in conjunction with the Soviet development of her capabilities for power projection into more distant areas during this period, that the Soviets felt they now had more freedom to support "national liberation movements" in Third World countries.

Finally, the Soviets were increasingly recognizing the likelihood of waging both nuclear and conventional limited wars without an undue risk of escalation to strategic nuclear war. This was conceded in such publications as *Voennaia Mysl'* and also, though less directly, in publications intended for foreign audiences. The U.S. flexible response doctrine undoubtedly impressed the Soviet leadership with its use of "nuclear superiority" to enhance the use of U.S. conventional forces in opposing the Communist insurgency in Vietnam and convinced them that a similar range of capabilities was desirable for the Soviet Union in order to support her more aggressive foreign policy goals. This was substantiated by Soviet military programs after the accession of the Brezhnev-Kosygin regime to power in 1964, particularly the major efforts devoted to augmenting Soviet airlift and sealift capabilities.

More specifically, the great increase in Soviet naval power and sealift capability improved the Soviet ability to support "national liberation movements" in more distant areas, or to lend logistical support to its allies, such as North Vietnam.[1] The Soviets increased their capabilities for amphibious landings by adding helicopter and landing ships and boosting the size of Soviet marine forces from 6,000 to 12,000 men by 1969.[2]

Soviet airlift capacity was also significantly enlarged, as evidenced by its successful resupply of Nasser's forces after the Arab-Israeli war, followed by smaller-scale airlifts to Yemen later in 1967 and 1968. The trend toward the development of air-landing and assault techniques, already in evidence during the Khrushchev period, was even more pronounced under Brezhnev.[3]

The most dramatic increases, however, came in the area of strategic deployments of land-based intercontinental ballistic missiles and submarine-launched ballistic missiles. If one can assume a lead time of about 18 months, the decision to accelerate the construction and deployment of ICBMs and SLBMs was probably made shortly after Brezhnev and Kosygin came to power. By October 1966 the number of land-based ICBMs reached 340, and a year later the total stood at 720. Soviet ICBM levels passed the U.S. total of 1,054 by September 1968.[4] By 1970, the number of operational Soviet ICBMs had reached 1,300.[5] The number of long-range SLBMs rose dramatically with the deployment of Soviet Y-class submarines comparable to the U.S. Polaris in 1968. By 1970, these missiles numbered roughly 300.[6]

The Soviet policy of peaceful coexistence (later "detente"), as it emerged under the Brezhnev-Kosygin regime, reaffirmed the Soviet intent to avoid thermonuclear war with the United States but nevertheless to unremittingly support "national-liberation movements" in the Third World.[7] This increased scale of the use of Soviet military power in support of her foreign policy objectives was reflected in the presence of Soviet "advisers" in such places as Indonesia and Cuba in 1962, the Middle East during the late 1960s and early

1970s, and in Vietnam during the same period.[8] Although Soviet ground forces were not committed in a direct intervention during the 1960s except for Czechoslovakia (where the Soviets acted in accordance with their sub-sequently declared "Brezhnev Doctrine," which basically stipulated that the Soviet Union would intervene in any socialist nation that it believed was threatened by "counterrevolutionary" forces), the Soviets undoubtedly be-lieved that the risk of confrontation with the United States was being reduced enough to justify their increased support of "national liberation movements" in a more direct way. This behavior will be shown as having stemmed from their perception and evaluation of the U.S. doctrine of flexible response.

The Soviet Propaganda Line

In keeping with the Soviet "disinformation" strategy of declaratory deter-rence, many Soviet statements regarding flexible response were highly propa-gandistic in nature. While some were the same used against massive retalia-tion back in the 1950s, other statements were tailored for use against flexible response.

1. *The ultimate goal of flexible response still remains the unleashing of a total nuclear war against the Soviet Union. Flexible response envisions the use of limited wars as a preparation for unleashing such a war.*

This assertion had, even by the early 1960s, become a standard theme of Soviet propaganda. A statement typical of this kind was in an article by Col-onel General N. Lomov, author of several books and articles on Soviet mili-tary doctrine following the publication of *Military Strategy*. Writing in *Kom-munist Vooruzhennykh Sil* in May 1962, Lomov claimed that the "contem-porary military doctrine of the United States of America" was "an expression of the imperialist policy 'from positions of strength,'" and that "the course of imperialism had not changed."[9] Reflecting Soviet strategic thinking con-cerning the value of surprise, he argued that the basis of U.S. strategy was "the striving for the establishment of world domination, for the unleashing of a world nuclear rocket war *by means of a surprise attack* on the Soviet Union and the other nations of the socialist camp."[10] (Emphasis added.)

Commenting on the limited wars aspect of the flexible response doctrine, Lomov quoted Khrushchev's contention that "small imperialist wars" may (or may not, we might observe) "escalate into a world nuclear war." Lomov maintained that since the United States saw that "a world war may result in the complete collapse of capitalism," the imperialists would attempt to achieve "their aggressive and reactionary goals by means of waging not only world, but also 'limited,' 'local' wars." Thus, he concluded that "a new world war may arise as a result either of a surprise attack on the part of an ag-gressive bloc, or the escalation of a local war." However, Lomov's assertion was contradictory, because starting a strategic nuclear war by escalation from a limited war would have sacrificed the element of surprise, something Soviet analysts thought was as important to U.S. planners as it was to them. This same thinking was reflected in the following passage from the first edition of Marshal Sokolovskiy's *Military Strategy*, published in April 1962:

> They are afraid to take the initiative in unleashing a nuclear war, since this would be disadvantageous from a political standpoint and extremely dangerous from a military standpoint. The whole point of their plans in this regard is to use nuclear weapons in the course of expanding local conflicts, particularly at critical moments, in order to alter the situation (locally) in their favor. They expect to be able to limit the employment of nuclear weapons to their satellites and to defend their own territory, at least at the beginning of the war, from a crushing nuclear blow. This is the essence of their aggressive plans to initiate a new world war, using local wars and conflicts.[11]

The implication of the above was that the United States planned to use limited wars as a disguise for unleashing a nuclear war against the Soviet Union, since an outright nuclear strike was supposedly too dangerous for the United States itself. This, however, made little sense, since the Soviets could still launch a retaliatory strike regardless of whether it was preceded by a limited war. Also, this contradicted the Soviets' earlier perception that the United States placed great emphasis on surprise. Proof of this was Sokolovskiy's discussion within *Military Strategy* of alleged U.S. preparation for a preventive war by means of a "preemptive strike."

The editors of *Military Strategy* also implied that the United States did not intend to refrain from escalation unless the circumstances were unfavorable. This was a nonfalsifiable argument; when the United States failed to escalate a local war by using nuclear weapons, as Soviet propaganda claimed it would, this did not mean that the United States had somehow become more "responsible," but that "the forces of peace" had stopped the United States from further escalation. Soviet military commentators found this line especially useful, since it was a ready-made rationalization for "maintaining vigilance" and for further strengthening Soviet military power. This call for maximum military preparedness is illustrated in the following passage:

> Only the fear of a powerful retaliatory strike will stop the imperialists. Therefore the Soviet Union and all the socialist countries are compelled to have in readiness the necessary forces and weapons for instantaneous retaliation to aggression.[12]

As implied in the above passage, the emphasis of Soviet strategy was still based on a nuclear strike, although the pre-emptive aspect of such a strike was not directly stated. The reason for this emphasis was that Soviet missile deployment was still slow, not being accelerated appreciably until 1966. The stress was therefore on deterrence of U.S. strategic power through such declaratory statements.

2. *It is not possible to establish "rules of the game" for waging limited wars using nuclear or conventional weapons. Every limited war may therefore escalate into a total war.*

This was a continuation of the first theme, namely, that since the United States allegedly intended to unleash a total nuclear war using limited wars, there was constant danger that such wars would escalate into total wars. An example of this was an article in the August 1964 issue of *KVS*:

> All discussions concerning small, limited, and local wars only mask preparation for a total, global war. In the same regard, where is the guarantee that a small war does not escalate into a big one? To the point, the military ideologists of imperialism see such a guarantee in the capacity of the warring states to conduct "limited" along with "unlimited" war.... Consequently, the discussions about a "local" war are being used as a cloak for the preparation for a large thermonuclear war.
>
> Any war, if the imperialists unleash it, has a tendency to escalate into an unlimited war.[13]

An integral part of this propaganda theme was the alleged impossibility of distinguishing neatly between military targets and populated areas in the employment of tactical nuclear weapons, whether in a European war, a strategic exchange, or a local war in the Third World. Nor would Soviet commentators have wanted to admit publicly that both sides would find it advantageous, or even be able, to restrict themselves to the means and areas designated for a limited nuclear war:

> War has its own laws. Its logic forces each side to defeat the other completely. Now the losing side is unlikely to abide by some restrictions. Similarly, the victorious side will try to finish the war as soon as possible. Can ... the Pentagon guarantee that the U.S. generals will, in the heat of the battle, judiciously identify each object as a military or civil target?[14]

In understanding the logic behind this propaganda, one should remember that it was (and still is) a uniquely American strategic concept that increased civilian damage is a primary consideration in determining the escalation of a war. The Soviets realized this and used it in their arguments against U.S. doctrine in an effort to make their statements appear more credible to a Western audience. For their own part, the Soviets never adopted this concept. Instead, it was the political goals of the war in question that determined the level of military force to be employed. Furthermore, such statements were a contradition of the Soviets' own historical experience in conducting wars with limited political objectives. The Soviets had had such experience against Finland in 1939-40 and against the Japanese in Manchuria in 1945, and they are having it at the present time in Afghanistan. In each of these conflicts, the limited nature of the political objectives the Soviets sought (and seek) imposed its own restraints on the level of military force necessary to achieve their political objectives.

3. *The nature of flexible response is essentially no different from that of massive retaliation.*

The claim being made in this instance was that flexible response was merely a continuation of the "positions of strength" policy, using different military means. This was a distortion of the actual Soviet recognition that flexible response represented a U.S. attempt to increase its range of available options to deter the widest possible range of Soviet threats. Elements of this view are illustrated in the following passage from the November 1965 issue of *Soviet Military Review*:

> One feature has been common to all the post-war phases in the evolution of the U.S. military doctrine: a steady expansion of the arsenal of American militarism. Every "new" prevalent conception of war and every new twist in the development of the armed forces have, in accordance with the aggressive "policy of strength," had the purpose of providing such ways and means of prosecuting a war that, in the opinion of the U.S. leaders, would bring imperialism victory over socialism and over the national-liberation and revolutionary movement of the peoples.[15]

4. *The use of military force by the United States is an inappropriate response to the "national-liberation movements" in the Third World.*

This theme was used most often by Soviet commentators in reference to the U.S. intervention in Vietnam. This was correctly perceived by the Soviets as the premier example of flexible response in practice, but one that did not pose a direct threat to the Soviet Union itself or threatened nuclear escalation.[16] But rather than admit such a thing publicly or concede the potential effectiveness of flexible response, they instead claimed that "the doctrine overestimates the U.S. potential and underestimates the strength of the world socialist system and the international Communist, labour, and national-liberation movement."[17]

Moreover, U.S. efforts at counterinsurgency were derided as "absurd" because they ignored "the deep social and economic roots of national-liberation movements. The local wars strategy, therefore, and the operations being mounted on its principles are doomed to failure because the U.S. ruling classes are incapable of correctly assessing the role of these factors supporting the national-liberation struggle, and unable to understand the nature and sociopolitical substance of the struggle.''[18] In view of the difficulty the Soviets have been experiencing in bringing the guerrillas in Afghanistan under complete control, one wonders how the author of this statement would apply his reasoning to that conflict.

The standard Soviet line concerning U.S. involvement in Vietnam was that the United States was using sheer military power to crush what essentially was a guerrilla movement (one supported quite heavily by North Vietnamese regular forces and supplied by the Soviet Union and China). No matter what level of force called for by flexible response was used, the Soviets maintained, it would do no good because armed intervention was an inappropriate response to a ''national-liberation'' war. In reality, however, the Soviet leadership was well aware that sufficient military power could suppress any ''national-liberation movement,'' and in its recent experience had used such power to crush so-called counterrevolutions in Hungary and Czechoslovakia.

The first three themes discussed above were basically carried over from the massive retaliation period, whereas the fourth theme was applied specifically to U.S. involvement in Vietnam. This last theme, however, was additionally intended to deter all U.S. efforts to oppose ''national-liberation movements'' with armed intervention.

The general pattern of the actual Soviet evaluation of flexible response revealed a fairly realistic recognition of its nature and purpose. However, as with massive retaliation, Soviet analysts continued to interpret the precepts of U.S. doctrine within the context of their own strategic mindset.

The Real Soviet View

1. *Flexible response was designed to increase the ability of the United States to suppress the "national-liberation movement." This required a broad buildup of conventional as well as nuclear capabilities, which signified that the United States was becoming more active in opposing the establishment of new communist regimes.*

One of the initial expressions of this notion was in a Soviet radio broadcast in English to Europe on July 26, 1961:

> The aims of the new program in foreign policy announced by Kennedy have nothing in common with the talk about protection of the ''freedom'' of West Berlin, which nobody has been or is threatening. Washington simply needed a pretext for aggravating general international tension, for trying to enhance its role as the gendarme of the ''free'' world. This is factually supported by the *New York Times*, which points out that the new plan is primarily aimed not at the defense of the former German capital, but at increasing the ability of the Western allies to wage any kind of war in any part of the world.
>
> Active opposition to the national liberation movement in Africa, Asia, and Latin

> America is of course what is chiefly meant [i.e., local wars]. Only this can ex-
> plain the words of the President about the need for creating a ''sea and airlift
> capable of moving forces quickly and in large numbers to any part of the
> world.''[19]

The broadcast also claimed that the military program announced by Kennedy in his speech ''was outlined a long time ago'' (possibly in reference to
the proposals made by General Maxwell Taylor in his book *The Uncertain
Trumpet*, although the commentator was not specific), and that the ''long-
term buildup'' of U.S. strength ''has been underway since January'' (of
1961). This illustrates that the Soviets were aware of a fundamental shift in
the U.S. doctrinal stance at this time, even though no formal pronouncement
acknowledging the shift had yet been made.

The Soviets also recognized early that the United States was building up its
conventional capability to cope with Soviet-supported insurgency movements
in Third World countries. This was commented on in *Izvestia* on May 24,
1962.

> The ''grand strategy'' primarily means a further stepping up of the arms race. It
> is openly stated in Washington that it envisages reinforcement of naval and air
> transport facilities, formation of nuclear units in the army which could be
> swiftly transferred to any area where in the opinion of the American military the
> possibility arises for triggering military gambles. The masterminds of this
> ''strategy'' loudly declare that it would be wise for the United States to organize
> for so-called special warfare. This means armed punitive action against peoples
> fighting for or defending their national independence.[20]

The Soviet recognition of the defensive nature of flexible response could be
found even in statements that were otherwise propagandistic. One such statement claimed that ''when the USA has built up its forces to wage limited
wars, it will not stop at armed intervention in the internal affairs of any country whose Government pursues a policy the US imperialists do not like.''[21]
Stripped of its rhetoric, the statement simply meant that the United States
might become more willing in the future to oppose the establishment of new
communist regimes. The statement is also of interest in that it argues that
''power tempts policy,'' a theme that has been in vogue with certain U.S.
analysts in well as Soviet. Briefly, the argument runs that, given increased
capability and power to carry out certain actions, the United States would
therefore be tempted to intervene in instances in which it would not otherwise
have considered doing so. However, even though power might ''tempt'' policy to some degree, it is self-evident that policy cannot be carried out without
power. The argument is therefore simplistic, since it ignores the objectives
and purposes of such intervention.[22]

The genuineness of this particular Soviet perception is reflected in the fact that it has been restated in official declarations of Soviet military doctrine such as the three editions of Sokolovskiy's *Military Strategy*,[23] as well as in publications written after the end of the flexible response period. An example of such confirmation in retrospect was *Scientific-Technical Progress and the Revolution in Military Affairs*, a book in the Soviet Officer's Library series. The author stated that the flexible response strategy "was also aimed at preventing the transition of the peoples in the young developing nations to a path of non-capitalist development, and at restoring the capitalist system in the socialist nations without involving the United States in a catastrophic thermonuclear war."[24] This amounted to a tacit recognition of the inherently defensive nature of flexible response as a means of enforcing the overall grand strategy of containment perceived by the Soviets.

2. *Changes in the strategic balance in favor of the Soviet Union forced the United States to modify its strategic doctrine. The United States was trying to expand its range of options to deal locally with Soviet direct or indirect expansion.*

This theme of Soviet perception was one of the elements of continuity from the massive retaliation period. One analyst, writing in the July 1962 issue of *International Affairs*, saw flexible response as a hybrid strategy combining elements of massive retaliation and limited war:

> The doctrine put forth by Taylor and others who think as he does is a kind of cross-pollination between Massive Retaliation and the theories of limited wars, and is an attempt to strike a balance in the effort to develop all types of armed forces and especially to increase appropriations for ground forces without relaxing attention to rocket, air and naval forces. . . . The description of the "new" doctrine shows that it lays claim to being a synthesis of all earlier Western theories of modern warfare, and proceeds on the false premise that the political and social problems arising in the world today can be solved in favour of imperialism by military methods.[25]

The same analyst also noted that the limited wars aspect of flexible response had been regarded in the United States as a forced expedient for the period in which the United States perceived a mutual "balance of terror" to have existed between the superpowers. Flexible response was "rooted in the change in the relation of forces [a mistranslation; "relation" should instead read "correlation"] and is in effect designed to serve through the period until that balance becomes 'favourable' for U.S. imperialism."[26] The United States then, according to Soviet analysis, not only had been forced to reconsider its doctrine, but had also recognized, if reluctantly, the factors responsible for forcing this change.

One of the most authoritative early analyses of flexible response along this line was made by a regular observer of U.S. doctrinal developments, Major General M. Mil'shtein, in the August 1962 issue of *MEMO*:

> The onset of the third stage of the overall crisis of capitalism showed the funda-
> mental change in the correlation of forces in the world arena, which was accom-
> panied by a sharp weakening of the economic and political positions of Ameri-
> can imperialism. The former military-strategic concepts of the United States
> suffered failure, and American military policy as a whole reached a crisis.
> Under these conditions, not wishing to come to terms with the objective laws of
> history, the ruling circles of the United States are taking a decisive stand on the
> further acceleration of the arms race and new military-strategic concepts, trying
> in this manner to "modernize" nothing more than the method of realizing all of
> that more than once bankrupted policy, "from a position of strength."[27]

Mil'shtein also recognized U.S. efforts to increase its conventional warfare capabilities "as concrete means for realizing one of the basic principles" of the flexible response doctrine, that "of 'raising the threshold' for the conduct of war with the use of conventional means of destruction." He argued that the reason for the "threshold" concept was "the maximum widening of the sphere and possibilities of waging such wars in which the United States could get by without the use of nuclear weapons."[28] He therefore clearly recognized that the United States was trying to make its doctrine more usable for carrying out the aims of U.S. foreign policy, and that the United States was matching its military capability to the requirements of its doctrine. He also saw that the United States was trying to restore the inviolability of U.S. territory and pre-serve a sense of invulnerability.[29]

This theme was confirmed privately in the August 1967 issued of *Voennaia Mysl'*. The author's main argument was that the United States was periodi-cally compelled to modify its strategic doctrine so as to better adjust to changing international conditions:

> The main thing that worries the U.S. imperialists is the alignment of political
> forces in the world arena: the growing power and prestige of the Soviet Union
> and the other socialist countries, the increase in the number of states taking the
> path of socialist development, the shrinking of the system of imperialism, and
> the active struggle of peoples against colonialism and imperialism. Therefore,
> the world gendarme which has military bases on every continent of the world
> and is conducting a struggle for its world supremacy, has to periodically change
> and modernize its aggressive strategic concept, adapting it to the concrete con-
> ditions of the international situation.[30]

This statement confirmed the validity of the viewpoints being expressed in the open Soviet press during this period about the development and nature of U.S. strategic doctrine. The tone of the article concerning the "struggle" of the United States for its "world supremacy" suggested that the Soviets recognized that the U.S. objective was not the destruction of the Soviet Union, but rather the containment of her expansionistic efforts. And the Soviets, of course, gave credit to "objective" changes in the overall balance of forces (i.e, changes the United States had no volitional control over) for producing a situation that, in their view, was lessening the danger of a strategic nuclear war.[31]

The main "objective factor" responsible for forcing change in U.S. strategic doctrine, particularly in compelling the United States to reconsider its flexible response doctrine, was the attainment of strategic parity with the United States in land-based ICBMs in 1969. Such were the words of Major General Simonyan, a prominent Soviet military analyst of the late 1960s and 1970s, in the January 1969 issue of *Soviet Military Review*:

> Although these military plans remain unchanged, the US ruling circles are compelled to modify their military-strategic concepts. From the military-technical point of view, these changes have been and still are decisively influenced by the growing defence potential of the countries belonging to the socialist community, above all the Soviet Union, its indomitable nuclear-missile might, which has basically changed the balance of strategic forces between the United States and the Soviet Union.[32]

3. *The Soviets continued to project their own strategic mindset onto U.S. doctrine.*

Mil'shtein was again the earliest authoritative Soviet analyst to show this mirror-imaging tendency, evaluating the U.S. discussion of "atomic survival" as the precursor of a nuclear war. This strategy was supposedly embodied, according to Mil'shtein, in "the famous pronouncement of Kennedy concerning the 'initiative of the United States in an atomic conflict with the Soviet Union.'" (Kennedy's statement was taken out of context; the reference was probably to an interview in the *Saturday Evening Post* of March 31, 1962, in which President Kennedy implied the threat of a U.S. first strike "under certain circumstances" in which the United States would have "to seize the initiative.")[33]

Even the most prominent Soviet military analysts and writers were not immune to the mirror-imaging tendency, as demonstrated in this passage from Marshal Sokolovskiy's *Military Strategy*:

> In accordance with the above military strategy of the United States and NATO [i.e., flexible response], there has been vast preparation of the imperialist camp, primarily the United States, for various wars against the countries of the socialist camp, primarily for a general nuclear war. Since such a war would entail the tremendous danger of mutual annihilation, the American aggressors exert all effort to assure victory in the event of the unleashing of a war, with the least los-

ses and destruction. They see the possibility of such an outcome of a war and in achieving surprise in the creation of strong and the most combat-ready forces which technically would be considerably superior to the armed forces of the enemy.[34]

The best proof of Soviet mirror imaging however, was in a December 1962 issue of *Kommunist Vooruzhennykh Sil*, the Soviet military theory journal published by the Main Political Administration, the organization through which the CPSU maintains control over the Soviet Armed Forces.[35] The author perceived the United States as striving for a nuclear warfighting doctrine and outlined the alleged U.S. "projections" concerning the nature of a future war. Upon careful examination, these projections are virtually identical to a similar Soviet discussion of a future war in Sokolovskiy's *Military Strategy*:[36]

1. There would be no essential differences between front and rear areas.
2. The first few days of the war would be the period of maximum military activity, and hence of the greatest destruction.
3. The war will be intercontinental as well as being waged on several continents.
4. It will be necessary to have forces in peacetime prepared for such a war.
5. Plans for a future war will be based on the primary employment of forces deployed at the start of the war.[37]

4. *The U.S. buildup of its strategic forces provided a "nuclear umbrella" for the waging of local conflicts.*

This appraisal accurately described the deterrence purposes of U.S. strategic nuclear forces and undoubtedly had a decisive influence, in combination with the results of the Cuban missile crisis, on the Soviet decision to launch a massive buildup of its strategic nuclear forces after 1964. One such analysis along this line was by Candidate of Military Science V. Larionov, a member of the Sokolovskiy study group, in the July 1963 issue of *International Affairs*, not long after the Cuban missile crisis. Noting statements by U.S. generals to the effect that the United States still intended to devote its major efforts to improving its strategic nuclear arsenal, he undoubtedly had the Cuban missile crisis on his mind when he concluded that:

> The U.S. nuclear potential continues to be regarded as an instrument of political blackmail and a means of ensuring freedom of action in a limited war. Even after the "flexible response" doctrine had been approved, the essential aims of U.S. policy in no way changed. The new doctrine merely takes into account the need to act cautiously in the changed conditions, to appraise every foreign policy action in the light of the possibilities of U.S. military strategy and to take a "flexible initiative" in unleashing either a full-scale nuclear war or limited wars.[38]

Soviet commentators did not picture the United States as being effectively restrained from using military power across the entire spectrum of conflict. Although the Soviets correctly understood that the United States was deterred from initiating an all-out nuclear war, they were much less sanguine about their capacity to dissuade the United States from taking action against Soviet-supported "national-liberation movements." The three editions of Sokolovskiy's *Military Strategy* (in 1962, 1963, and 1968) had portrayed a United States with a powerful and still growing military capability. This respect was especially reflected in their description of the U.S. strategic arsenal.[39] It was this superior strategic arsenal, from the Soviet perspective, that enabled the United States to use its conventional military power without fear of the Soviet threat of uncontrolled escalation.[40]

5. *The Soviets increasingly recognized, both publicly and privately, the likelihood of limited wars being waged with both nuclear and conventional weapons without escalation to strategic nuclear war.*

Even as early as the mid-1960s, the Soviets were admitting the possibility of having to conduct limited wars, even with the use of nuclear weapons, without escalation. One such reference was made in *Nedelia* in April of 1965 by a Soviet military analyst. Contending that "the development of the military might of the USSR and the socialist camp has influenced the evolution of the military doctrine of the imperialist countries, particularly the United States," he further argued:

> This is why not only principles of military docrine more flexible in form and contents have emerged in Washington—principles such as the "strategy of flexible reaction" and the "counterforce strategy"—but there are more and more frequent references to a war without nuclear weapons or in which only tactical nuclear means will be used within the framework of "local" and "limited" wars. *Soviet military doctrine does not exclude such wars*, but we are against the use of any nuclear weapons in general and in the talk of the imperialist militarists about tactical nuclear weapons we see only a trick intended somehow to help motivate and help legalize the use of the atom against mankind.[41] [Emphasis added]

This was corroborated in part by Sokolovskiy in the April 1965 issue of *Soviet Military Review*, contending that "the possibility of a relatively protracted war cannot be excluded, particularly a war involving no nuclear weapons, for instance, a local war." Although Sokolovskiy did not speak directly of the possibility of a limited *nuclear* war, he was at least admitting that a conventional local war could be waged without escalation. The prolonged U.S. involvement in Vietnam, just then coming into greater prominence with the commitment of significant numbers of ground troops, was a clear demonstration of this. Furthermore, Sokolovskiy stated that "preparations for a relatively protracted war should not be neglected.''[42] This was an apparent call for the Soviet Union to develop a more flexible military capability similar to what the United States already had.[43]

The most definitive proof, however, could be found (or, rather, *not* found) in the third edition of Sokolovskiy's *Military Strategy*, published in 1968, in which there was a significant omission. The part left out talked about the difficulties involved in keeping a limited war from escalating to strategic nuclear war. This discussion, which had been in the 1962 and 1963 editions, was much in keeping with Khrushchev's practice at the time of denying the possibility of conducting a limited war. Its omission in the 1968 edition seems to have reflected the Brezhnev regime's acceptance of limited war without escalation, coupled with the idea that it was necessary to develop a similar military capability.[44] This was confirmed by an article in the October 1968 issue of *Voennaia Mysl'* by Marshal Sokolovskiy and Major General M. Cherednichenko, in which they discussed various problems of military strategy, including that of being able to conduct a *limited nuclear war*:

> Along with this the possibility is not excluded of wars occurring with the use of conventional weapons, *as well as the limited use of nuclear means in one or several theaters of operations*, or of a relatively protracted nuclear war with the use of capabilities of all types of armed forces. To maintain in peacetime massive armed forces for conventional war, and in the case of escalation, nuclear war, is impossible, and inexpedient primarily for economic reasons. Therefore, it is necessary to develop appropriate plans for mobilization deployment.[45] [Emphasis added]

Thus, even though Soviet commentators would continue to stress that there could be no such thing as a limited nuclear war in their public declaratory deterrence statements, the above passage demonstrates that the Soviets in fact did not believe their own propaganda.

6. *The collapse of the flexible response doctrine was caused by the failure of the United States to achieve decisive results in Vietnam, in combination with the Soviet attainment of strategic parity with the United States.*

When President Nixon proclaimed the Nixon Doctrine shortly after he took office in 1969, the Soviets quickly recognized that U.S. strategic doctrine was undergoing another change. Since Nixon had publicly acknowledged the attainment by the Soviets of strategic nuclear parity with the United States, Soviet analysts were all the more eager to proclaim it as having been a decisive factor:

> US imperialism is finding it more difficult and dangerous to place all its hopes on world nuclear war. The US strategists realise that a head-on armed clash with the USSR would be suicidal for the USA. Understandably enough, all US doctrines for the 1970s are based on the so-called ''nuclear balance'' which, they say, exists today in US-Soviet relations.[46]

This notion was reaffirmed more explicitly by G. Trofimenko, a prominent Soviet analyst of U.S. strategic doctrine during the 1970s, in an article in *International Affairs* written well after the demise of flexible response (October 1975):

> To sum it up, the balance of world forces had further shifted in socialism's favour by the early 1970s as evidenced, for example, by the attainment of Soviet-American nuclear and missile parity and the awareness by the USA of its limited possibilities to influence diverse events in the world by means of military forces. This made the US ruling class start a "reappraisal of values" and acknowledge the need to reconcile the reality of competition between the two systems with the imperative of coexistence.[47]

Although the Soviets also called the war in Vietnam a major factor in the demise of flexible response, it was not given the repeated emphasis that the attainment of strategic nuclear parity was given, which was an accurate indicator of what the Soviets thought was the stronger influence on U.S. doctrinal development. G. Arbatov, a prominent observer of U.S. docrinal developments during the 1970s and up to the present time, claimed that "the war in Vietnam showed that military might alone can no longer bring the United States victory not only in the struggle against the "main" enemy, but also on the periphery."[48]

The Effect of Flexible Response

The Soviet response to the U.S. doctrine of flexible response during this period unmistakably reflected a strong Soviet conviction that qualitative and quantitative improvements in Soviet strategic power yielded substantial political returns. This belief was directly reflected in Soviet usage of military power during the latter half of the 1960s, the period when Soviet ICBM levels were increasing the fastest. Whereas the Soviet leadership under Khrushchev in the 1950s and early 1960s felt sufficiently restrained by U.S. strategic superiority to have used only threats and military maneuvers for the most part, the scale of Soviet military support was gradually increased during the 1960s to include logistical efforts in support of her Vietnamese and Arab allies. The greater degree of freedom for the United States to use its military power under cover of its nuclear umbrella was an object lesson that was not lost on either the Soviet military or the political leadership.

Despite the Soviet perception that the restraints on the use of her own military power were being steadily weakened, Soviet analysts were always wary of new U.S. strategic concepts, examining them from the standpoint of their usefulness in a warfighting strategy. Soviet analysts read their own thinking into all such concepts, even though certain concepts such as assured destruction were obviously not designed for warfighting from the U.S. viewpoint.

The Soviet perception of the ideas set forth by McNamara in the 1960s had important implications for future U.S. doctrine, which will be examined in the next chapter.

Notes

1. T. Wolfe, *Soviet Power and Europe, 1945-1970* (Baltimore: Johns Hopkins, 1970), pp. 442-447.
2. Ibid., p. 450.
3. Ibid., pp. 448-449.
4. Ibid., pp. 432-433.
5. R. Bonds, ed., *The Soviet War Machine* (New York: Chartwell, 1976), p. 210.
6. Wolfe, *Soviet Power*, p. 434.
7. F.D. Kohler et al., *Soviet Strategy for the Seventies: From Cold War to Peaceful Coexistence* (Coral Gables, Fla.: Center for Advanced International Studies, 1973), pp. 76-78.
8. Wolfe, *Soviet Power*, p. 449.
9. N. Lomov, "On Soviet Military Doctrine," *KVS*, No. 10, May 1962, p. 14.
10. Ibid., pp. 16, 19.
11. H. Dinerstein, L. Gouré, and T. Wolfe, *Soviet Military Strategy* (Santa Monica, Calif.: RAND, R-416-PR, April 1963), pp. 396-397. See also Y. Oleshchuk, "Small Wars and the Aggression in Vietnam," *International Affairs*, No. 5, May 1966, p. 36.
12. Dinerstein, Gouré, and Wolfe, *Soviet Military Strategy*, p. 397.
13. N. Ponomarev, "Crisis of Bourgeois Theories of War and Peace." *KVS*, No. 16, August 1964, p. 13.
14. V. Mochalov, "Concerning the Theory of Limited Wars," *Soviet Military Review*, No. 2, February 1965, p. 41.
15. V. Glazov, "The Evolution of US Military Doctrine," *Soviet Military Review*, No. 11, November 1965, p. 57.
16. V. Zavyalov, "Flexible Response Strategy: Theory and Practice," *Soviet Military Review*, No. 5, May 1965, pp. 36-38. See also S. Malyanchikov, "On the Nature of Armed Struggle in Local Wars," *Voennaia Mysle'*, No. 11, November 1965, trans. FBIS, FPD, No. 953, 8 March 1966, pp. 12-24. See also K. Bochkarev, "On the Character and Types of Wars of the Contemporary Epoch," *KVS*, No. 11, June 1965, pp. 8-17.
17. Glazov, "US Military Doctrine," p. 57.
18. Oleshchuk, "Small Wars," p. 36. See also Y. Melnikov, "U.S. Foreign Policy: A Threat to Peace," *International Affairs*, No. 1, January 1967, pp. 64-70.
19. Radio broadcast by Moscow TASS in English to Europe, 1610 GMT, 26 July 1961, FBIS, *USSR and Eastern Europe*, 27 July 1961, p. BB6.
20. Radio broadcast by Moscow TASS in English to Europe, 1539 24 May 1962, FBIS, *USSR and Eastern Europe*, 25 May 1962, p. BB4. See also Glazov, "US Military Doctrine," p. 57.
21. V. Pechorkin, "Crisis of Imperialism's Military Doctrines," *International Affairs*, No. 7, July 1962, p. 33. See also V. Larionov, "The Doctrine of 'Flexible' Agression," *International Affairs*, No. 7, July 1963, pp. 46-51.
22. R.A. Aliano attempted to argue this thesis in relation to the decision to intervene

in Vietnam in *American Defense Policy from Eisenhower to Kennedy: The Politics of Changing Military Requirements, 1957-1961* (Athens: Ohio University Press, 1975). See also N. Prokopyev, "Problems of War and Peace in Our Age," *International Affairs*, No. 12, December 1967, p. 59; R. Simonyan, "Doctrine of the American Aggressors," *Soviet Military Review*, No. 1, January 1969, p. 50.

23. V.D. Sokolovskiy, *Soviet Military Strategy*, ed. and trans. H.F. Scott (New York: Crane, Russak, 1975), p. 66.

24. N.A. Lomov, ed., *Scientific-Technical Progress and the Revolution in Military Affairs*, trans. U.S. Air Force (Washington, D.C.: U.S. Government Printing Office, 1973), p. 254. See also B. Teplinsky, "US 'Grand Strategy,'" *International Affairs*, No. 2, February 1964, p. 25.

25. Pechorkin, "Crisis of Imperialism's Military Doctrines," p. 33.

26. Ibid., pp. 33-34. See also the Russian-language version in *Mezhdunarodnaia Zhizn*, No. 7, July 1962, p. 44.

27. M. Mil'shtein, "Certain Strategic Military Concepts of American Imperialism," *MEMO*, No. 8, August 1962, p. 85.

28. Ibid., p.94.

29. See S. Konstantinov, "The Military Doctrine of American Imperialism," *KVS*, No. 23, December 1962, p. 83.

30. Kh. Dzhelnaukov, "The Evolution of U.S. Military Doctrine," *Voennaia Mysl'*, No. 9, September 1967, trans. FBIS, No. 0132/68, 5 September 1968, p. 94.

31. Ibid., pp. 97-98. See also Wolfe, *Soviet Power*, pp. 452-453.

32. Simonyan, "Doctrine of the American Aggressors," p. 50. See also Lomov, *Scientific-Technical Progress*, p. 253.

33. Mil'shtein. "American Imperialism," p. 87. Kennedy's remarks were taken out of context. See Stewart Alsop, "Kennedy's Grand Strategy," *The Saturday Evening Post*, March 31, 1962, pp. 11, 13. Quoted in Dinerstein, Gouré, and Wolfe, *Soviet Military Strategy*, p. 166.

34. Scott, *Soviet Military Strategy*, p. 117. See also Simonyan, "American Aggressors," p. 52.

35. J. Dziak, *Soviet Perceptions of Military Power: The Interaction of Theory and Practice* (New York: Crane, Russak, 1981), pp. 9-10.

36. Scott, *Soviet Military Strategy*, pp. 201-211.

37. Konstantinov, "American Imperialism," p. 80.

38. Larionov, "'Flexible' Agression," p. 46.

39. Scott, *Soviet Military Strategy*, pp. 74-100.

40. This is alluded to in Lomov, *Scientific-Technical Progress*, p. 254.

41. S.M. Shtemenko, "The Queen of the Battlefield Yields Her Crown," trans. and quoted in W. Kintner and H.F. Scott, *The Nuclear Revolution in Soviet Military Affairs* (Norman: University of Oklahoma Press, 1968), p. 55.

42. V.D Sokolovskiy, "On the Soviet Military Doctrine," *Soviet Military Review*, No. 4, April 1965, p. 8.

43. R. Kolkowicz, "Strategic Parity and Beyond," *World Politics,* Volume 23, No. 23, No. 3, April 1971, p. 439. See also W.F. Scott and H.F. Scott, *The Armed Forces of the USSR* (Boulder, Colo.: Westview, 1979), pp. 54-56. See also Wolfe, *Soviet Power,* pp. 451-452.

44. Scott, *Soviet Military Strategy*, pp. 378-379. See also B. Teplinsky, "U.S. 'Grand Strategy,'" *International Affairs*, No. 2, February 1964, p. 25: idem, "U.S. Military Programmes," *International Affirs*, No. 8, August 1967, p. 48.

45. V.D. Sokolovskiy and M. Cherednichenko, "Military Strategy and Its Prob-

lems,'' *Voennaia Mysl'*, No. 10, October 1968, trans. FBIS, No. 0084/69, 4 September 1969, p. 37.

46. A Baryshev, "New US Doctrines: Same Old Aims," *International Affairs*, No. 12, December 1969, pp. 12-13. See also Lomov, *Scientific-Technical Progress*, p. 254; G.A. Trofimenko, "Some Aspects of US Military and Political Strategy," *SShA: Ekonomika, Politika, Ideologia*, No. 10, October 1970, trans. Joint Publications Research Service (hereafter JPRS) No. 51895, 1 December 1970, p. 19.

47. G. Trofimenko, "From Confrontation to Coexistence," *International Affairs*, No. 10, October 1975, p. 38. See also the Russian version of Trofimenko's article in *Mezhdunarodnaia Zhizn*, No. 9, September 1975, p. 42.

48. G.A. Arbatov, "American Foreign Policy at the Threshold of the 1970's," *SShA: Ekonomika, Politika, Ideologia*, No. 1, January 1970, trans. JPRS No. 49934, 26 February 1970, p. 19.

6.
Soviet Reaction to the McNamara Concepts

The public Soviet reaction to the concepts of counterforce, damage limitation, and assured destruction have just as much relevance to the current discussions of nuclear strategy as they did at the time when former Secretary of Defense Robert McNamara first enunciated them in 1962. This is so because, although the concept of damage limitation was dropped not too long after its inception (largely because of McNamara's reasoning that it would be more cost-effective to carry out an assured destruction strategy than one based on damage limitation), the concepts of counterforce and assured destruction still dominate much of the dialogue in nuclear strategy today. In addition, it was during this same period of time that Herman Kahn, in his book *On Escalation: Metaphors and Scenarios*, introduced the 44-step escalation ladder that was to dominate U.S. strategic thinking through the present day. The Soviet response to this notion, although it proved erroneous, foreshadowed their reactions to later developments in U.S. strategic doctrine.

Most of the public Soviet response to the so-called McNamara concepts focused on the notion of counterforce. Counterforce, in its simplest terms, is merely the targeting of the enemy's nuclear forces in the event of a nuclear war in an effort to reduce his capacity to inflict massive damage on either U.S. nuclear forces or U.S. cities. Soviet observers tended to read into the counterforce concept their own notions of nuclear warfighting based on a preemptive strike; in fact, as will be seen later in this chapter, they did the same thing with the assured-destruction concept, even though it was intended more to support arms control than a nuclear warfighting doctrine. Since the Soviets tended to interpret counterforce as indicative of a U.S. attempt to move towards a strategic doctrine similar to their own, they directed the majority of their declaratory deterrence statements towards the discrediting of the usefulness of counterforce.

The Soviet Propaganda Line

This section addresses five major themes of the Soviet declaratory deterrence strategy, four of which dealt with counterforce. The fifth theme covers the predominant Soviet line regarding the escalation concept.

1. *The Soviets implied a high readiness to "launch on warning" or "launch under attack," a capability that nullified the effectiveness of counterforce.*

One Soviet analysis in *International Affairs* implied that upon receiving word via radar and other sources that an attack was in progress they would immediately launch the vulnerable portion of their strategic forces (bombers and ICBMs) rather than wait for the missiles to strike and then retaliate with the undestroyed part of their forces:

> The element of surprise, rather important in past wars, now has a different character. Even such weapons as instant-action rockets, launched at any time of day or night and in any weather, can be detected in the first section of their flight path by ever vigilant radars and other instruments. In this age of radioelectronics and targeted ready-to-fire rockets, a counterstrike will follow the first strike in a matter of minutes. The first rockets and bombers of the side on the defensive would take off *even before the aggressor's first rockets, to say nothing of his bombers, reached their targets.*[1] [Emphasis in original]

The authors also recognized the fact that, even to achieve a modicum of surprise, an attacker "would have to use in his very first salvo a small but most efficient part of his means of attack." In response to such a move, they said that "after the aggressor's strike the attacked [sic] could discount the element of surprise and would use all his counterstrike means set in motion before the first explosions on his territory or remaining intact after the start of the enemy's nuclear bombardment."[2]

However, it is important to note that the U.S. concept of launch on warning describes a high state of readiness of strategic forces. In the case of the Soviets, their strategic forces in the 1960s were not in such a high state of readiness, particularly at the time the above statement was made (November 1963). Indeed, it has not been until recently that the Soviet level of strategic readiness has significantly increased.[3] Consequently, much of what was said in the early and mid-1960s was largely academic, and indicated a Soviet reliance on early warning and preemption rather than on the concepts of launch on warning or launch under attack. An example of this kind of indirect statement was in an article in the April 1965 issued of *Soviet Military Review* by Sokolovskiy, which implied such a preemptive strategy:

> Imperialist atom-mongers [sic] pin their hopes on a surprise attack and here lies the main danger. Consequently, the important, the primary mission of the

Soviet Armed Forces is to be ready to *nip in the bud any attempts* by aggressors at launching a surprise attack against the USSR and other socialist countries.[4] [Emphasis added]

2. *Since a U.S. counterforce strike cannot guarantee the destruction of all Soviet missiles, it is ineffective. Relative superiority in missiles is therefore meaningless, since the Soviet Union possesses an assured capacity for "crushing" retaliation.*

This was an obvious Soviet attempt to reduce the deterrent value of U.S. strategic nuclear superiority by publicly declaring that nuclear superiority had no real meaning, not even if a counterforce strategy was employed. In the April 1962 issue of *International Affairs*, less than two months before Mc-Namara actually announced the counterforce strategy, and six months before the onset of the Cuban missile crisis, Major General N. Talensky was the first to argue that a successful surprise attack could not possibly knock out all of a major power's means of nuclear delivery. This was supposed to be due to the high level of so-called nuclear saturation that then existed.[5] This was obvious propaganda on Talensky's part, since Soviet strategic forces in 1962 were still quite small in absolute numbers, as well as being quite numerically inferior relative to those of the United States.[6] Talensky repeated his argument in a later issue of *International Affairs* on the eve of the Cuban missile crisis:

> To unleash war with the use of such weapons clearly implies suicide, for no one can ever guarantee the aggressor from a retaliatory blow with similar weapons. Western military theoreticians, the apologists of "preventive war," seek to prove the advantages of this type of war by claiming that a preemptive attack would greatly lessen the effect of the retaliatory blow from the attacked side. A surprise attack naturally would inflict greater losses and destruction on the target state but it would not save the aggressor from a retaliatory blow. *At the present day there is as yet practically no possibility of preventing a retaliatory blow or of diminishing its power to any considerable extent.*[7] [Emphasis in original]

Talensky was trying to make two propaganda points: (1) it is not possible to carry out an effective counterforce attack, and (2) the United States might be able to make such an attack successfully and must therefore be told that it cannot hope to do so. Talensky conveniently did not mention Soviet antiballistic missile (ABM) development efforts during this time, since this would have detracted from his arguments against the likelihood of limiting damage. Much of the remainder of his article was devoted to pointing out the technical difficulties involved in carrying out a counterforce attack, such as accuracy and the uncertainty of strategic intelligence.[8] The overall impression one gets from Talensky's statements is that they were principally for their propaganda value, using weak arguments for lack of better ones.

What must be remembered above all else, though, is that at the time this statement was made, Soviet strategic forces were relatively greatly inferior with respect to the numbers of nuclear weapons and delivery systems available. This kind of "mutual vulnerability" argument was natural coming from a power that was inferior in the above respects. The obvious aim of these statements was to negate the value of U.S. nuclear superiority as an effective instrument of political leverage. However, Soviet behavior during the Cuban missile crisis proved that the Soviet leadership did perceive more actual U.S. political leverage than they were willing to admit, as well as their self-perceived need to make up for their lack of intercontinental capability by trying to move their intermediate-range ballistic missiles (IRBMs) forward into Cuba.

The editors of *Military Strategy* also tried to discredit the counterforce strategy by using a combination of "strategic bluffing" with the "all-or-nothing" argument that if you could not destroy *all* of an opponent's missiles, the strategy was ineffective:

> The ruling circles of the imperialist states, especially of the United States, recognize that, in conditions where *the Soviet Union has superiority in strategic missiles* [Note the exercise in strategic bluffing.], a surprise nuclear strike would be even more dangerous, since it would not obviate a crushing retaliatory missile-nuclear strike from the Soviet Union.[9] [Emphasis added]

The thrust of the editors' argument against counterforce was that, since the United States was not capable (allegedly) of executing a counterforce strike with any reasonable hope of success, the Soviet Union automatically possessed the ability to retaliate in kind. This made any attempts to establish nuclear superiority meaningless. This line of propaganda, however, did not square with the statements of Soviet military spokesmen concerning the necessity for preparing to fight a nuclear war with the idea of attaining victory. It was an attempt by Soviet propagandists to use American arguments as a means of making Soviet declaratory deterrence statements more believable to U.S. observers. This kind of argument was typified in the May 1966 issue of *International Affairs*:

> Superiority has become a concept which has no bearing on war. No superiority can save the aggressor from retribution. Any efforts of an aggressor to achieve *relative* nuclear superiority are neutralized in advance by the fact that the other side possesses *absolute* power which guarantees the destruction of the aggressor. For the same reason, the aggressor can gain nothing from a nuclear war or even from nuclear blackmail. . . . Although these conclusions logically follow from recognition of the impossibility of victory in a nuclear war and from arguments about a guaranteed destruction potential, Washington sacrifices logic to military considerations.[10] [Emphasis in original]

One does well to be skeptical of this kind of statement asserting the uselessness of superiority and the impossibility of attaining victory in a nuclear war. These arguments were simply a carbon copy of similar ones being made in the United States concerning the "nonutility" of nuclear superiority. The aim was to create in the minds of U.S. analysts a picture of a Soviet Union whose strategic outlook was similar to that of the United States. When you also consider the fact that the Soviet strategic buildup was rapidly accelerating at the time of this article, it is clear that it was designed to persuade U.S readers and analysts that the Soviets were not trying to attain nuclear superiority, but would be satisfied with parity. Unfortunately, this aspect of Soviet declaratory deterrence worked all too well.

3. *It is not possible to establish "rules of conduct" for a nuclear war by making arbitrary distinctions between civilian and military targets, as implied by counterforce.*

The corollary of this assertion was that it was not possible to separate military targets from civilian ones reliably because of the great destructive power of nuclear weapons. An early example of this line was given in an article by Major General Talensky in *International Affairs*. He doubted McNamara's contention that "in a nuclear-missile war blows would be struck primarily at military targets and not at cities and industrial areas," arguing that historical experience with very powerful weapons tended to prove that one could not reasonably expect to exclude cities from nuclear attack.[11]

Another Soviet commentator, writing in a January 1963 issue of *New Times*, maintained that making a distinction between purely military as opposed to civilian targets would be very difficult, and that McNamara was not considering the effects of radioactive fallout:

> But how is he [McNamara] going to distinguish between military and non-military targets? And what does he intend to do about the lethal radioactive fall-out which, originating from an attack on a military objective would doom every living being for miles around?[12]

It should be pointed out that the Soviets were already hard at work trying to solve this problem with their civil defense efforts.[13] A similar argument was made on a more sophisticated level in the November 1963 issue of *International Affairs*. The authors emphasized the difficulty of hitting a relatively small military target with a weapon designed to devastate a much larger area (a reference to the question of yield versus accuracy) without resulting in heavy collateral damage among the civilian populace:

> It is self-evident that any belligerent, if only to reduce his own losses, will first strive to knock out the enemy's military targets, especially his nuclear strike means. This does not at all mean that in the massive use of nuclear weapons cities and their inhabitants would be able to escape without huge losses. How can a multi-megaton bomb strike be limited to selected military targets when their area usually runs to no more than two figures, and the area directly hit by

the bomb blast, to tour or five figures? Besides, many important military objectives are located in cities or in their vicinity, and in heavily populated areas. [This is an exercise in sophistry; it depends upon where the weapons that constitute military targets are located. The Soviets always made up for poor accuracy with large yields.] All this quite apart from the spread of radioactive fallout, fire storms, and the disruption of supply systems and medical services.[14]

The authors further argued that "to accept the Western doctrine of limiting the use of nuclear weapons to geographical areas, specified targets, or size of warheads would be to recognise [sic] as lawful the annihilation of millions of people through the use of dozens or hundreds of 'small' nuclear missiles or rockets." Moreover, they contended that any effort to set any sort of rules of the game for nuclear war was unrealistic, "because nuclear war differs in principle from all previous wars in that it *cannot be limited*" (emphasis in original).[15] The deterrence value of this assertion should not be ignored, since it was in the Soviet interest to weaken the credibility of U.S. deterrence, especially with regard to the conduct of a limited nuclear war in defense of NATO, by creating as much uncertainty as possible in the minds of U.S. planners as to the willingness of the Soviet Union to resort to a strategic nuclear strike against the United States in the event of a confrontation in Europe in which the U.S. resorted to a limited use of nuclear weapons.

The Soviets were therefore claiming that counterforce was unworkable on the grounds that it was impossible to make the necessary fine distinctions between civilian and military targets. This, however, was a phony argument. For one thing, Soviet missile deployment was such that Soviet ICBMs, the likely targets of a counterforce strike, were not near large population centers.[16] Furthermore, even if strikes against military targets caused limited civilian damage, this by itself would not justify making a retaliatory strike against the enemy's cities. In fact, Soviet targeting doctrine does not target cities per se.[17] Missiles and submarines would be the targets for counterforce attacks, and since these targets are not located in cities, this Soviet argument was based on a false assumption. As stated by Soviet analysts themselves, the problem was a matter of defining what constituted a military target.

4. *Counterforce is merely another name for a preemptive strike, and merely conceals preparations for a preventive war by the United States.*

This propaganda line was a carryover from the late 1950s. It was given notoriety by such commentators as Major General Talensky. The likely reason that the Soviets made such prominent use of Talensky in their declaratory deterrence strategy is that he was known in the West as the previous editor of *Voennaia Mysl'*. As such, his statements would therefore carry more credibility than most other commentators of lesser reputation. His basic argument was that the idea of a counterforce strategy was inseparable from that of a preventive war, and that the United States was actively planning for this contingency.[18] As we saw in chapter 4, the Soviets had long since been aware of the difference between a preemptive strike, as implied by the counterforce concept, and a preventive war. Soviet commentators were claiming that the latter notion was the real intent of counterforce, while American analysts such as Bernard Brodie, whom the Soviets were citing to support their claims, were vigorously denying it.[19]

The theme of U.S. preparation for preventive war by means of the counterforce strategy was reiterated in *Military Strategy* as well:

> The strategy of "counterforce" primarily stems from the necessity for preventive war and the achievement of surprise. A strategy which contemplates attaining victory through the destruction of the armed forces cannot stem from the idea of a "retaliatory blow"; it stems from preventive actions.[20]

Although the distortion of the terms "preemptive strike" and "preventive war" is fairly obvious, this passage also reflects a substantial degree of Soviet projection of their own thinking on nuclear war onto U.S. doctrine and intentions. This is evidenced in the Soviet attribution to U.S. planners of the goal of victory in a nuclear war and the emphasis on surprise.

Another member of the Sokolovskiy editorial staff for *Military Strategy*, V. Larionov, asserted that attempts to wage war according to "agreed rules" was "contradictory to the principle of excluding war as a means of deciding international questions."[21] He further contended that the counterforce strategy, "from the political point of view, bears an openly aggressive character, because it may be considered to be operational only under conditions of a preventive strike."[22] But Larionov had little cause to doubt the nature of Soviet strategic doctrine, which advocated a preemptive strike.[23] While Soviet commentators made much complaint about the U.S. strategy of counterforce, they omitted mentioning that they had a similar doctrine. The fact that demonstrates the falsity of this propaganda theme is that, since this particular article was written in June 1966, the author by this time was well aware of the unilateral U.S. freeze on further strategic buildup.

5. *The escalation concept is a means for the United States to unleash a total nuclear war.*

The main theme of Soviet propaganda regarding the concept of "escalation" was that the United States was planning to unleash a total nuclear war by means of escalation of local conflicts up the 44 rungs of Herman Kahn's escalation ladder. This, of course, assumed that Kahn's escalation theory had actually been adopted as a tenet of the U.S. doctrine of flexible response, which in fact it had not, although Kahn's ideas influenced U.S. thinking on nuclear strategy considerably.

Soviet commentators claimed to find evidence of Kahn's escalation theory's being put into practice in the U.S. conduct of the Vietnam war. A prime example of this was in the April 1967 issue of *Soviet Military Review*, when the U.S. involvement in Vietnam was approaching its peak intensity. The author attempted to demonstrate that "the US war in Indo-China is the most typical example of how imperialism is broadening out aggression in the spirit of the escalation theory."[24] The author then matched up the events in the chronology of initial U.S. involvement in Vietnam with the steps in the escalation ladder.[25] He then claimed that the United States was continuing to climb the escalation ladder not only by increasing the scale of violence in Vietnam, but also by initiating conflicts in other areas so as to further exacerbate the situation:

> Recklessly climbing the escalation ladder, the US imperialists are drawing their military bloc partners into adventure. They are seeking to provoke other conflicts in South-East Asia and elsewhere. It is considered that the unleashing of new conflicts when those already started are in the stage of aggravation is a key proposition of the theory of escalation. . . . The aggressive theories of the US military theoreticians thus conform with the aggressive objectives of imperialism. This is freshly borne out by the escalation theory.[26]

In retrospect, though, there was little real evidence that the United States was attempting to spread the conflict throughout Southeast Asia, unless the author was referring to U.S. air actions in Laos or the limited actions at that time on the Cambodian border. The argument that the escalation theory was inherently aggressive because it conformed to the inherently aggressive tendencies in imperialism has long been a standard part of the Soviet declaratory deterrence strategy against all previous U.S. strategic doctrinal concepts. It should therefore be considered accordingly.

Although Soviet analysts were able to make connections between the stages of U.S. involvement in Vietnam and the steps in Kahn's escalation ladder, Soviet observers failed to realize that the escalation ladder was *descriptive* rather than *prescriptive* in its intentions regarding potential crises. Although the editors of *Military Strategy* did not go so far as to attribute Kahn's theory as being part of U.S. strategic doctrine, it is clear that they also had difficulty in telling the difference between mere academic discussion and analysis of real doctrine, tending to assume that all such theoretical analyses reflected doctrine to some extent. The propaganda line against escalation can easily be dismissed if one considers it in conjunction with the growing Soviet admission of the likelihood and necessity of having to wage limited conflicts of both nuclear and conventional types. Given also the Soviet emphasis on surprise and their tendency to assume the same for U.S. doctrine, it is not at all likely that they seriously believed the United States to be preparing to unleash a total nuclear war through escalation of limited conflicts, as this would obviate the chances of surprise. This argument was similar to that used against the strategy of limited war and foreshadowed the argument that would later be used against Secretary of Defense James Schlesinger's proposed strategy of limited nuclear options.

The Real Soviet View

Continuing the tendency from the 1950s, Soviet analysts projected their own nuclear warfighting mindset onto U.S. doctrine in analyzing the intent and rationale behind the McNamara concepts, as well as Herman Kahn's theory of escalation. Two of the following four themes pertain to the concepts of McNamara's nuclear strategy, while the latter two deal with the Soviet perception of escalation.

1. *The Soviets initially perceived the United States as attempting to adopt a nuclear warfighting doctrine as embodied in the concepts of counterforce and damage limitation.*

As first illustrated in chapter 4, Soviet analysts viewed U.S. strategic doctrine within the context of their own nuclear warfighting doctrine. This tendency did not change with U.S. doctrine.[27] This was proven in the first serious academic analysis of the new concepts by Major General M. Mil'shtein in the August 1962 issue of *MEMO*. (However, Soviet commentators had made reference to the McNamara concepts in statements predating this article, even though the depth of analysis was lacking.)[28] Mil'shtein argued that the phraseology of U.S. strategists regarding "the enemy's attack" or "the retaliatory blow" was merely camouflage "by which the accelerated formation of the [so-called] 'second strike force' is justified."[29] Considered with the following passage, Mil'shtein apparently believed the U.S. counterforce strategy to be based on carrying out a first strike. As can also be seen, though, he recognized its retaliatory aspects as well:

> First of all, the American military command, under the pretense of creating a "counterforce" and "second strike force," is in fact creating at a forced rate and is holding in a high state of readiness the necessary means for inflicting not the second but the first strike.
>
> The second conclusion: American strategists admit that as the result of a *counterblow* [i.e., a preemptive strike] on the part of the Soviet Union, many means of atomic attack of the United States, especially those which require fixed installations, will either be fully destroyed or so badly damaged that they cannot be used in the future. Therefore, they hope to preserve mobile weapons of such types as nuclear missile-launching submarines, Minuteman missiles on mobile launchers [!], a part of their strategic aviation, etc., and thereby attain, *in the course of war*, atomic superiority over the Soviet Union. Such are their hopes.[30] [Emphasis added]

Although Mil'shtein tried to prove that the United States was in fact contemplating a first-strike and not a second-strike capability, he contradicted himself almost immediately. He recognized that the U.S. was trying to deny success to a Soviet preemptive strike by emphasizing the survivability of its strategic forces, which would not have been an important consideration if the United States was really committed to a first-strike strategy. Mil'shtein's own nuclear warfighting orientation was reflected in his contention that the U.S. sought to gain, "in the course of war, atomic superiority over the Soviet Union" by means of increasing the survivability of its strategic forces.

Mil'shtein also took note of the debate within the U.S. military regarding the objectives to be emphasized in a nuclear attack. According to Mil'shtein, "Adherents of one point of view, primarily representatives of the Army and Navy, consider that the primary objectives should be the 'key centers' or large cities."[31] In other words, this was an argument in favor of deterrence by the threat of a countervalue attack, a consideration unrelated to a warfighting strategy. On the other hand, the counterforce advocates "consider that they should be primarily military objectives, more precisely, the enemy's atomic means: rocket bases, launching sites, airports, storage sites for atomic ammunition, etc."[32] What is interesting about this latter statement is that it is identical to the *Soviet* targeting priorities later given in Sokolovskiy's *Military Strategy*, a comprehensive statement of Soviet strategic doctrine.[33]

As an "answer" to the U.S. counterforce strategy, Mil'shtein strongly implied the use of a Soviet preemptive strike.[34] In this sense, Mil'shtein used the same formula as Sokolovskiy did later for the determination of a Soviet "counterblow": Soviet "retaliatory" strikes are to destroy enemy strategic forces *before* they are launched.

Another military analyst, writing only a few months after Mil'shtein in *Kommunist Vooruzhennykh Sil*, reflected the mirror-imaging tendency as well, emphasizing U.S. discussions of the necessity to attain surprise in order to support his propagandistic assertion that the United States intended to undertake a preventive war against the Soviet Union.[35]

Soviet analysts also recognized the difficulties inherent in a counterforce strategy. In the second edition of Sokolovskiy's *Military Strategy*, which appeared in December 1963,[36] the authors discussed the difficulty of attempting to destroy well-dispersed and hardened forces. In addition, it was pointed out that a decision about what type of objectives should be attacked was dependent to a great extent on the type and accuracy of the weapons involved:

> The launching of nuclear strikes against enemy strategic weapons is a more difficult task in comparison with the launching of strikes against large cities. These difficulties are caused primarily by the fact that, first of all, there are significant numbers of such weapons, and, secondly, by the fact that the majority of them, especially rocket weapons, in modern conditions are *an absolute weapon* [This

phrase was incorrectly translated by the editor. Taken in the context of the passage, a better translation would be "the *perfect* weapon."], located in underground bases of low vulnerability, on submarines, etc. In this connection, there is a growing tendency toward the increase of their invulnerability.

The decision as to which objectives should be the ones against which nuclear strikes are launched—against strategic weapons or cities—depends to a considerable degree on the weapons system on hand and on its quantity. If the weapon is so inaccurate that it cannot be used to destroy small-dimension targets such as ballistic missile launching pads or airports, and there is not enough room for them, it can only be used against large objectives, for example, cities.[37] [Emphasis added]

The Soviets at this time did not seem to anticipate (nor, for that matter, did the United States) the great improvements that would be made in missile accuracy by both themselves and the U.S., thus increasing the vulnerability of the land-based ICBM.[38] Soviet analysts correctly doubted the effectiveness of a counterforce strategy at the time these statements were made in the early 1960s. The number of U.S. land-based ICBMs, though at the time much more numerous than what the Soviets had, were still too few in absolute terms to pose a genuine threat to destroy Soviet nuclear forces with a high degree of reliability. This was because these ICBMs were still highly inaccurate compared with those of later years.[39] Just because the Soviets recognized this fact, though, does not mean that they did not appreciate the warfighting aspects of counterforce; it did mean that their line that the United States was planning a first strike as a prelude to a "preventive war" was sheer propaganda, since they had little confirmation of this from U.S. strategic capabilities. A considerable amount of mirror imaging went into these propaganda claims, as demonstrated in the following passage from an article in the March 1965 issue of *International Affairs*:

But from the standpoint of warfare it was valid only in case the United States was to start war first. Indeed, the aggressor is above all interested in knocking weapons out of the hands of his victim and in this way saving himself from a retaliatory blow. *The counterforce strategy is unsuitable for defense.* [But it is apparently suitable for preemption.] What is the sense in destroying the launching pads if the missiles are already heading for their targets? Counterforce is only another name for the selfsame idea of the first strike.[40] [Emphasis added]

2. *The Soviets interpreted the later abandonment of counterforce and damage limitation as a U.S. move away from a warfighting doctrine towards a deterrence-oriented strategy.*

Since the concept of damage limitation was abandoned rather quickly by the United States in favor of assured destruction shortly after its enunciation by McNamara in 1963, the Soviets made very little mention of it in their writings, with the exception of the third edition of Sokolovskiy's *Military Strategy*.[41] Soviet analysts were apparently confused by the assured destruction concept at first, mainly because they viewed it as part of the requirements for a warfighting strategy instead of perceiving its true nature as an arms-control requirement. This was demonstrated by the following passage from an analysis in *Kommunist Vooruzhennykh Sil*:

> US Defense Secretary McNamara set forth the notorious "counterforce strategy," the basic thinking of which amounts to the use of nuclear weapons in a future war only on the main groupings of armed forces, but not on the industrial-economic centers and civilian population. . . . Indeed, McNamara himself repeatedly declared that the United States of America "through necessity" uses nuclear weapons on the "military-industrial complex" of any opponent and that the essence of the "strategy of counterforce" is to have a few American rockets for the "assured destruction" of each Soviet rocket.[42]

The author had definitely misread the assured destruction concept, in that he implied that it applied only to Soviet strategic forces, rather than to the ability specified by McNamara of being able to inflict unacceptable damage on the Soviet population and industry. As has been discussed in a previous chapter, counterforce and assured destruction were not compatible with each other as part of a warfighting strategy. The former notion was correctly interpreted as a possible move towards a nuclear warfighting strategy. Assured destruction, however, was actually an arms-control assessment of the requirements for credible deterrence.[43]

Conversely, the Soviets realized that the United States was actually moving more in the direction of a deterrence posture because of the growing U.S. emphasis on the assured-destruction concept, coupled with the decline of counterforce and damage limitation in U.S. strategic doctrine. Even in the third edition of Sokolovskiy's *Military Strategy*, however, the Soviets still tended to attribute warfighting goals to U.S. nuclear planners:

> Thus, the strategic concepts of "assured destruction" and "damage limitation," considered together, suppose the delivery by the strategic strike forces of the U.S. and their allies of massive nuclear strikes on a whole complex of objectives *that make up the military-economic potential of the enemy* [a projection of Soviet targeting doctrine], and at the same time an active and passive defense of the U.S. so as to limit to a maximum degree the damage from a decisive retaliatory strike by the enemy. The realization of these strategic concepts, according to the military-political leadership of the USA, *requires a balanced combination of strategic offensive forces, defensive forces, and means of passive defense* [This was really the *Soviet* view of what was logically required from strategic doctrine.]. This fact is characteristically acknowledged in the West, that an all-out nuclear rocket war, no matter how it is unleashed, will be destructive for both sides.[44]

Found within the same work was an interesting new passage on the alleged intent behind the notion of assured destruction:

> The *military circles* of the USA openly admit that the basic principle of the American strategy is the achievement of victory in a war by means of destroying the industrial potential and undermining the morale of the civilian population of the enemy . . . the aim of the US strategic nuclear forces is said to be the assurance of the "guaranteed destruction" of the enemy. It is also flatly stated how many millions of the population of the socialist countries can be annihilated, as well as what percentage of the industrial potential can be destroyed.[45] [Emphasis added]

It is interesting that Soviet military analysts attempted to find analogous ideas of attaining victory in a nuclear war in U.S. strategic thinking. They apparently did not understand initially that the notion of assured destruction was primarily designed as a means of achieving war *avoidance* as opposed to attaining a warfighting objective. Instead, they perceived it as a postulation of military goals in the event of an actual nuclear war.

It should be remembered, however, that the third edition of *Military Strategy* was not set in type until November 1966.[46] The Soviets by this time were well aware of the freeze on further U.S. strategic buildup and the virtual abandonment of a national civil defense program. This recognition of the real nature of the shift in emphasis of U.S. strategic concepts was more explicitly recognized almost a year later in the August 1967 issued of *Voennaia Mysl'*. Although the subject of the article dealt with the evolution of U.S. military doctrine in general, the author's comments on the intent behind the counterforce strategy and the reasons for its subsequent decline are somewhat revealing:

> And here we see the striving of the U.S. militarists to represent their aggressive strategy as defensive, although in reality, counting on the supposedly invincible forces of the "retaliatory strike," American strategists intend to *blackmail* their enemies and *impose their will upon them within the limits of a limited nuclear war*. . . . As a result of the evaluation of the nuclear capabilities of the Soviet Union and criticism inside the country, the concept of "counterforce" gradually lost its significance as a new position of U.S. military doctrine. The strategy of "flexible response" . . . received further recognition as the leading strategic concept.[47] [Emphasis added]

Three main points should be gleaned from the above passage. First, the author implies that it is indeed possible to conduct a limited nuclear war, a point that has been proven in the previous chapter. Second, he projects Soviet estimations of the political utility of nuclear weapons and of "victory" in the context of a nuclear war, whether limited or not, onto U.S. doctrine. Third, and most important, he stated that one of the factors responsible for the demise of counterforce was the U.S. recognition of the growing nuclear capabilities of the Soviet Union. It is difficult to believe that the Soviets would not have known of the discussions in the United States regarding the limitations of U.S. strategic forces for counterforce strikes, particularly the U.S. problem with Circular Error Probable (CEP) margins that were still too large for an effective counterforce strategy. Circular Error Probable, by way of definition, is the measure of the accuracy of land- and sea-based ballistic missiles. It represents the area of impact within which there is a 50% probability of a hit by a given missile. If 20 missiles with a CEP of 0.2 miles each are fired at a target, then it is expected that 10 of these missiles will land within a radius of 0.2 miles from the target, with the remainder landing outside this radius at varying distances.[48] Because of the limited capability of U.S. ICBMs and SLBMs to destroy Soviet missiles in their silos, the United States continued moving in the direction of a pure retaliatory concept, which made counterforce less desirable from the standpoint of the arms-control advocates.

Soviet analysts therefore seemed inclined to take the "best-case" analysis, so to speak, in explaining why the U.S. was emphasizing assured destruction over the concept of counterforce. Their conclusion was that the United States was abandoning the counterforce strategy only because it was *compelled* to do so by the growth of Soviet strategic power as the chief factor among those that made up the correlation of forces.[49]

3. *The Soviets interpreted the escalation concept as an actual part of U.S. strategic doctrine.*

On some occasions Soviet analysts had difficulty making a proper distinction between academic discussions of strategic concepts never officially or completely adopted as doctrine, and those that were eventually adopted (such as Maxwell Taylor's arguments for the flexible response doctrine in *The Uncertain Trumpet*). The premier example of this kind of error was the overemphasis given to Herman Kahn's escalation concept, interpreted by the Soviets as the logical extension of flexible response. It is no surprise, then, that the Soviets would pay a lot of attention to the writings of its chief exponent, Herman Kahn. His writings first drew attention in *Voennaia Mysl'*. In the September 1965 issue, two Soviet officers analyzed the escalation concept, giving particular weight to the model of the escalation ladder with its 44 rungs of conflict intensity. They first quoted Kahn as to the precise definition of "escalation":

> A consistent, gradual increase of threats and military efforts in carrying out the strategy of "flexible response" should be, in the opinion of US military theoreticians, the basis of carrying on "protracted conflict." This has been more clearly formulated in the so-called theory of "escalation," which is applied both to the hot and cold war. As H. Kahn says, escalation is a consistent

increase of the scale of threats and military pressures in a limited conflict under
conditions where it not possible for the opposing side, at each given moment, to
counter with even greater pressure. In other words, escalation is "competition
in risk to be taken by one's own side."[50]

As one might expect, the Soviets looked for evidence that escalation was
actually being applied. According to the authors of the above article, "Escalation finds application primarily in conditions of international military-political crises and military intervention in the affairs of underdeveloped countries.
A typical example of putting this theory into practice is the U.S. intervention
in Vietnam."[51] From the Soviet perspective then, the U.S. involvement in
Vietnam was the prime example and definitive proof that the escalation concept was being put to a practical test.

In more open Soviet publications, Soviet treatment of escalation was more
general, stressing mainly the application of "strategy" in Vietnam. Although
such references were almost always couched in propagandistic rhetoric, the
implication was still that "the 'strategy of flexible response' has been put to a
practical test in Vietnam in the form of the escalation strategy, where the
American brasshats are constantly extending the scale of their aggression."[52]

4. *The Soviets saw the escalation concept as evidence that the United
States might not be deterred from the increased use of force by the Soviets'
implied threat of uncontrolled escalation.*

In an extensive public analysis by V. Larionov (a member of the
Sokolovskiy group that produced the three editions of *Military Strategy*) in the
June 1966 issue of *MEMO*, he stated that the principles of the escalation ladder were those that guided the U.S. intervention in Vietnam, as well as continuing U.S. efforts to "escalate" the conflict.[53] The other conclusions drawn
by Larionov about the nature of the escalation theory were as follows:

1. The 44-step escalation ladder made the process of unleashing a nuclear war
   "smoother."
2. The intent of the escalation ladder was to disarm world public opinion and
   to paralyze those who opposed universal nuclear war.
3. The escalation theory served to "open the door to the unleashing of war
   with the use of nuclear weapons."
4. The concept of escalation, along with the concepts of graduated deterrence
   and the "nuclear threshold," are a logical continuation of the flexible response doctrine.[54]

These conclusions agreed with those expressed in *Voennaia Mysl'*, and
confirmed that Soviet analysts placed considerably more emphasis on Kahn's
escalation ladder than was justified. This is really not surprising, since the implication of escalation, like the later concept of limited nuclear options as
enunciated by Schlesinger, was that the United States may not be deterred

from the use of force by the Soviet implied threat of uncontrolled escalation. This was quite a disturbing prospect for Soviet analysts, as illustrated by the tone of the following passage from an article in the April 1967 issue of *Soviet Military Review*:

> Even a cursory examination of the Kahn theory allows one to draw at least two fundamental conclusions. The first is that the purpose of this theory is not to *avert* but to *kindle* another world war. The second is that it tries to prove that today a world war cannot break out without a preliminary and gradual development of a conflict. The aggressors thereby plan to dull the peoples' vigilance by making believe that the danger of the hotbeds of tension created and fanned by US militarism in various parts of the world is not very great. There is hardly any need to dwell on the deadliness of this camouflage.[55] [Emphasis in original]

Although the second "conclusion" could be dismissed as propaganda, the first conclusion reflected the Soviet fear of the possibility of a United States undeterred by the threat of uncontrolled escalation. The author of the above passage, commenting on the "step" of officially declaring nuclear war with one or two atomic bombs, objected to such a step with the assertion that "no person is naive enough to believe that the Pentagon seriously intends to announce nuclear strikes beforehand. It is well known that the surprise factor does not by any means figure last in the aggressive plans of the top US brass."[56] (Yet this type of warning by the U.S. is included as part of the later Schlesinger doctrine involving limited nuclear options.) As in all earlier cases, the author once again projected Soviet thinking regarding the value of surprise onto U.S. military planners. Later Soviet analysis, however, conceded the possibility of a limited strategic exchange.[57]

An analysis in the August 1967 issue of *International Affairs* contradicted the Soviets' own propaganda line regarding the escalation "strategy." Instead of asserting that the United States was planning to unleash a global nuclear conflict at a propitious moment by escalating local conflicts, the author contended that the so-called strategy had the more limited objective of exhausting the "national-liberation movement":

> The US imperialists think that a long, strenuous struggle carried on through small, "limited," local wars and conflicts will sap the material resources and demoralise the peoples [of the third World involved in national-liberation movements]. They want to achieve their aims by the old "strategy of attrition," extending on a global scale over decades.[58]

In other words, the United States was not "recklessly" climbing the escalation ladder ostensibly for the purpose of unleashing global nuclear war. Rather, the argument was that the U.S. sought the suppression of the national liberation movement by means of localized armed intervention.

Surprisingly, there is practically no reference to Kahn's escalation ladder in the third edition of Sokolovskiy's *Military Strategy*. This could be partially explained by the fact that the third edition was not set in type until November 1966, perhaps not allowing the editors of *Military Strategy* enough time to formulate an official pronouncement. A more likely explanation, however, is that they saw the Kahn theory as just that, a theory, and little more. Their uncertainty over how to treat such theories was reflected in their statement that many military theories "often . . . reflect the opinion of the individual military theoreticians and practitioners. However, in these opinions, there is probably also some reflection of official doctrine."[59] From the above statements, it is clear that the Soviets saw far more of the Kahn escalation theory being reflected in U.S. strategic doctrine and practice than the available evidence supported.

Conclusion

Whereas we were able to say with some certainty in the last chapter that U.S. doctrine had a definite influence on Soviet military planning and programs, it is not as clear in determining the influence of the McNamara concepts on Soviet doctrine or programs, or both. Certainly the Soviets never adopted anything resembling the assured-destruction concept, because this would have meant denying the political utility of nuclear weapons. If the Soviets had really believed that nuclear superiority carried no political leverage advantages, they would never have embarked on such an extensive strategic buildup past the point of "parity" with the U.S. to the verge of strategic superiority in the early 1980s. This was the fatal error of the arms-control theorists and advocates in the United States—in order for arms control to have a chance to succeed, both sides would have to have similar strategic outlooks and foreign policy goals that were intended to preserve the international status quo. And if this situation were indeed the case, then arms control would never have become an issue, since neither side would either have felt threatened or have desired to take advantage of the other's passivity to expand its influence and power at the expense of the other. In other words, in order for arms control to have succeeded between the United States and the Soviet Union, both sides would have to be basically peace-loving and nonexpansionistic, which would remove the problem all by itself.

As far as counterforce was concerned, the Soviets already had their own equivalent of it in their own doctrine; that is, if you interpret counterforce in its strictest military application as a preemptive strike against the enemy's warmaking capability, particularly his strategic nuclear forces, then the Soviets had a counterforce concept. It is also clear, judging from the Soviet civil defense program that was extensive even during this period, that the

Soviets had their own notions of how to achieve damage limitation (see note 13).

Overall, then, it cannot be said that the McNamara concepts had any appreciable effect on Soviet doctrine, military programs, or even on Soviet uses of military power in support of its expansionistic foreign policy objectives. The reasons for this are quite clear. Soviet strategic doctrine had been, and still is, formulated and carried out by professional military men operating in complicity with the political objectives of the Communist party of the Soviet Union. As such, military considerations such as nuclear warfighting, war survival, and the attainment of victory in the traditional Clausewitzian sense of having the ability "to compel the opponent to fulfill your will" were predominant. On the other hand, U.S. nuclear strategy during the 1960s was formulated by a man whose primary concern was cost effectiveness—a distinctly managerial consideration that was anathema to the essence of grand strategy. The available means and resources should not have determined the objectives of U.S. strategic doctrine; rather, it should have been the objective that determined the means to be obtained for achieving it with available resources. This may seem like a mere word game, but it accurately describes the backwards logic of the managerial school of strategic thought. Many military programs that would have contributed significantly to the U.S. ability to defend against a nuclear attack as part of a war survival strategy were not considered cost-effective by McNamara; e.g., programs such as civil defense and a large-scale antiballistic missile system. To McNamara's way of strategic thinking (such as it was), offensive systems were cheaper and easier to develop than defensive systems and could be produced in greater numbers for the same amount of resources assigned to them. Therefore, a strategic doctrine based on an ability to inflict assured destruction on the Soviet Union, at a level that McNamara considered would be unacceptable to them, was the most cost-effective way to deter nuclear war. Unfortunately, McNamara assumed a like strategic mindset on the part of both Soviet as well as U.S. strategic planners. The Soviets, for their part, saw the advantages that could be attained by convincing the U.S. that they too did not perceive any political leverage in the possession of nuclear superiority. Their declaratory deterrence strategy during this period was designed to create this impression in the minds of unwary U.S. strategic analysts who were inclined to interpret all public Soviet statements at face value without considering them in the context of other factors. Ironically then, the asymmetry between U.S. and Soviet strategic thinking helped to stimulate the very kind of arms buildup that U.S. strategic doctrine under McNamara had hoped to prevent.

Moreover, as the Soviets increasingly admitted the likelihood of more limited conflicts occurring, along with their perception of the U.S. move away from the warfighting-oriented concepts of counterforce and damage limitation towards the deterrence-oriented concept of assured destruction, they reached an important conclusion. They reasoned that this change in the nature of U.S. strategic doctrine was mainly due to the growth of Soviet strategic power, which served as a self-sustaining motivation for a continued Soviet military buildup of both strategic as well as conventional capabilities of all kinds. Following this reasoning, the more strategic nuclear power that the Soviets possessed, the more that U.S. strategic doctrine would have to change in order to accommodate itself to an unfavorably altered strategic balance. This would insure greater freedom for the Soviets' own use of military power to support their objectives, a freedom that the Soviets had perceived the U.S. as having when it had possessed a large margin of nuclear superiority. As can be seen from Appendix B, the Soviet use of military power had increased in scale from the 1950s during the 1960s as a direct result of this Soviet perception of increased restraints on U.S. freedom of action.

Finally, the Soviets saw a decreased risk of escalation involved in the limited use of force by either side. The exception to this was the Soviet misreading of the escalation concept as espoused by Herman Kahn. Mistaking it as having been part of U.S. strategic doctrine, they were disturbed by the prospect of the United States being undeterred by the implied Soviet threat of uncontrolled escalation. This point is important because if foreshadows the later Soviet response to the proposed Schlesinger doctrine of limited nuclear options, which would irritate the Soviets even more.

By the end of 1968, the Soviets were fast approaching a state of strategic parity vis-à-vis the United States. The attainment of nuclear parity, from the Soviet view, was one of the fundamental shifts in the overall world correlation of forces in favor of socialism and the Soviet Union. Ironically, then president Lyndon Johnson had reached an agreement with the Soviet leadership to begin the first round of the Strategic Arms Limitation Talks, which would actually take place after President Nixon took office in 1969. Nixon would also bring with him a new U.S. strategic doctrine that would eventually come to be known as realistic deterrence. What discernible effect would the advent of SALT and the realistic deterrence doctrine have on the Soviet perception of U.S. doctrinal intentions and development? This will be the subject of part 4.

Notes

1. I. Glagolev and V. Larionov, "Soviet Defense Might and Peaceful Co-existence," *International Affairs*, No. 11, November 1963, p. 32.
2. Ibid.
3. J. Collins, *American and Soviet Military Trends since the Cuban Missile Crisis* (Washington, D.C.: Center for Strategic and International Studies, 1978), pp. 84-85.

4. V.D. Sokolovskiy, "On the Soviet Military Doctrine," *Soviet Military Review*, No. 4, April 1965, p. 8. See also H.F. Scott, *Soviet Military Strategy* (New York: Crane, Russak, 1965), p. 210.

5. N. Talensky, "The 'Absolute Weapon' and the Problem of Security," *International Affairs*, No. 4, April 1962, p. 25. See also I. Glagolev and V. Larionov, "Soviet Defense," p. 32.

6. For ICBM figures see R. Bonds, ed., *The Soviet War Machine* (New York: Chartwell, 1976), p. 210.

7. N. Talensky, "'Preventive War'—Nuclear Suicide," *International Affairs*, No. 9, September 1962, p. 14.

8. Ibid.

9. V.D. Sokolovskiy, *Soviet Military Strategy*, trans. and ed. H.S. Dinerstein, L. Gouré, and T. Wolfe (Santa Monica, Calif.: RAND, R-416-PR, April 1963), p. 395. See also Glagolev and Larionov, "Soviet Defense," p. 33.

10. G. Gerasimov, "Pentagonia, 1966," *International Affairs*, No. 3, May 1966, p. 28. See also V. Pechorkin, "About 'Acceptable' War," *International Affairs*, No. 3, March 1963, pp. 20-23.

11. Talensky, "Preventive War," pp. 14-15.

12. V. Zorin, "The Three McNamara Doctrines," *New Times*, No. 3, January 1963, p. 13.

13. For an accounting and description of Soviet civil defense efforts during the sixties, see L. Gouré, *Civil Defense in the Soviet Union* (Berkeley: University of California Press, 1962). For a later analysis coupled with a discussion of its place in Soviet warfighting/war survival doctrine, see idem, *War Survival in Soviet Strategy* (Coral Gables, Fla.: Center for Advanced International Studies, 1976).

14. Glagolev and Larionov, "Soviet Defense," p. 31.

15. Ibid.

16. For Soviet ICBM deployment see Collins, *Military Trends*, p. 90.

17. Scott, *Soviet Military Strategy*, p. 210.

18. Talensky, "Preventive War," p. 14.

19. See B. Brodie, *Strategy in the Missile Age* (Princeton: Princeton University Press, 1959), pp. 229-241, for a complete discussion.

20. Scott, *Soviet Military Strategy*, p. 61.

21. V. Larionov, "The Development of the Armed Means and Strategic Concepts of the USA," *MEMO*, No. 6, June 1966, p. 78.

22. Ibid., pp. 78-79.

23. Scott, *Soviet Military Strategy*, p. 210.

24. V. Glazov, "Strategic Concept of the Aggressors," *Soviet Military Review*, No. 4, April 1967, p. 49.

25. Ibid., pp. 49-50.

26. Ibid.

27. G.A. Trofimenko, *SShA: Politika, Voina, Ideologia* (Moscow: Izdatelstvo "Mysl," 1976), pp. 234-244.

28. See for example the Izvestia article by Matveyev broadcast by the Moscow Domestic Service in Russian, 1500 GMT, 25 June 1962, trans. FBIS, *USSR and Eastern Europe*, 26 June 1962, pp. BB3-BB5,

29. M. Mil'shtein, "On Certain Military Strategic Concepts of American Imperialism," *MEMO*, No. 8, August 1962, p. 91.

30. Ibid., pp. 91-92.

31. Ibid., p. 92.

32. Ibid.

33. Scott, *Soviet Military Strategy*, p. 288.
34. Mil'shtein, "On Certain Military-Strategic Concepts of American Imperialism," pp. 91-92. See also N. Krylov, "The Nuclear Missile Shield of the Soviet State," *Voennaia Mysl'*, No. 11, November 1967, FBIS, FPD No. 0157/68, pp. 13-21.
35. S. Konstantinov, "The Military Doctrines of American Imperialism," *KVS*, No. 23, December 1962, p. 84.
36. Scott, *Soviet Military Strategy*, ·p. xvi.
37. Ibid., p. 59.
38. As an example of such argumentation against the case for the likelihood of a successful first counterforce strike, see J. Fallows, "Muscle-Bound Superpower: The State of America's Defense," *The Atlantic*, September 1979, pp. 66-72. For a counterpoint, see Collins, *Military Trends*, pp. 75-154.
39. Collins, *Military Trends*, pp. 88-96.
40. G. Gerasimov, "The First Strike Theory," *International Affairs*, No. 3, March 1965, p. 41. See also Larionov, "Armed Means," pp. 78-79.
41. Scott, *Soviet Military Strategy*, pp. 62-63.
42. V. Shmuratov, "Doctrines of Aggression and Piracy," *KVS*, No. 15, August 1965, p. 78.
43. This was recognized later in Trofimenko, *SShA*, pp. 245-248. See also Scott, *Soviet Military Strategy*, p. 63.
44. Scott, *Soviet Military Strategy*, p. 63.
45. Ibid., p. 277.
46. Ibid., p. xvi.
47. Kh. Dzhelaukhov, "The Evolution of U.S. Military Doctrine," *Voennaia Mysl'*, No. 9, September 1967, trans. FBIS, FPD No. 0132/68, p. 97. See also Scott, *Soviet Military Strategy*, p. 63.
48. R. Bonds, ed., *The US War Machine* (New York: Crown), 1978, p. 65. See also Collins, *Military Trends*, pp. 93-94, for a comparison of the CEPs of U.S. and Soviet missiles.
49. R. Simonyan, "Doctrine of the American Aggressors," *Soviet Military Review*, No. 1, January 1969, p. 50.
50. A. Kvitnitskiy and Ym. Nepodayev, "The Theory of the Escalation of War," *Voennaia Mysl'*, No. 9, September 1965, trans. FBIS, FPD No. 952, 2 March 1966, pp. 16-17.
51. Ibid., p. 17.
52. V. Glazov, "The Evolution of U.S. Military Doctrine," *Soviet Military Review*, No. 11, November 1965, p. 57.
53. Larionov, "Armed Means," p. 79.
54. Ibid.
55. Glazov, "Strategic Concept," p. 48.
56. Ibid., pp. 48-49.
57. S. Ivanov, "Soviet Military Doctrine and Strategy," *Voennaia Mysl'*, No. 5, May 1969, trans. FBIS, FPD No. 0116/68, 18 December 1969, p. 47.
58. B. Teplinsky, "U.S. Military Programme," *International Affairs*, No. 8, August 1967, p. 51.
59. Scott, *Soviet Military Strategy*, p. 279.

PART IV

REALISTIC DETERRENCE PERIOD (1969-1982)

7.

The Crisis of Capitalism: Soviet Views of the Nixon Doctrine

Shortly after the coming to power of the Nixon administration in January 1969, President Nixon outlined the tenets of a new U.S. strategic doctrine that was to become known as the Nixon Doctrine. At the foundation of the Nixon Doctrine was the strategy of realistic deterrence, which Defense Secretary Melvin Laird outlined later in a report to the House Armed Services Committee on March 9, 1971. Laird specified that the realistic deterrence strategy rested on the fulfillment of three important criteria:

1. Preservation by the United States of a sufficient strategic nuclear capability as the cornerstone of the Free World's nuclear deterrent.
2. Development and/or continued maintenance of Free World forces that are effective, and minimize the likelihood of requiring the employment of strategic nuclear forces should deterrence fail.
3. An international security assistance program that will enhance effective self-defense capabilities throughout the Free World, and, when coupled with diplomatic and other actions, will encourage regional security agreements among our friends and allies.[1]

Although similar points of this strategy had been implied in earlier statements during the Nixon administration, the Soviets had recognized the retreat in the U.S. doctrinal stance as early as 1969. But although Soviet analysts accurately saw the real nature of the Nixon Doctrine and realistic deterrence as a U.S. retreat from a higher level of military commitment abroad, they still showed a marked tendency to look for nuclear warfighting trends in U.S. strategic doctrine. Since the United States was clearly moving not in the direction of a warfighting doctrine but in the direction of a pure deterrence strategy as symbolized by the notion of mutual assured destruction, Soviet analysts publicly concluded that the main cause was the growth of Soviet military power, particularly the attainment of strategic parity with the United States in 1969.

Given this kind of perception, the Soviets could not have been expected to restrain their own military buildup, particularly in the area of strategic nuclear weapons, since the posture that they had already attained as early as 1969 had produced such obvious benefits as a change in U.S. strategic doctrine, which was accommodating their foreign policy objectives, and a U.S. willingness to engage in arms-control talks. This was a signal to the Soviets, however unintentional on the part of the United States, that their military buildup had wrung these concessions from an otherwise unwilling and "aggressive" adversary. It was difficult for the Soviets to conclude otherwise, since the U.S. was at the height of its involvement in Vietnam at that time. Logically, from the Soviet perspective, if the military buildup that they had already completed could produce such a U.S. willingness to make concessions, then further military buildup, even while the Soviets ostensibly were engaging in arms-control limitation talks, would reap even greater benefits. SALT, viewed within this context, was therefore not a means for achieving and maintaining strategic stability but was merely another weapon in the Soviet military-political arsenal for the attainment of its expansionistic goals. The Soviets well understood, however, that it was still necessary to project a semblance of an attitude similar to that of the United States toward nuclear weapons and their political utility. This became the focal point of the Soviet declaratory deterrence strategy during this period. It was expressed in their foreign policy declarations through the vehicle of detente. While many Americans hailed the concept of detente as signaling a new era in Soviet-American relations and an end to the days of the Cold War, there were few who bothered to take a serious look at the nature of the Soviet statements concerning detente.[2] What we called "detente" was still "cold war" as far as the Soviets were concerned; the only difference was that there was now a greatly reduced danger of strategic nuclear war as seen by the Soviets.

In their evaluations and pronouncements on the various aspects of the Nixon Doctrine, Soviet analysts saw elements of continuity between it and previous U.S. doctrine. This tendency to look for continuity and consistency was in part a reflection of these same things that the Soviets saw within their own doctrine; that is, U.S. objectives remained the same, but the strategy to achieve them changed depending upon the correlation of forces. One should remember then, that the Soviets have consistently attributed far more rationality and purposefulness to U.S. strategic doctrine and its development than some of us might think justified. This is an error on the conservative side; when one is not sure of an adversary's intentions, the safest thing to do is to assume that he knows what he is doing, and not that he is aimlessly blundering along. U.S. analysts, of course, have done the same thing with regard to Soviet strategic doctrine, although probably with better reason.

The body of Soviet views on the nature of the Nixon Doctrine and realistic deterrence was amply reflected in their military programs and foreign policy behavior during the period from 1969 to 1981. The use of threats and military maneuvers, as employed during the 1973 Yom Kippur War, was a carryover from the massive retaliation period. Likewise, the use of Soviet sea and airlift capability to mount logistical operations during the flexible response period to Egypt and North Vietnam was still very much in evidence during this period. But the single greatest escalation in the Soviet use of military power in her aggressive foreign policy strategy was the introduction of the use of proxy troops to do the actual fighting, thus taking the onus of physical intervention off Moscow. First the Cubans, and later the Ethiopians, Yemenis, and East Germans, were to be employed in this role, supported by Soviet logistical efforts. Again, the singular exception to this trend was in December 1979 when Soviet troops invaded Afghanistan to prop up a tottering pro-Soviet regime. But unlike the earlier Soviet interventions in Hungary and Czechoslovakia, the Afghanistan invasion represented yet another important escalation in the Soviet use of military power, since it took place outside her recognized sphere of influence in Eastern Europe. This increase in scale of the use of military power matches up very closely with what one could expect from the Soviet perception of U.S. strategic doctrine during these years and demonstrates that the Soviet leadership has indeed been influenced by, and has acted upon, these perceptions.

Even though this perception was being communicated in public Soviet sources, the Soviet leadership still had to mask its real views as much as possible so as not to alarm U.S. observers. Therefore, the aim of Soviet declaratory deterrence statements during this period was to portray the United States in the most aggressive light possible vis-à-vis the Soviet Union in addition to undermining the credibility of realistic deterrence. This propaganda campaign had the beneficial (for the Soviets) effect of drawing attention away from the Soviet military buildup and toward U.S. efforts to merely stay close.

The Soviet Propaganda Line

1. *United States military power is not usable for the attainment of its political goals.*

G. Trofimenko, an analyst for the Institution for the Study of the U.S.A. and Canada, was a prominent spokesman for this line. When considered within the context of Soviet military doctrine, however, his statement clearly referred to a hoped-for "reality" rather than the real situation:

> Understanding that the possibilities for the United States' direct utilization of military force in today's world are seriously limited . . . the U.S. leadership apparently cannot and is not prepared to renounce the traditional philosophy which believes the accumulation of "military hardware" to be the chief means of "insuring security."[3]

Other Soviet analysts claimed that the United States had taken on commitments that were beyond its real capacity to fulfill. This was obviously not entirely sincere, since the Soviets would not have wished to acknowledge publicly the political utility of U.S. military power.[4] Soviet English-language publications, such as *Soviet Military Review, New Times,* and *International Affairs* (Moscow), all stressed this theme heavily. These English-language periodicals often used arguments that had their origins in the American press in order to make their statements seem more plausible to Western readers.

Even though the Soviets had recognized that they had achieved strategic parity with the United States and that the latter was not undertaking any massive strategic buildup in response on the scale of that in the early 1960s, Soviet commentators such as Trofimenko nevertheless maintained that the United States still intended to attempt to gain advantages over the Soviet Union regardless of how defensive its new strategic doctrine seemed:

> Finally, proceeding from the formal recognition of the strategic equality an parity of the United States and the USSR, this strategy nonetheless does not want to come to terms with the fact of this equality and is aimed at searching for crafty, devious ways to nonetheless achieve for the United States some military advantages compared with the USSR.[5]

The real proof, however, that this was not a genuine Soviet perception was that it did not coincide with the Soviets' own behavior and attitudes toward military power and its support of "national-liberation movements" in the Third World.[6] As noted at the beginning of this chapter, the Soviet use of military power definitely increased in scale during a period when Soviet commentators were asserting that military power allegedly was not a viable instrument for the attainment of foreign policy objectives.

2. *The U.S. failure in Vietnam showed that flexible response was not a reliable doctrine because of its emphasis on military force. In addition, this failure in Vietnam was the main reason for the lowering of the U.S. conventional force requirement from "two and a half wars" to "one and a half wars."*

This was a more subtle theme of Soviet declaratory deterrence, since it contained elements of truth mixed with distortion. G. Arbatov was one of the first to argue this theme in the first issue of *SShA: Ekonomika, Politika, Ideologia* in January of 1970:

> The basis of this strategy [flexible response] always was reliance on military force. The war in Vietnam showed that military might alone can no longer bring the United States victory not only in the struggle against the "main" enemy, but also on the periphery. . . . It became clear that even the tremendous military power created by the United States has its limits, in which respect these limits are much narrower than required by the political plans of Washington.[7]

Arbatov also claimed to perceive ostensible contradictory behavior in U.S. military allocations in that "on the one hand, it is proceeding towards some reductions in the current military budget, and on the other, it is making a decision on building new, expensive weapons systems."[8] Such behavior, however, was not contradictory in the context of U.S. deterrence strategy and posture;[9] rather, it was contradictory in Soviet eyes to the way they would have wanted the United States to behave.

In an article in *MEMO* in August 1971, Lieutenant General Mil'shtein observed that the concept of one and a half wars was a step back from the previous requirements of being able to wage two and a half wars, although he was not specific about why the United States had stepped back from the requirements.[10] The apparent explanation given was that "the government and military commands of the USA calculated the 'Vietnam conflict' only as a 'half war.' . . . Yet after some time the complete baselessness of such calculations became evident."[11] The miscalculation of the probable scale of the war in Vietnam was so great, according to Mil'shtein, that it was the main factor responsible for the demise of the two-and-a-half-wars concept.[12]

It is unlikely, however, that Mil'shtein actually believed the explanation that he offered. The clear implications of the U.S. deterrence strategy and posture was that the United States did not expect the Soviet Union and the People's Republic of China to ally with each other against the United States in the event of a major conflict in Europe or Asia.[13] Given that the political split between the Soviet Union and the PRC was quite unmistakable by this time, the two nations having had border clashes along the Ussuri River as recently as 1969, and that President Nixon at the time of this article (August 1971) was effectively exploiting the rift with overtures to China, the Soviets were not about to acknowledge the fact in their analyses of U.S. doctrine. Instead, they rationalized the U.S. lowering of its force requirements by claiming that it was a forced development resulting from Vietnam:

> The fiasco in Vietnam served as a powerful catalyst for Washington's reassessment of the strategic situation because: (a) it fostered the coming to power in the U.S. government of a different party, the Republicans, and the logic of the interparty struggle was obligated to a certain "change of landmarks" and (b) it forced new people in a new government to make a critical analysis of the weaknesses and shortcomings of the Kennedy-Johnson strategy of "flexible response," the unsoundness of which had been revealed in Vietnam.[14]

3. *The realistic deterrence concept of "sufficiency" was no different from the previous flexible response concept of assured destruction. It is such an open-ended concept that it can be used to justify a continued arms race and other attempts to gain "one-sided advantages."*

This third major theme of the Soviet declaratory deterrence strategy had previously been directed towards U.S. strategic doctrine in general and was now a very prominent theme in Soviet discussions of SALT. When the Soviets did discuss SALT, however, it was as a separate entity. It was almost never mentioned in Soviet military writings and very rarely was discussed at any length in conjunction with Soviet analyses of U.S. strategic doctrine. That the Soviets would compartmentalize their analysis in such a fashion demonstrates their perception of SALT as an offensive propaganda weapon, rather than as a serious alternative. Soviet propagandists still wished to portray the United States as inherently aggressive, even though their actual perception (to be discussed later) was that the United States was retreating from its previously higher level of military commitment while trying to enforce its containment strategy.

Soviet commentators and analysts alike concentrated on the notion of sufficiency in trying to prove that U.S. "aggressive intentions" had still not changed. G. Trofimenko noted the seemingly deliberate open-endedness of sufficiency, citing American military leaders in support of his claim that the United States was still striving for superiority.[15] Another analyst asserted that sufficiency was little different from the McNamara concept of assured destruction. He claimed that "the new aggressive concept opens the way for the utilization of strategic nuclear weapons not only on targets of a global scale, but also for the attainment of advantage in periods of local crisis situations."[16] Mil'shtein made a similar argument, saying that sufficiency "in fact proceeds from the necessity of creating superiority in the strategic nuclear forces and keeping them in such a state of preparedness, which would have allowed the USA to continually threaten the world with the prospect of a nuclear blow on a global scale."[17]

In reality, however, the Soviet emphasis on the vagueness of the sufficiency concept was more an attempt to paint the United States as the instigator of the arms race than a real indicator of Soviet belief. For one thing, Soviet observers were well aware of the large body of opinion in the United States that was against trying to keep a clear-cut superiority in nuclear weapons, which was restricting U.S. freedom of action to maintain the levels of spending on strategic forces necessary to maintain superior numbers.[18] Another point is that they had already recognized the fact that the United States was cutting back on the level of forces it was willing to commit or support. Given that the Soviets believed the United States to be relying more on its allies, they would not at the same time believe that the United States was embarking on another massive buildup recalling the early 1960s. A variation on this was that the United States was striving for "qualitative" superiority. They argued that while realistic deterrence rejected "the thesis of absolute military superiority, it nevertheless stressed the significance of technical military superiority."[19] And, of course, the Soviet leadership emphasized the need for the Soviet

Union to attain and maintain "military-technical supremacy" over the United States.[20]

The Real Soviet View

1. *The Soviets saw realistic deterrence as a retreat from the flexible response doctrine, seeing the new doctrine as signifying a lower level of U.S. military commitment. Nevertheless, Soviet analysts saw much more similarity between realistic deterrence and flexible response than between flexible response and massive retaliation.*

Soviet analysts, even in publications primarily directed at Western audiences, did not fail to make the point that they considered the Nixon Doctrine to have been a retreat from previous periods:

> The military-political activity of the Nixon Administration since it was installed has outlined with sufficient clarity the conception which, it may be assumed, is to shape US foreign policy and military strategy over the immediate period ahead. It is a buildup of the armoury [sic] and the maintenance and strengthening of military commitments and greater wariness over participation in local conflicts.[21]

When compared with Secretary of Defense Laird's statements at the beginning of this chapter, one can see that this was an accurate assessment. The same analyst also recognized the defensive nature of the new doctrine and its implied retreat from the previous doctrine of flexible response. The same analyst observed that the new doctrine "envisages primarily suppression of the national liberation movement and the mounting of local wars," and that it was by such means that "US strategists hope to change the world balance of strength in favor of the USA and to fortify the positions of imperialism as a whole."[22] Such a statement is in contrast with earlier pronouncements during the massive retaliation and flexible response periods that pictured the United States in a much more aggressive foreign posture.

This theme was more explicitly stated by Georgi Arbatov, director of the Institute for the Study of the USA and Canada, in the February issue of *SShA: Ekonomika, Politika, Ideologia:*

> But in the 1960's it was revealed that even the limited wars undertaken within the framework of the doctrine of "flexible reaction" can prove to be very difficult for the United States, and can prove to be such that the United States, in essence, is incapable of winning any kind of decisive victory. These lessons were becoming more and more obvious and had to find some kind of reflection in the doctrines that were formulated by the new administration.[23]

An even more incisive analysis was found in the May 1971 issue of the above publication. The author recognized the altered strategic situation that necessitated the change in U.S. domestic constraints, such as increasing public American protests against the war, which were forcing change upon U.S. leadership:

> The Nixon Doctrine, as we can see, by no means signifies U.S. abandonment of those positions which it has seized abroad. It is only a change in the method of retaining them dictated by the altered situation. Remarking that ''over 25 years the American people have become tired of the international burden,'' the message's authors openly declare that the Nixon Doctrine is intended ''to satisfy the demands within the country concerning the manifestation of restraint in our international role without sacrificing our interests abroad.''[24]

Soviet analysts saw the primary change in U.S. strategic doctrine as being a reduced U.S. willingness to commit its own military forces as a means of enforcing the grand strategy of containment. This was a clear signal to the Soviet leadership that an increase in the scale of Soviet military power employment in support of its foreign policy would not be met directly by U.S. military opposition, particularly in the Third World; i.e., the United States was less willing to use its own military power to enforce its grand strategy of containment.

The Soviets saw far less difference in the specifics of the realistic deterrence strategy in comparison with flexible response. One of the few distinguishing features was the change in force level requirement from two and a half wars to one and a half wars.[25] Under the concept of one and a half wars, according to one Soviet analyst, ''the United States must be ready to simultaneously wage an aggressive war against the socialist countries in Europe or Asia and to resolve an 'emergency situation in any other place.' What is meant by the latter case is the suppression of the national liberation movement in different regions of the world.''[26] It was also contended that the new strategic doctrine of realistic deterrence was merely an updated version of flexible response:

> What has been set out . . . leads to the conclusion that the ''realistic restraint'' strategy does not in fact reject the ''flexible response'' doctrine, as some leading Washington figures say. It only brings it up to date. The anti-communist trend—the basis for all American military-political concepts—is fully preserved in this strategy. It is essentially distinguished from its predecessor in that it relies on a broader military-technical and military-organizational base, and this endows it with a character which is still more dangerous for the cause of peace.[27]

Culling out the rhetoric in the above passage regarding the ''dangerous character'' of realistic deterrence, Soviet observers saw little change in the broader aspects of U.S. doctrine. This was further corroborated by Lieutenant General Mil'shtein in the August 1971 issue of *MEMO*:

> The difference of the strategy of "realistic deterrence" from the strategy of "flexible response" consists mainly in the means and methods of attaining objectives. Beyond these limits "realistic deterrence" and "flexible response" are in fact identical. The new strategy is called the strategy of "realistic deterrence," yet the English word "deterrence" may also have another meaning, for example, "intimidation." [Note: the Soviets do not have a word for "deterrence" in the Russian language!] Therefore the new strategy is sometimes called the strategy of "realistic intimidation," that, perhaps better reflects its actual direction.[28]

It is interesting that Mil'shtein leaned toward "intimidation" as more descriptive of the intent behind the notion of deterrence. The Russian word *sderzhivania,* meaning literally a "holding in check," implied a more defensive connotation than the Russian word *ustrashenia,* which could best be translated as "intimidation." Mil'shtein may have been trying to make a propaganda point by ascribing a more aggressive intent to the idea of deterrence. In any event, Mil'shtein's point, propaganda or not, was contradicted in the November 1971 issue of *SShA: Ekonomika, Politika, Ideologia* by Colonel V. Larionov, a member of the editorial group of Soviet officers for *Voennaia Strategia (Military Strategy).* In his article, he stated that "much of what the United States believed feasible (even if only speculatively so) a few years ago is now discarded by Washington as impractical."[29] Larionov, therefore, confirmed the overall Soviet perception of realistic deterrence as basically defensive. As the U.S. withdrawal program from Vietnam was well underway by this time, there was ample corroboration for this perception in U.S. behavior, not to mention U.S. willingness to participate in SALT negotiations.

2. *The United States was adapting itself to the growth of Soviet strategic power.*

This theme was one that was stated across the board in English-language Soviet publications as well as in Soviet military and academic journals. For example, in the September 1971 issue of *Soviet Military Review,* the authors accurately observed that realistic deterrence was simply an attempt to increase the utility of U.S. military power in a situation of nuclear parity as opposed to the previous condition of nuclear "superiority":

> This above all explains Washington's attention to the "realistic deterrence strategy." Carried out in the framework of the "flexible response" concept, it has as its aim to consolidate the leading position of the USA in the capitalist world, galvanise NATO and other military blocs, make the "allies" shoulder an additional burden of militarisation, and extend the scale of their participation in US imperialism's aggressive ventures. . . . In short, the "realistic deterrence strategy" is another attempt to find more effective means for solving military-political tasks from "positions of strength" in the situation when the new world balance of forces is no longer favorable for imperialism.[30]

G.A. Trofimenko, author of several books and articles on U.S. and NATO doctrine, was one of the most prominent spokesmen for this theme. He characterized the central problem of postwar U.S. foreign policy as the resolution of the dilemma between "seeking ways to retain war as an instrument for implementing U.S. imperialism's foreign policy aims, on the one hand, and to utilize military force in such a way that its application does not threaten the United States' very existence on the other."[31] He claimed to see a great deal of continuity in the evolution of U.S. strategic doctrine, asserting that "each subsequent strategy has emerged not in a vacuum but has been organically linked with the preceding one."[32] In explaining the shift by the U.S. from flexible response to realistic deterrence, Trofimenko named what he believed were the main factors in the shifting correlation of forces, among them the growth of Soviet military power:

> The U.S. defeat in Vietnam—a defeat which has called the fundamental postulates of the "flexible response" strategy into question—the new correlation of forces in the world—a correlation linked with the intensification of the Soviet Union's economic and military might and with the further development of the world revolutionary process, on the one hand, and the Peking leaders' definite about-face in foreign policy on the other—all made the latest revision of U.S. military-political strategy inevitable.[33]

Soviet analysts recognized that the Nixon Doctrine was "a modification of various elements of the policy of 'containment' in a new situation, with a correction for those reduced capabilities that the United States has at its disposal today."[34] By "reduced capabilities" the Soviets did not actually mean that the United States had declined in the level of its *absolute* military power, but that its relative position of superiority with respect to the Soviet Union had been eliminated, and therefore greater restraints were now placed on the use of U.S. military power. This, according to Arbatov, was one of the main factors compelling the United States to reappraise its strategic doctrine:

> To a greater degree than his predecessors, Nixon has been forced to adapt American foreign policy to the changing ratio of forces in the world, to the new conditions that have been created as a result of the further weakening of the military-political and economic positions of the United States, on the one hand, and the increase in the might of the Soviet Union and the entire socialist community with their increasing influence upon the course of world events, on the other. . . . The admission that the United States is incapable of fulfilling the role of world policeman in all conflicts and critical situations is not a voluntary course, but a forced line governing the conduct of the American ruling circles.[35]

Other analyses were still more blunt, arguing that the Soviet attainment of strategic parity with the United States had been primarily responsible for the change. Furthermore, Trofimenko argued that it was the possession of such nuclear parity that was effectively restraining the United States from first use of its nuclear weapons against the Soviet Union:

> But since, in reality, it was a question all these years not of restraining the USSR from attacking the United States but, on the contrary, of the USSR restraining U.S. imperialism from unleashing a big thermonuclear war, the U.S. concept of "deterrence" signifies, in fact, a recognition that the Soviet Union possesses such strategic strength which effectively restrains the United States from direct use of its nuclear missile arsenal against the USSR. This is how the situation of the well-known nuclear balance between the USSR and the United States arose, which is characterized by the second part of the formula of the new strategy, that is, by the word "deterrence."[36]

Trofimenko showed good perception of the real nature of U.S. doctrine, noting that realistic deterrence "officially proceeds from U.S. reluctance to be the initiator of unleashing such a conflict and stipulates only the U.S. right and resolve to inflict a counterstrike in the event of an attack on itself."[37] Examining its conventional aspects, he contended that "by expanding military partnership and promoting U.S. allies as the main and, according to the optimum variation, the only suppliers for waging 'local wars,' the Washington leaders are trying to create freedom of action for themselves in critical situations."[38]

In other words, an ongoing struggle was perceived in U.S. strategic planning between the weakening power positions of the United States relative to the Soviet Union on the one hand, and U.S. efforts to counter such a trend by modifying its strategic doctrine to meet the needs of a changing situation on the other hand. This was spoken of as "the contradiction between the desire to preserve war as a political means and imperialism's ever narrowing opportunities for waging a successful war which brings results."[39] Such a statement should be viewed with some skepticism, however. Although the relative-power position of the United States had indeed declined, and though Vietnam-style interventions had proven to be counterproductive, the utility of U.S. military power had not declined to the extent ostensibly believed by Trofimenko, who claimed that realistic deterrence was "a futile search for ways and means of waging war which are without danger for the United States."[40] In a state of strategic parity, the use of military power by the Soviets would have been as risky for them as they said it was for us. But since the Soviets themselves had increased the scale of their use of military power, then it was logically still possible for the United States to use its military power in similar fashion without undue risk of escalation to a strategic exchange.

Another analysis by Trofimenko, while criticizing the use of the word "deterrence" as mere camouflage, nevertheless conceded that the statement by Secretary Laird to Congress (March 9, 1971) describing the U.S. military position for 1972-1976 "can be viewed as a very frank description of the forms of and conditions for U.S. participation in future military conflicts provoked by the forces of imperialism."[41] One of the main differences noted between flexible response and realistic deterrence was that the latter implied that the level of military response made by the United States would not necessarily match that used by an adversary, either in kind or degree:

> Generalizing, it can be said that while under Kennedy and Johnson "flexibility" consisted in creating a capability for using American armed forces in a braod range of variations of force with inflexibility in the military obligations taken on by the USA, under Nixon the "flexibility" is interpreted primarily as preserving great freedom for the USA to decide whether it will or will not become involved in a particular military conflict, with greater rigidity in the use of military force if the USA all the same decides to use it.[42]

By changing the meaning of "flexibility," therefore, the United States was trying to resolve "the dilemma of how to keep war as an instrument of U.S. foreign policy and at the same time do it in such a way that if the war does break out, it is not a catastrophe for the USA itself." It must be emphasized that the Soviets saw the Nixon Doctrine and realistic deterrence as forced developments, not as a manifestation of any basic pacifism in the nature of U.S. society. Their rationale was that because of "the sharp qualitative improvement and the quantitative growth in the nuclear missile arsenals of the main rivals, and the improvement in the strategic arsenals of other nuclear powers, the current leaders in Washington have been forced to develop their military concepts with due regard for current realities."[43]

The culmination of U.S. reassessment of its strategic doctrine was said to have taken place in the May 1972 summit meeting between President Nixon and Party Secretary Leonid Brezhnev in Moscow. This development was stressed in the October 1973 issue of *International Affairs,* which stated that "the recognition by the US ruling circles of the nuclear parity between the Soviet Union and the United States was recorded in the documents signed during the May 1972 summit meeting in Moscow."[44] The most important conclusion the Soviets drew from this series of events was that the growth of its own strategic power was a decisive factor in the global "correlation of world forces," which was asserted by Trofimenko in the October 1975 issue of *International Affairs:*

> To sum it up, the balance of world forces had further shifted in socialism's favour by the early 1970's as evidenced, for example, by the attainment of Soviet-American nuclear and missile parity and the awareness by the USA of its limited possibilities to influence diverse events in the world by means of military forces. This made the US ruling class start a "reappraisal of values" and

acknowledge the need ''to reconcile the reality of competition between the two systems with the imperative of coexistence.''[45]

3. *The United States, despite the adaptation of its strategic doctrine to the growing strategic nuclear power of the Soviet Union, still is attempting to incorporate a nuclear warfighting strategy into its doctrine.*

Notwithstanding the general accuracy of the Soviet appraisal of U.S. doctrinal developments during this period, there was nevertheless a marked inclination by Soviet analysts to look for warfighting characteristics in the realistic deterrence strategy. A U.S. move toward such a doctrine would be the very kind of ''reactionary reversal'' in U.S. strategic doctrine that the Soviets feared most. Such fears would later be confirmed by the proposal of the limited nuclear options strategy by Defense Secretary James Schlesinger. Because this mirror-imaging tendency has been noted and documented considerably in previous chapters, only a few representative examples need be used here.

One example of Soviet mirror-imaging was in an article by Soviet military analyst Major General R. Simonyan. He claimed that realistic deterrence, ''like its predecessor, stems from the need to prepare and wage wars of different scales: from local wars to all-out nuclear war.''[46] The reasons for such mirror-imaging are not as strange as we might think, since the Soviets believed that there exist certain ''laws'' governing military science and strategy. Since these laws supposedly hold true regardless of the circumstances surrounding a potential conflict, it would be foolish from the Soviet perspective for an adversary to knowingly violate them.[47] Since the Soviets consistently credited U.S. actions with a certain degree of rationality, it follows that Soviet analysts would expect U.S. planners to adopt a strategy the Soviets considered rational.

Even with the Soviet recognition of a U.S. retreat in its doctrine, they continued to look for warfighting orientations in U.S. doctrine. Major General Simonyan, writing for *New Times* in March of 1977, claimed that ''Pentagon and NATO strategists see in surprise attack the best way to start a general nuclear war, since this could substantially weaken retaliatory strikes, give the strategic initiative to the attacker and sharply shift the balance in his favor.''[48] One might be tempted at first to dismiss such statements as pure propaganda designed to portray the United States in the most aggressive light possible. However, when considered within the context of Soviet strategic doctrine, which emphasized surprise and the notion of a preemptive strike, it becomes merely another instance of Soviet mirror-imaging of their own strategy onto U.S. doctrine. If the Soviets themselves considered a preemptive strike an optimum strategy to adopt, then they would have considered it optimum for the United States as well. This is why Soviet declaratory deterrence statements were designed to convince the United States that such a strategy could not possibly work; the last thing the Soviets wanted was for the United States to adopt a nuclear warfighting doctrine similar to their own, since this would have negated much of the benefit that the Soviets were getting from the U.S. deterrence posture in terms of freedom to use their own military power in support of their objectives.

In the April 1977 issue of *Voenno-Istoricheskii Zhurnal* an article appeared that analyzed the development of U.S. strategic doctrine in the postwar period. As illustrated by the following passage, much of the thinking attributed to U.S. planners concerning a future nuclear war could just as easily have been taken from Soviet statements concerning their own doctrine:

> In accordance with present actual military doctrine, the basis on which the strategy of "realistic deterrence"["ustrashenia," meaning "intimidation" in the literal sense] is composed, the USA should be prepared for the waging of total, as well as limited nuclear war. The doctrine considers total nuclear war as a war between two opposing social systems—capitalist and socialist. It is considered, that a future war will be coalitional, short and decisive, with the mass use of nuclear-rocket weapons. A total nuclear war may be unleashed by two means: by a surprise nuclear attack or gradual engagement in war, by the escalation of a local war into a total, nuclear war.[49]

The words regarding the "clash between two opposing social systems," with emphasis on the "coalitional, short and decisive," nature of a nuclear conflict, is reminiscent of some of the characteristics of Soviet military doctrine as it was originally stated by Khrushchev and Malinovskiy in 1960, and as it remains today.

Conclusion

On the whole, leaving out the rhetoric, the Soviet analysis of the Nixon Doctrine and realistic deterrence was quite accurate. By 1969 the strategic balance had changed (see Appendix A), and opposition to the Vietnam war was mounting in the United States. Clearly the United States was no longer able to engage in Vietnam types of containment actions, and now sought a new "formula" whereby the other countries would take the responsibility of defending themselves and the United States would be more selective in its intervention. The Nixon Doctrine played a part in the eventual move to the 1972 detente. It signaled an important retrenchment in U.S. policy and obviously a greater readiness on the part of the United States to seek some form of cooperation with the Soviet Union. Of course, certain propagandistic themes such as the aggressive nature of capitalism, U.S. reliance on military power and responsibility for the arms race, the danger of a reactionary reversal in U.S.

policy, and fundamental U.S. "anti-Sovietism" remained constant themes of Soviet declaratory deterrence strategy, as was shown in the first part of this chapter. But the Soviets, for the most part, saw the Nixon Doctrine and realistic deterrence as a retreat, as indeed they were.

In 1974, however, there would be a proposal in U.S. strategic doctrine set forth by Defense Secretary James Schlesinger that would produce a surprisingly worried reaction from Soviet commentators, who saw certain elements of his proposed limited nuclear options strategy as the very kind of "dangerous reversal" in U.S. strategy that they had feared. These particular elements, and the Soviet reaction to the proposed doctrine in general, will be the focus of the next chapter.

Notes

1. See M. Laird, *Statement of Secretary of Defense Melvin R. Laird before the House Armed Services Committee on the Fiscal Year 1972-1976 Defense Program and the 1972 Defense Budget* (Washington, D.C.: U.S. Government Printing Office, March 1, 1971), p. 15.
2. An examination of the Soviet view of détente in their foreign policy strategy is found in F. Kohler et al., *Soviet Strategy for the Seventies: From Cold War to Peaceful Coexistance* (Coral Gables, Fla.: Center for Advanced International Studies, 1973), p. 87.
3. G.A. Trofimenko, "some Aspects of US Military and Political Strategy," *SShA: Ekonomika, Politika, Ideologia,* No. 10, October 1970, trans. in JPRS No. 51895, December 1, 1970, p. 30. See also A. Baryshev, "New US Doctrines, Same Old Aim," *International Affairs,* No. 12, December 1969, p. 12.
4. G.A. Arbatov et al., "The Nixon Doctrine: Declarations and Realities," *SShA: Ekonomika, Politika, Ideologia,* No. 2, February 1971, trans. FBIS, *USSR Daily Report,* March 5, 1971, p. A34.
5. G.A. Trofimenko, *SShA: Ekonomika, Politika, Ideologia,* No. 12, December 1971, trans. JPRS No. 54971, January 19, 1972, p. 15.
6. Kohler et al., *Soviet Strategy for the Seventies: From Cold War to Peaceful Coexistence,* pp. 76-78. See also ibid., pp. 83-88 for Soviet commentary on the need for continued military buildup.
7. G.A. Arbatov, "American Foreign Policy at the Threshold of the 1970's," *SShA: Ekonomika, Politika, Ideologia,* No. 1, January 1970, trans. JPRS No. 49934, February 26, 1970, pp. 16, 19.
8. Ibid., p. 24.
9. J.E. Endicott and R.W. Stafford Jr., *American Defense Policy* (New York: Johns Hopkins University Press, 1977), pp. 80-81.
10. M. Mil'shtein, "American Military Doctrine: Continuity and Modifications," *MEMO,* No. 8, August 1971, pp. 34-35.
11. Ibid., p. 35.
12. Ibid., p. 36.
13. Endicott and Stafford, *American Defense Policy*, p. 81.
14. G.A. Trofimenko, "Military-Strategic Aspects of the Nixon Doctrine," *Doktrina*

Niksona, ed. Yu. Davydov (Moscow: Izdatelstvia Nauka, 1972), trans. JPRS No. 58317, February 26, 1973, p. 49.

15. Trofimenko, "US Military and Political Strategy," p. 19. See also idem, "Nixon Doctrine," p. 54.

16. O. Bykov, "Concerning Some Features of the Foreign Policy Strategy of the USA," *MEMO*, No. 4, April 1971, p. 57.

17. Mil'shtein, "American Military Doctrine," p. 33. See also V. Larionov, "The Transformation of the 'Strategic Sufficiency' Concept," *SShA: Ekonomika, Politika, Ideologia*, No. 11, November 1971, trans. JPRS No. 54676, December 10, 1971, p. 38. See also pp. 39-40 of the same article for the Soviet definition of the U.S. concept of "sufficiency."

18. Mil'shtein, "American Military Doctrine," pp. 35-37.

19. V.F. Petrovskiy, "The Evolution of the 'National Security' Doctrine," *SShA: Ekonomika, Politika, Ideologia*, No. 11, November 1978, trans. FBIS, *USSR Daily Report Annex*, November 17, 1978, p. 5.

20. Kohler et al., *Soviet Strategy*, pp. 86-89.

21. B. Teplinsky, "Some Aspects of US Global Strategy," *International Affairs*, No. 5, May 1970, p. 70. See also G.A. Trofimenko, "Anti-Communism and Imperialism's Foreign Policy," *International Affairs*, No. 1, January 1971, p. 53. See Soviet admission of limited war possibility in Editorial, "On Guard for Peace and the Building of Socialism," *Voennaia Mysl'*, No. 12, December 1971, trans. FBIS, FPD No. 0003/74, January 17, 1974, p. 12.

22. Teplinsky, "US Global Strategy," p. 70.

23. Arbatov et al., "Nixon Doctrine," p. A3. See also Trofimenko, *SShA: Ekonomika, Politika, Ideologia*, No. 12, December 1971, trans. JPRS No. 54971, January 19, 1972, p. 3.

24. D.Z. Khoskin, "Labyrinth of Contradictions," *SShA: Ekonomika, Politika, Ideologia*, No. 5, May 1971, trans. JPRS No. 53268, June 2, 1971, p. 80. See also A. Migolat'yev, "The Aggressive Essence of the Military-Political Strategy of American Imperialism," *KVS*, No. 10, May 1971, p. 84; P. Zhilin and Y. Rybkin, "Militarism and Contemporary International Relations," *International Affairs*, No. 10, October 1973, p. 28.

25. J. Collins, *American and Soviet Military Trends since the Cuban Missile Crisis* (Washington, D.C.: Center for Strategic and International Studies, 1978), pp. 157-58.

26. R. Simonyan, "A Strategy Doomed to Failure," *Pravda*, August 14, 1971, p. 4, trans. FBIS, *USSR Daily Report*, August 25, 1971, p. A5.

27. Ibid., p. A6.

28. Mil'shtein, "American Military Doctrine," pp. 40-41. See also Trofimenko, "Nixon Doctrine," p. 60.

29. Larionov, "Strategic Sufficiency," p. 33.

30. V. Perfilov, "New Doctrine—Old Aims," *Soviet Military Review*, No. 9, September 1971, p. 57. See also B. Dmitriev, "Policy of Détente," *New Times*, No. 43, October 1971, p. 7.

31. Trofimenko, "US Military and Political Strategy," p. 15.

32. Ibid., p. 18.

33. Ibid., p. 19. See also I. Potapov, "The Evolution of the Strategic Concepts of Imperialism in the Post-War Period," *Voenno-Istoricheskii Zhurnal*, No. 5, May 1971, pp. 44-49, passim.

34. Arbatov et al., "Nixon Doctrine," p. A7.

35. Ibid.
36. Trofimenko, *SShA: Ekonomika, Politika, Ideologia,* No. 12, December 1971, trans. JPRS No. 54971, January 19, 1972, pp. 8, 14. See also similar statements by Brezhnev and Grechko quoted in L. Gouré, F. Kohler, and M. Harvey, *The Role of Nuclear Forces in Current Soviet Strategy* (Coral Gables, Fla.: Center for Advanced International Studies, 1975), p. 49.
37. Ibid.
38. Ibid., p. 10.
39. Ibid., p. 13.
40. Ibid., pp. 14-15. See also idem, "Nixon Doctrine," pp. 47-49.
41. Trofimenko, "Nixon Doctrine," p. 55.
42. Ibid., p. 60.
43. Ibid., p. 68. See also Petrovskiy, "National Security Doctrine," p. 3.
44. Anat. Gromyko and A. Kokoshin, "US Foreign Policy Strategy for the 1970's," *International Affairs,* No. 10, October 1973, p. 69.
45. G. Trofimenko, "From Confrontation to Coexistence," *International Affairs,* No. 10, October 1975, p. 38. See also P. Sergeyev and V. Trusenkov, "Evolution of the US Military Doctrine," *Soviet Military Review,* No. 11, November 1976, p. 52.
46. Simonyan, "Doomed to Failure," p. A6.
47. For an example of Soviet commentary regarding the laws of armed conflict, see *The Philosophical Heritage of V.I. Lenin and Problems of Contemporary War* (Moscow: Voennoe Izdatelstvo, 1972), trans. U.S. Air Force (Washington, D.C.: U.S. Government Printing Office, 1972), pp. 95-116. See also Sergeyev and Trusenkov, " US Military Doctrine," p. 52.
48. R. Simonyan, " 'Realistic Deterrence': The Real Implications," *New Times,* No. 10, March 1977, p. 18. See also idem, "The Pentagon's Nuclear Strategy," *New Times,* No. 35, August 1977, pp. 22-24.
49. N. Nikitin, "The Evolution of the Military Doctrine and Strategic Concepts of the USA after the Second World War," *Voenno-Istoricheskii Zhurnal,* No. 4, April 1977, p. 66.

8

Dangerous Reversal: Soviet Reaction to the LNO Strategy

Why the Soviet Reaction Is Important

Soviet analysts were clearly disturbed by the announcement of the strategy of limited nuclear options as an important part of the proposed Schlesinger doctrine, because it signaled the possibility of the very kind of ''dangerous reversal'' in U.S. strategic doctrine that the Soviets had long feared might take place. They expressed this fear even though they were claiming at the same time that the likelihood of strategic nuclear war had been greatly reduced, largely because they perceived the United States as restrained in its ability to threaten escalation by the growth of Soviet strategic power.

The timing of the LNO strategy was especially disturbing, since it came in January 1974, a time when the United States had just about extricated itself from the quagmire of Indochina. U.S. willingness to commit its military power in support of anything was at an all-time low, particularly because of the domestic turmoil being stirred up by the Watergate affair. The Soviets were at the stage of considering the use of proxy troops in more overt fashion to support their supposed national liberation movements in Third World countries. It is not surprising then, that the Soviets would have been nervous over the possibility that the United States might actually respond to an increased use of Soviet military power with a limited strategic strike on Soviet territory using only one or a few nuclear weapons.

The reasons behind this kind of Soviet reaction can be clearly understood if we look at the logic behind the Soviet declaratory deterrence strategy from previous periods. Soviet reaction in the past to any declared U.S. attempts to limit conflict on either a conventional or a nuclear scale had always consisted of statements designed to give the impression that such attempts might lead to uncontrolled escalation to strategic nuclear war. Despite the public Soviet use of this threat, other analyses from both public and private Soviet sources had been increasingly admitting the likelihood and necessity of having to wage a limited, localized conflict *without* escalating to strategic nuclear war. By the use of their declaratory deterrence strategy, however, the Soviets were hoping to encourage the United States to remain in its pure retaliatory posture based on mutual assured destruction and to believe that any attempts to use its nuclear weaponry for any other purposes were too dangerous.

But with the LNO strategy, the United States was threatening to wipe out the entire basis for the Soviet declaratory deterrence strategy in one stroke. The earlier Soviet reaction to Herman Kahn's escalation ladder provides the reason why. Both public and private Soviet evaluations of Kahn's escalation concept indicate that the Soviets were highly disturbed by the apparent U.S. willingness to escalate in complete disregard of Soviet implied threats of further escalation to dangerous levels. The Soviets were counting on the United States' remaining in its defensive retaliatory posture so that they might have more freedom to use Soviet military power to aid in the attainment of her political and strategic objectives. A United States that apparently was willing to disregard the dangers involved in escalation was a great restraint on Soviet freedom of action, from their point of view, because the Soviets themselves were afraid of the consequences of such escalation. Although it is true that the nuclear balance was more in favor of the Soviets at the time of the LNO strategy as compared to the mid-1960s (see Appendix A), there were enough similarities in the Soviet response to escalation and limited nuclear options to suggest that the actual adoption of an LNO strategy might have improved the U.S. ability to discourage Soviet use of her military power later on.

This point, however, cannot be proven or disproven. Since the Schlesinger Doctrine was never wholly adopted, Schlesinger having been fired by President Ford in 1976, the LNO strategy fell by the wayside. Some features though, such as increased targeting flexibility and accuracy, were picked up later and incorporated into U.S. strategic planning. In fact, they were to show up in the U.S. "countervailing strategy" announced during the Carter administration (a subject for the next chapter). Since the LNO strategy never became an operational part of U.S. strategic doctrine, it is not practical to compare Soviet foreign policy behavior with their stated views on LNO. The reason for this is that the doctrine actually in force during this brief period (1974-1976) was at best an attenuated version of the Nixon Doctrine. Examining the Soviet perception of the LNO strategy is still useful, nevertheless, since the nature of the Soviet response provides important clues to what the Soviets might find deterring or restraining to them. As will be seen in the course of this chapter, the Soviets reacted most strongly to those features of the LNO strategy that looked like moves towards a nuclear warfighting doctrine similar to what the Soviets themselves adhered to.

The Soviet Propaganda Line

As was the case with previous U.S. strategic doctrines that had been implemented, the primary purpose of the Soviet declaratory deterrence strategy was to discredit the feasibility of limited nuclear options. Soviet commentators used basically these three lines of argument:

1. *The use of limited strategic strikes against military targets in the Soviet Union carried the danger of uncontrolled escalation to total nuclear war. Such a limited strike would not be conducted according to the rules of the game envisioned by Schlesinger and would not remain confined for long to limited exchanges.*

Even before the LNO strategy had been set forth in January 1974, at least one Soviet military analyst foresaw the possibility of a limited strategic exchange for purposes of political intimidation. Army General S. Ivanov, in the May 1969 issue of *Voennaia Mysl'*, pointed out this possibility even while saying that such an exchange could not characterize the entire war:

> Of course, theoretically it can be assumed that for the purpose of scaring one another the belligerents will limit themselves to inflicting some selected nuclear attacks on secondary objectives, but will not dare to expand the nuclear conflict any further. But such an exchange of individual nuclear attacks, even if it should take place, cannot characterize the war in entirety.[1]

This assertion reflected the warfighting mindset of the Soviet military, which was not inclined to think of nuclear attacks as a means of political "signaling" or incremental coercion, even if they were on a limited scale.

Soviet propagandists once again borrowed from the Western press in their selection of arguments that would appear most credible to unwary Western readers. For example, then lieutenant general M. Mil'shtein and Colonel L. Semeyko, in the November 1974 issue of *SShA: Ekonomika, Politika, Ideologia*, claimed that "even having begun by inflicting strikes on several selected military targets, such a conflict will not develop in accordance with the 'rules of the game' now being drawn up in Pentagon offices but will most likely develop into a general war which does not lend itself to 'flexible response.'"[2] In other words, regardless of U.S. efforts to impose limits on the kind of targets that were to be attacked, there was no guarantee that the war would not escalate further. What Soviet commentators were careful not to say, though, is that there was also no guarantee that the war *would* escalate.

Arbatov reiterated this Soviet propaganda theme in *Soviet Military Review*, arguing that it is "hard to assume that nuclear war, once it begins, will remain within the artificial 'rules' and not grow into a universal war."[3] Notice that the Soviets never tried to provide any solid argumentative evidence that an LNO strategy would lead to strategic nuclear war; they asserted it flatly and without elaboration, as if it were an unchallengeable tenet of faith. Also,

Schlesinger never said that war would not escalate, but he did say that the president should have the option to initiate a U.S. response at various levels of intensity.

2. *The United States is striving to derive unilateral advantages from the LNO strategy through a lowering of the nuclear threshold.*

The Soviets tried to argue that any lowering of the so-called nuclear threshold was destabilizing. Such was the case in the May 1975 issue of *Mezhdunarodnaia Zhizn*, the Russian-language version of *International Affairs*:

> In substantiating the need for the strategy of "retargeting," the US military theoreticians assert that the United States' possession of the ability to wage "limited" nuclear wars intensifies the "deterrent" effect and strengthens international stability. But in reality, this theory, which preaches the permissibility of the use of nuclear weapons, leads to an erosion of the differences between conventional and nuclear wars and creates an illusion of the legitimacy of a war in which nuclear missile means are used. Therefore the US researcher Barry Carter is profoundly correct when he writes that the concept of "retargeting" in fact contains a "tendency to overcome arguments against the use of nuclear arms—in essence a tendency toward lowering the nuclear threshold."[4]

Of course, what the Soviets did not say was the fact that the ability of the *defender* to "lower the nuclear threshold" by means of an LNO strategy was highly destabilizing for Soviet planning. It introduced still more uncertainty into the calculus of Soviet strategic planning by confronting the Soviets with the hitherto excluded possibility (at least in public discussions) of a series of nuclear strikes on Soviet territory that were limited in scope and number; that is, a low-level counterforce war. By increasing the range of possible U.S. responses in this way, Soviet planners would have had to exercise more caution in their evaluation of the US intent in the event of a confrontation.

The author of the above article also argued that the LNO strategy represented an "arbitrary convention" between "nuclear wars of various degrees of intensity," and thus was "extremely unstable and mobile." He argues further that "once used, nuclear missile weapons set off a chain reaction which, taking into consideration the distinctive features of modern military equipment and the military-ideological doctrines of the United States which envisage the direct participation of strategic forces in the implementation of the tasks of a 'limited war,' could prove to be totally uncontrolled and extremely rapid."[5] This was a presumptuous statement on the author's part, since there has never been a military conflict in which nuclear weapons have been used on anything resembling a large scale, nor one in which nuclear weapons were possessed by more than one side. So it is difficult to take seriously a statement that baldly asserts that the use of nuclear weapons will in fact set off a chain reaction.

It was Arbatov who put forth one of the most refined propaganda arguments against LNO in a July issue of *New Times*. In the following passage, he basically argued that neither side could be expected to restrain itself during a crisis to highly circumscribed rules of the game that were arbitrarily defined by the United States:

> For example, even if one were to suppose that a situation emerged in which the threat of the escalation of a nuclear conflict right up to a massive ("spasmodic," to use Schlesinger's term) strike against cities did not prevent the hypothetical "enemy" from carrying out a "limited attack," then the enemy would be deterred still less by the threat of a "selective retaliatory strike." On the contrary, it would create the impression that such actions are less risky and more acceptable. Furthermore, if we were to suppose that a "limited nuclear war" had nevertheless started, the other side could not be requested to hold its missiles meant for a retaliatory strike (including a strike against cities) "in reserve" in the silos—after all, these missiles, according to Schlesinger's ideas, are in fact the main target of a "limited" (essentially, disarming) strike by the foe's nuclear forces.[6]

The problem with Arbatov's argument was that LNO was not intended to have included a "disarming" strike, but was designed to be a means of incremental coercion to persuade the opponent to end the war quickly at minimum loss to the United States and its allies. If one looked at the LNO strategy in terms of its usefulness in an actual nuclear warfighting doctrine, then it made little sense. If a nation adopts a warfighting strategy, then it follows that it must have conditions or objectives that define "victory." On the other hand, if the national objective (as in the case of the United States) was the avoidance of nuclear war in the first place or the early termination of the war at minimum loss should deterrence fail, then it was not necessary to define victory. Since the Soviet strategic culture was (and continues to be) dominated by nuclear warfighting concepts, the Soviets saw the LNO strategy as evidence that the United States was trying to break out of its strategic impasse, which had been imposed by the growth of Soviet military power:

> Since the strengthening of the USSR's defense put an end to hopes that a nuclear war was possible and safe for the United States, the military-industrial complex and its patrons in the United States have repeatedly tried to break out of the deadlock that had developed. They created increasingly refined strategic concepts. Of course, this did not reduce the threat of general war.[7]

3. *No nuclear conflict can be limited because of the very nature of the weapons involved.*

Typical of this kind of propaganda is the following excerpt from a Radio Moscow commentary. Since this theme was the simplest, it was used most often and most widely by Soviet commentators:

It is always said that it wouldn't be a total strike but rather a selective one with small nuclear warheads, as though that changes anything. A nuclear war is a nuclear war, with all its horrors and untold suffering, especially when it is started against a country in possession of equal means to make a return strike.[8]

A variation of this argument was that the destructive power of nuclear weapons was so great that it was not possible to use them against isolated military targets without causing heavy casualties among the civilian population. This allegedly made it impossible to have a limited nuclear war. The following passage from an article by Major General Simonyan in a March 1979 issue of *New Times* was typical:

Actually, as the U.S. press has noted, the location of military installations is such that nuclear strikes at them, however "selective," would inevitably cause enormous loss of life among the civilian population. For instance, Pentagon experts have estimated that a nuclear strike at the Whiteman air base in Missouri could take a toll of 10.3 million lives. The consequences of "limited" nuclear warfare would be still more disastrous if massive strikes with scores or perhaps hundreds of warheads in the megaton class were used against military targets.[9]

This was a false argument, since the Soviets deliberately omitted the fact that the United States had the technology to produce low-yield warheads and to deliver them with sufficient accuracy to minimize the collateral damage inflicted. The implication that LNO would involve a "massive strike" with "hundreds of warheads" was also false, since the strategy was originally intended to provide a number of lesser options short of such a massive strike.[10] This kind of argument was really little more than a word game, since its validity rested on the basis of the Soviets' having defined nuclear weapons beforehand as unlimited by their very nature.

The Real Soviet View

The period of the most active Soviet response to the strategy of limited nuclear options dated from November 1974 to the end of 1976, by which time it had become fairly obvious to the Soviets that the Schlesinger Doctrine with its attendant strategy of LNO was not going to be adopted as part of U.S. strategic doctrine. (This was especially so in light of the fact that Ford had fired Schlesinger as secretary of defense by this time.) Between the time of Schlesinger's initial statements on LNO in January 1974[11] and the first comprehensive response to LNO in the Soviet press in November 1974, there was an unusually long pause, during which there was little real attempt at serious public analysis of LNO. The Soviets were undoubtedly using this time to analyze its implications before going public with their preferred line. Unfortunately, unclassified issues of *Voennaia Mysl'* after 1973 are not available and so there is currently no way of using this publication as a check on open sources. However, there was a considerable amount of discussion of LNO in the East European press during the early part of 1974, the very period when the Soviets themselves were silent on the subject for the most part.[12]

1. *Soviet analysts saw LNO as a move towards a nuclear warfighting doctrine similar in some respects to their own, equating it with the counterforce strategy formerly espoused by McNamara. The Soviets further believed that this strategy was an abandonment of a pure retaliatory posture in favor of a possible U.S. first use of nuclear weapons.*

The Soviet preference for viewing U.S. strategic doctrine through the prism of their own nuclear warfighting strategy was still fully evident during this period, even in some of the most authoritative and comprehensive analyses. For example, Lieutenant General Mil'shtein, in the first major analysis of LNO, in the November 1974 issue of *SShA: Ekonomika, Politika, Ideologia*, showed this mirror-imaging tendency even while making the propagandistic assertion that possession of strategic power had little political utility:

> If we sum up the results of the period from the end of the forties through the six-ties, the main point which emerges is that, during that period, the focus of American military-political thinking and of official military-strategic aims was by no means the problem of the impossibility of nuclear war, despite the many loud statements made about the horrors such a war would entail, but, on the contrary, the problem of seeking ways of using that power and *seeking out forms and methods of waging war which would enable the United States to survive and win in a nuclear clash*. [This is a virtual mirror-image of what occurred in the Soviet Union during the late forties and up through the early sixties.] Emphasis was placed on this despite the growing awareness of the fact that attempts by the United States to use all or even part of its nuclear potential could have suicidal consequences. *It took a fundamental change in the Soviet-American strategic nuclear balance and in the correlation of forces in the world as a whole for the political realism which enabled the agreement on the prevention of nuclear war to be signed with the USSR in 1973 to begin to gain the upper hand in the United States.*[13] [Emphasis added]

Soviet military publications disregarded the political signaling aspects of the LNO strategy, looking instead at its warfighting applications. For example, in the July 8, 1975, issue of *Krasnaia Zvezda* (Red Star), two military officers looked at the possible application of the Schlesinger LNO strategy to the NATO alliance, particularly in regard to limited nuclear war in Europe. As can be seen in the following passage, the authors emphasized the warfighting applications of Schlesinger's ideas:

> The Atlantic strategists are not only looking at ''limited nuclear war'' on the theoretical plane. They are engaging in direct preparations for waging such a

war. Its prospects were discussed at the recent meeting of the NATO Nuclear Planning Group. That meeting decided on a fundamental modernization of American tactical nuclear weapons in Europe. In addition, the United States promised to allocate additional Poseidon missiles . . . to strengthen the bloc's nuclear might.[14]

But if the Soviets were indeed projecting their own notions of nuclear warfighting onto the LNO strategy, then they probably found that it was very awkward as a nuclear warfighting doctrine. The LNO strategy was never designed to support a nuclear warfighting posture; this was because the U.S. lacked the strategic defenses in the form of civil defense and an antiballistic missile system that would have given the United States the credible war survival-recovery capability necessary for such a warfighting doctrine. Instead, the goal of LNO was to strengthen the credibility of U.S. deterrence, with the goal of "early war termination" should deterrence fail instead of pressing for any sort of victory. It should also be noted that early war termination is not a recognized military objective; instead, it is a political objective that does not fall under the jurisdiction of military operations. It is therefore not hard to see that Soviet military planners would have a hard time understanding or accepting such an objective as interpreted within the context of their own doctrine.

An important reason for this difficulty the Soviets had in understanding the reasoning behind the Schlesinger LNO strategy is the distinctively different sources of strategic thinking in the two countries. American strategic thinking, particularly since the early 1960s, has been heavily influenced by highly abstract, "game theory" concepts such as compellence and incremental coercion. These concepts were completely ahistorical and apolitical in their methodology and analysis. When historical examples were used (a rare occurrence), they were carefully selected and interpreted in such a way as to support the assumptions of the game theorists. On the other hand, Soviet military strategy has been developed for the most part by professional military officers, with heavy emphasis on the study of military history and political theory (albeit Marxist-Leninist political theory); therefore, the influence of such "traditional" notions as military effectiveness and warfighting is predominant.[15] If we accept the premise that Soviet political and military analysts of U.S. doctrine are as equally vulnerable to the mirror-imaging fallacy as their U.S. counterparts, then the Soviet reaction becomes much easier to understand.[16]

Soviet observers were plainly not happy about the possibility implied by LNO that the United States might be moving back to a counterforce strategy. Even more unsettling was the prospect of the United States' using nuclear weapons first in a crisis situation, thus abandoning its former retaliatory stance. This fear was expressed in the July 12, 1975, issue of *Pravda*, in which it was asserted that "while talking about some 'hypothetical circumstances' in which the United States might utilize nuclear weapons, Schlesinger is essentially orienting his department not toward the implementation of the agreement on the prevention of nuclear war, *but toward a strategy of the possible utilization of nuclear weapons by the United States in any crisis situation*"[17] (emphasis added).

The LNO strategy provoked such dismay among Soviet observers that it constituted one of the few instances in which the Soviets began linking it to arms control in one way or another. In the November 1974 issue of *SShA: Ekonomika, Politika, Ideologia*, it was Mil'shtein who equated the LNO strategy with the McNamara strategy of counterforce, claiming that LNO was an attempt "to return to ten-year-old concepts and to apply them under the new conditions on the pretext that a 'limited strategic war' under modern conditions is 'more advantageous' and is supposedly aimed at preventing a nuclear disaster and limiting its scale in every possible way."[18] More specifically, it was claimed that the introduction of LNO would stimulate the arms race in the qualitative sphere, as opposed to merely building large numbers of weapons, and would eventually lead to the U.S. development of a first counterforce strike capability:

> Despite these explanations, it is obvious that the desire to create nuclear forces capable of inflicting effective blows on "military targets" can serve only to encourage the arms race and not to limit arms. And it is understandable why: The introduction of military sites among the primary targets of nuclear weapons justifies the demand to increase the number of warheads, all the more so since anything one pleases can be classed as such targets. [It is interesting that these analysts implied that targeting military installations was somehow a new idea, since Soviet military literature assumed that the U.S. would target military installations.] What is more, the destruction of small military sites will inevitably require the creation of highly accurate nuclear attack facilities, that is, their continuous qualitative improvement. And this is nothing other than the arms race in its most complex and perhaps, most dangerous—QUALITATIVE—sphere.[19] [Caps in original]

Indeed, Arbatov went even further in arguing this point. He contended that any withheld Soviet missiles, "according to Schlesinger's ideas, are in fact the main target of a 'limited' (essentially, disarming) strike by the foe's nuclear forces."[20] In other words, LNO was not only equivalent to counterforce, but to the long-held Soviet concept of the preemptive strike as well,[21] and any qualitative arms improvements made by the United States "are directly linked with the new theory of J. Schlesinger, the Pentagon chief, concerning the 'possibility of making the first nuclear strike, and of a limited nuclear war with the exchange of highly accurate strikes.'"[22]

Well-known military analysts such as Major General R. Simonyan also drew comparisons between LNO and counterforce. According to Simonyan, the original purpose of the counterforce strategy "was aimed at creating the kind of strategic nuclear forces and at maintaining them at the kind of degree of combat readiness which would enable the United States to deliver a preemptive nuclear strike and achieve victory on this basis. That was its essence."[23] A more clear-cut example of Soviet mirror imaging would be difficult to find. He then asserted that the LNO strategy "differs little from the essence of the counterforce strategy."[24] This once again illustrates the difficulty Soviet military analysts had in understanding the signaling aspects of LNO, since LNO did not envision a disarming strike with the goal of victory but was instead a means of strengthening U.S. deterrence. Simonyan's argument was not an isolated one but was reiterated even in such publications as *Soviet Military Review*:

> In proclaiming the "targeting" concept the Pentagon leaders stated that it does not envisage the creation of forces of the so-called "first capability strike" [sic] but provides only for a more flexible use of the already available strategic offensive forces. It is not hard to see, however, that this statement is an attempt to camouflage the increase in nuclear potential for delivering a massive forestalling nuclear attack.[25]

2. *The Soviets believed that the United States might disregard the Soviet threat of uncontrolled escalation and in the event of a crisis employ the use of force on any scale it chose, including selected strategic strikes, without being deterred by the fear of escalation.*

This was the aspect of LNO that most profoundly disturbed Soviet analysts, since it added an element of unpredictability to U.S. behavior. This was something that the Soviets obviously felt was the last thing they needed from the United States, since they had enough difficulty making sense out of the public declarations on U.S. doctrine without adding still more uncertainty to it.[26] According to Mil'shtein and Semeyko in the November 1974 issue of *SShA: Ekonomika, Politika, Ideologia*, LNO was part of a continuing effort by U.S. strategists "to seek ways and opportunities to use nuclear weapons, striving here to implant the illusion that it is possible to find a means of doing so without risking the nuclear devastation of the United States itself."[27] This plainly concerned Soviet analysts, because LNO suggested that the United States might not be paralyzed by the fear of escalation and might accept the concept of first use of nuclear weapons, disregarding Soviet warnings of possible escalation. This concern was plainly expressed by Major General R. Simonyan in the September 28, 1976, issue of *Krasnaia Zvezda (Red Star)*. He argued that by proclaiming a strategic doctrine that emphasized flexibility of options, including a limited counterforce strike, "the strategists across the ocean are hoping not only to convince the potential enemy of the acceptability of a 'limited' nuclear war but also to make him wage it on terms advantageous to the United States.''[28] Although Simonyan implied that the new strategy was a move toward a warfighting posture, he apparently had his doubts about U.S. ability to carry out the strategy in a realistic way. As stated earlier, Soviet observers of U.S. doctrine were aware that the United States had not made any moves toward improving its own war survival capability, not even making anything more than the most perfunctory efforts at a civil defense program. In view of the U.S. lack of such protection for its own population and industry in comparison with the Soviet Union's, LNO seemed very awkward to Soviet analysts as a warfighting strategy.[29] Even so, the Soviet perception was still that LNO was a dangerous shift in U.S. doctrine from previous periods.

The reasons for this Soviet concern over LNO were less than unselfish. They had oriented their doctrine to take advantage of the retaliatory nature of U.S. doctrine, which had come to accept the premise for quite some time that nuclear war was both unthinkable and unwinnable.[30] LNO, however, was unsettling for the Soviets because it represented a rejection of many prior assumptions of U.S. doctrine. It postulated not only that the United States might indeed make a first strike on Soviet territory with limited numbers of weapons, but that the United States did not expect that such strikes would inevitably escalate to all-out nuclear war. In effect, the United States was telling the Soviets that it believed them to be as restrained by the fear of escalation as the United States was, and probably more so. Not only did this confront Soviet planners with an unanticipated set of U.S. responses to deal with, but it disrupted the entire picture the Soviets had constructed of expectations of U.S. behavior in a crisis. From the Soviet side of things the United States should have been behaving in a more restrained manner because of the attainment of strategic parity by the Soviet Union with the United States. But instead, the United States was saying that it might ignore such restraints. This concern was reflected in the April 1976 issue of *SShA: Ekonomika, Politika, Ideologia*:

> Discussions of new concepts are taking various directions. However, the main topic of debate in the United States on the revision of military strategic concepts is the new military-strategic concept known as the "Schlesinger doctrine." This concept and the "strategic retargeting" it envisages adds yet another kind of war—"limited strategic nuclear war"—to the spectrum of nuclear wars accepted by the "realistic restraint" doctrine. *"Limited strategic nuclear war" implies a limited exchange of strategic nuclear strikes against a small number of military targets*. The substantiation for this type of war is that both sides would have no interest in expanding the nuclear conflict and would prefer variations offering the possibility of localizing it since their strategic nuclear forces would retain a constant capacity for so-called "assured destruction"—a capacity

which has been and remains the basis of the development of strategic nuclear forces in the United States. *In other words, the "retargeting" doctrine provides for an increase in the flexibility and feasibility of the use of strategic nuclear weapons in war.*[31] [Emphasis added]

Of course, there was supposedly "a principal, determining factor exerting a decisive influence" on the evolution of U.S. doctrine in this particular direction. It was "the further shift in the correlation of forces in the world, including the military-strategic sphere." It was this growth in Soviet strategic power which was "compelling American strategists and politicians to engage in repeated analysis and forecasting taking into account the correlation of forces on both a global and a regional scale and to assess through this prism the effectiveness of previous military-strategic concepts and to formulate new ones."[32]

Although the unwary reader might be tempted to dismiss these Soviet allegations of a U.S. move towards a preemptive strategy as propagandistic, it is clear that the Soviets were reading the logic of their own nuclear warfighting doctrine as the only truly rational, objective, and scientific doctrine onto the LNO strategy. And assuming that the Soviets saw their U.S. counterparts as equally rational, it naturally follows that they would expect the United States to have been considering a preemptive strategy like their own.

Just how seriously Soviet analysts viewed the implications of the LNO strategy was revealed in an article in the April 1976 issue of *SShA: Ekonomika, Politika, Ideologia*. A group of Soviet analysts, among them Georgi Arbatov, the director of the institute that published this periodical, discussed the ramifications of the LNO strategy. Arbatov, in particular, voiced concern over LNO to the extent of proposing that the arms-limitation agreements also include a provision that would prohibit either side from altering its strategic doctrine. Absurd as the proposal was, it nevertheless reflected the degree to which Soviet analysts in general were perturbed by the "unpredictability" of the course of U.S. strategic doctrine. The following passage was a major exception to the general Soviet practice of compartmentalizing their discussions of SALT and U.S. strategic doctrine as separate considerations:

> It is also essential to stress that in works by our research workers the military detente which must reinfoce political detente is often solely identified with the limitation and reduction of arms and armed forces. A broader view obviously must be taken of this problem. *As we see it, the concepts of "military detente" must be extended to military doctrines and military-strategic concepts, which constitute a very important component of the entire mechanism of military policy and one of the factors influencing the arms race–both the quantitative and the qualitative arms race.* Of course, the struggle against imperialist military-strategic doctrines and concepts is a complex matter, but there is broad scope here for exposing the dangerous military-strategic theories being formulated by

reactionary U.S. circles—theories calculated to wreck the relaxation of international tension and the positive development of Soviet-U.S. relations.[33] [Emphasis added]

Conclusion

Although the anxiety evidenced in the Soviet reaction to the LNO strategy provides some promising clues to the kind of U.S. doctrine that will best strengthen our national security, it would be exceedingly trite to say that all the United States need do is declare that the LNO strategy is now a part of U.S. strategic doctrine and its problems are essentially solved.[34] The Soviets, as evidenced in this and preceding chapters, also look for signs that the United States is trying to match its actual capabilities to its declared doctrine. Since the LNO strategy incorporated certain aspects of the Soviet nuclear warfighting doctrine, the Soviets naturally looked for the United States to begin bolstering its strategic defenses so as to attain a credible war survival capability. When it was obvious that the United States had no intention of doing such a thing, LNO lost credibility in the minds of Soviet analysts. During the period in which the LNO strategy was under consideration (1974-1976) and until August 1980, U.S. strategic doctrine was a combination of the mutual assured destruction concept and a watered-down version of the Nixon Doctrine. To put it another way, the United States had the worst of both worlds during the period from 1974 to 1980; it had many security commitments and interests around the world that were vulnerable to Soviet expansionary efforts but at the same time lacked either the national will to use its military power in defense of these interests or the actual military capability. The Soviets, seeing their opportunity but not wishing to alarm the United States to the point where it might take decisive action, accelerated their use of proxy forces in support of ostensible national-liberation movements in various Third World countries in the Middle East and Africa. In some cases Soviet military advisers alone were present; in others it was a combination of proxy forces supported by Soviet logistics and advisers (see Appendix B). In all cases the Soviets managed to keep a profile low enough that their presence was not viewed as sufficiently threatening to elicit vigorous countermeasures from the West. At the same time, the Soviets kept up the pretense of detente by engaging in SALT talks, MBFR (Mutual Balanced Force Reductions) talks, and the Helsinki accords, and in general paying lip service in their pronouncements to the West on peace, security, respect for human rights, and anything else the Soviets felt the United States wanted to hear. The Soviets obviously felt sufficiently free in their ability to use military power that they decided to use their own troops in an actual intervention in Afghanistan in December of 1979 to support a collapsing pro-Soviet regime. Compared to previous periods, this was a definite escalation in the Soviet use of military power in support of foreign policy, and is definitive proof that the Soviet leadership was acting upon its perception of a United States restrained by the growth of Soviet strategic power to gradually expand the use of its own military power.

In July 1980, nearly seven months after the Soviet intervention in Afghanistan, the Carter administration announced another shift in U.S. nuclear strategy in the form of Presidential Directive 59. This "new" strategy supposedly emphasized the nuclear warfighting aspects of the U.S. strategic doctrine and posture by targeting such things as Soviet missile silos, command posts, and a Soviet warmaking capacity in general. Supposedly this was a step in the right direction; but were the Soviets genuinely convinced? This will be the question answered in the next chapter.

Notes

1. S. Ivanov, "Soviet Military Doctrine and Strategy," *Voennaia Mysl'*, No. 5, May 1969, trans. FBIS. FPD No. 0116/69, 18 December 1969, p. 49.
2. M. Mil'shtein and L. Semeyko, "The Problem of the Inadmissibility of a Nuclear Conflict (On New Approaches in the United States)," *SShA: Ekonomika, Politika, Ideologia*, No. 11, November 1974, trans. JPRS No. 63625, December 10, 1974. p. 9.
3. G. Arbatov, "Strength-Policy Impasses," *Soviet Military Review*, No. 1, January 1975, p. 48.
4. A. Karenin, "Détente and New Variants of Old Doctrines," *Mezhdunarodnaia Zhizn*, No. 5, May 1975, trans. FBIS, *USSR Daily Report*, 10 June 1975, p. AA7.
5. Ibid., p. AA8.
6. A. Arbatov and G. Arbatov, "Schlesinger's Ideas in Form and Content," *Novoe Vremia*, No. 30, 25 July 1975, trans. FBIS, *USSR Daily Report*, 14 August 1975, p. B3.
7. Ibid., p. B4. See also R. Simonyan, "The Concept of 'Selective Targeting,'" *Krasnaia Zvezda*, 28 September 1976, p. 3, trans. FBIS, *USSR Daily Report*, 1 October 1976, p. B4.
8. Moscow in English to North America, 2300 GMT, 4 July, 1975, FBIS, USSR Daily Report, 7 July 1975, p. B1.
9. R. Simonyan, "'Realistic Deterrence': The Real Implications," *New Times*, No. 10, March 1977, p. 19.
10. R. Bonds, ed., *The US War Machine* (New York: Crown, 1978), pp. 65-66. See also J.L. Snyder, *The Soviet Strategic Culture: Implications for Limited Nuclear Operations* (Santa Monica, Calif.: RAND, R-2154-AF, September 1977), pp. 1-3.
11. J. Endicott and R. Stafford, eds., *American Defense Policy* (Baltimore: Johns Hopkins University Press, 1977), p. 82.
12. The reader is referred to FBIS, *Eastern Europe Daily Report*, January-November 1974.
13. Mil'shtein and Semeyko, "Nuclear Conflict," pp. 6-7.
14. M. Ponomarev and V. Vinogradov, "The Atlanticists' Nuclear Ambitions," *Krasnaia Zvezda*, 8 July 1975, p. 3, trans. FBIS, *USSR Daily Report*, 14 July 1975, p. B2.

15. See John J. Dziak, *Soviet Perceptions of Military Power: The Interaction of Theory and Practice* (New York: National Strategy Information Center, 1981), pp. 20-28, for a detailed discussion of this point.
16. Snyder, *Soviet Strategic Culture*, p. 6. In his analysis of the Soviet perception of LNO, Snyder does not discriminate among the various Soviet statements on LNO, tending to take them at their face value.
17. "J. Schlesinger's Strange Position," *Pravda*, 12 July 1975, p. 4, trans. FBIS, *USSR Daily Report*, 15 July 1975, p. B4.
18. Mil'shtein and Semeyko, "Nuclear Conflict," p. 8.
19. Ibid.
20. Arbatov and Arbatov, "Schlesinger's Ideas," p. B3.
21. An excellent article showing the consistency of the Soviet "preemptive strike" concept through the present time is found in J.M. Caravelli, "The Role of Surprise and Preemption in Soviet Military Strategy," *International Security Review*, Vol. 6, No. 2, Summer 1981, pp. 209-236.
22. Yu. Gavrilov and V. Berezin, "The Pentagon: More Billions, More Programs," *Krasnaia Zvezda*, 14 September 1975, p. 3, trans. FBIS, *USSR Daily Report* 2 October 1975, p. B5.
23. Simonyan, "Selective Targeting," p. B5.
24. Ibid.
25. P. Sergeyev and V. Trusenkov, "Evolution of the US Military Doctrine," *Soviet Military Review*, No. 11, November 1976, p. 53.
26. For an in-depth analysis of this particular problem of Soviet analysis of U.S. doctrine, see L. Gouré, "The U.S. 'Countervailing Strategy' in Soviet Perception," *Strategic Review*, Fall 1981, pp. 51-64.
27. Mil'shtein and Semeyko, "Nuclear Conflict," p. 8.
28. Simonyan, "Selective Targeting," p. B3.
29. See Gouré, "U.S. 'Countervailing Strategy,'" pp. 56-57.
30. Bonds, *US War Machine*, pp. 62-63. See also J. Collins, *Military Trends* (Washington, D.C.: Center for Strategic and International Studies, 1978), pp. 76-78.
31. "Certain New Trends in the Development of U.S. Military-Strategic Concepts," *SShA: Ekonomika, Politika, Ideologia*, No. 4, April 1976, trans. FBIS, *USSR Daily Report Annex*, 30 April 1976, p. 3. See also Mil'shtein and Semeyko, "Nuclear Conflict," p. 5.
32. "New Trends," p. 3.
33. Ibid., p. 8.
34. Dziak seems to imply this in his closing remarks in *Soviet Perceptions of Military Power*, p. 68. But merely declaring a more "symmetrical" strategic doctrine vis-à-vis the Soviets is not enough; it must be supported by military programs which the Soviets themselves will find credible, otherwise the Soviets will quickly see through any such superficial declaration as a mere sham.

9.
Toward Nuclear Warfighting? The Soviet View of PD 59

Is It Nuclear Warfighting or Not?

The initial Soviet response to PD 59 was along the lines of their reaction to previous U.S. strategic doctrine: the United States was once again trying to break out of the strategic impasse that had been forced upon it by the growth of Soviet strategic power by devising a "new" strategy which the United States supposedly believed would bring it victory in the event of a nuclear confrontation with the Soviet Union. Soviet analysts allegedly saw indications that were more definitive to them than ever before that the United States was actively striving for a preemptive strike capability. On the surface, it seemed initially that PD 59, known later as the countervailing strategy, might actually give Soviet planners pause.

But there were signs during this most recent period, even in open Soviet publications, that the Soviets were not convinced of the genuine credibility of PD 59 as a serious U.S. move towards a nuclear warfighting doctrine. For one thing, Soviet observers were well aware by this time of the long lead times involved in the U.S. procurement of new weapons systems to support its doctrine and knew that the United States was moving even more slowly than usual to obtain the necessary weapons systems to carry out the highly accurate and selective strikes on Soviet missile silos, command posts, and other Soviet nuclear warfighting means called for by PD 59. Second, the U.S. concept of "victory denial" seemed illogical to the Soviets, and a contradiction to the principles of strategy in general and their own nuclear warfighting doctrine in particular. In fact, this latest U.S. proclamation was simply another in a long line of strategic concepts founded on the belief that nuclear war was unwinnable and therefore unthinkable except as a means of "punishing" the Soviets for having started the war. Third, and perhaps most important of all, the Soviets recognized that the U.S. version of nuclear warfighting, even though it envisaged a range of responses less than a massive one, was lacking in the kind of war survival capability necessary to make the strategy truly credible from the Soviet perspective. Moreover, as Leon Gouré has pointed out in a recent article,[1] what is convincing to the Soviets is whether there is a concerted effort to match capability to doctrine, and not mere sham declarations of a change in strategy. In fact, the United States was making no moves whatsoever, even during the first year of the Reagan administration, to initiate programs such as civil defense, ABMs, improved antiaircraft defenses, or even space-based defense systems, which would have gone a long way towards giving the United States a credible capacity for war survival and recovery.

This being the case, the Soviet use of its military power in support of its foreign policy objectives has gone on without hindrance from the United States. If the Soviets have been experiencing any setbacks or reverses in their foreign policy involving the use of military power as an instrument of political leverage, the United States cannot take credit for them for the most part. Critics who charge that the United States has been too paranoid about Soviet intentions and the Soviet military buildup have simply been ignoring the trends involving the escalation of the use of Soviet military power since the mid-1950s. It is a situation analogous to that of placing a frog in a pot of water and raising the temperature very slowly so that the change in temperature never enters the frog's threshold of awareness: eventually the frog is boiled alive. In much the same way, critics of the current administration's attempts to redress the balance pay little heed to the current level of Soviet military power usage, as if it were not significant. Viewed as isolated events at that given point in time, they may not seem so threatening. Viewed in relationship to the much lower level of employment of Soviet military power during the 1950s and early 1960s, when U.S. superiority was clearly recognized and unchallenged, current employment of Soviet military power is indeed part of a very threatening trend. This is especially so when it is compared with Soviet perception of our strategic doctrine as the result of a forced accommodation to the growth of Soviet strategic power.

Even during this most recent period of U.S. doctrinal development, Soviet propagandists were still trying to obscure their true strategic perceptions with a great deal of rhetoric aimed at the alleged aggressiveness of the countervailing strategy. The purpose here, of course, has been to draw attention away from the Soviets' own buildup and use of military power. The main thrust of the Soviet declaratory deterrence strategy will now be examined.

The Soviet Propaganda Line

1. *The essence of the countervailing strategy involves the use of a preemptive strike as part of a preventive war against the Soviet Union.*

This line was actually nothing new in the Soviet repertoire at all, as a glance back at chapter 3 will show. During the latter part of the massive retaliation period, when the United States was considering (albeit briefly) the merits of a preemptive strike strategy against the Soviet Union, this was an extensive theme of the Soviet declaratory deterrence strategy. Although the Soviets were well aware of the fact that a preemptive strike was based purely on military considerations and could be part of defensive doctrine (which the Soviets themselves advocated for their doctrine), they deliberately sought to distort the political intent behind U.S. doctrine and strategy by claiming that the so-called preemptive strike was really the opening phase of a preventive war against the Soviet Union. Although it is true that a preventive war, based on the political consideration of eliminating a potential long-term enemy by going to war while one still has military superiority, requires the use of a preemptive strike, it is not true that the mere advocacy of a preemptive strike strategy is an intent to undertake a preventive war. Nevertheless, this did not prevent Lieutenant General N. Chervov, in an interview with the Czech newspaper *Rude Pravo* on August 25, 1980, from claiming that "the practical plans for preventive nuclear warfare with the delivery of a preventive strike against the Soviet Union's military facilities have formed the basis of the United States' strategic course for a long time."[2]

An *Izvestiya* commentator argued much along the same lines only a couple of days earlier in the August 23 issue of that newspaper, contending that the aim of U.S. strategy was to create the necessary conditions for the undertaking of a preventive war against them:

> Contrary to what was said in Vienna and in complete contradiction with previous Soviet-American accords, the Washington administration has in effect announced as its main method of conducting international affairs the method of exerting pressure on the USSR in all its forms, including the possible use of nuclear weapons. At the same time attempts are being made to create a political and psychological climate favorable to the adoption by the U.S. leadership, when it is considered expedient, of a decision, in the guise of "defense," to deliver a "preemptive" nuclear strike against the Soviet Union.[3]

The commentator went on to say that world peace would be endangered if the United States were to adopt a preemptive strategy.[4] But since a preemptive strike, in the context of the U.S. countervailing strategy, would be made only if the United States saw that the Soviets were about to launch an attack of their own, there was in fact no increased danger of nuclear war at all. No danger, that is, if in fact that Soviets indeed had defensive and peaceful intentions, in which case they would not have had anything to worry about, since they would never fulfill U.S. conditions for the delivery of a preemptive strike. If, on the other hand, the Soviets harbored truly aggressive and warlike intentions, then a preemptive strike strategy would be the best possible deterrent against Soviet aggression, since the Soviets could not plan on beginning any sort of major war without having to worry about the possibility of U.S. disruption of their plans with a ''spoiling'' nuclear strike. In either case, the U.S. announcement of the possibility of launching preemptive strikes did not increase the likelihood of war, contrary to Soviet propaganda, since the Soviets alone controlled the trigger cause for the United States making such a strike.

2. *The U.S. countervailing strategy represents another attempt by the United States to stimulate the arms race and attain strategic superiority over the Soviet Union.*

U.S. responsibility for the arms race, as noted on chapter 8, has long been a standard Soviet theme. The main difference in this declaratory deterrence theme is that the Soviets were now emphasizing the fact that the United States had lost superiority and that attempts to regain it were futile. A standard example of this theme was an article in the January 1981 issue of *International Affairs* by Major General Slobodenko:

> The material base for the elaboration of this strategy is provided by the development and sophistication of diverse new arms systems in the United States, with which its government circles hope to achieve military superiority over the Soviet Union. This once again outlines the extreme danger stemming from the arms race, which is continuously being whipped up by aggressive imperialist forces, since the stockpiling and sophistication of weapons do not increase security but, on the contrary, as the ''new nuclear strategy'' demonstrates, increase the threat for all the peoples throughout the world.[5]

The way in which Soviet commentators have managed to conceal the true course of events in the so-called strategic arms race borders on the ingenious. For example, in a recent article, Arbatov noted how ''previously, the U.S. relied on its 'nuclear superiority' . . . in its approach'' to the political utility of nuclear weapons.[6] Yet he says later on in the article that ''the hopes of U.S. ruling circles for achieving an advantage in the strategic arms sphere as they move toward the 'countervailing' strategy are even less well founded, given the present correlation of forces, than the previous American plans of building 'nuclear superiority.' ''[7] This statement was corroborated in an article in *Izvestiya* in August 1980, in which the author boldly stated that ''the Soviet Union has never permitted anyone to talk to it from a 'position of strength' in the past, nor will it permit this in future. *It is evident that attempts to achieve military superiority over the USSR are even more unfounded now than formerly*'' (emphasis added).[8] In the case of these particular passages, it was not what was said, but rather implied, that demonstrated the falsity of this Soviet declaratory deterrence theme. In the first statement by Arbatov, it was conceded that the United States had possessed strategic superiority over the Soviet Union. But the latter two statements implied not only that the United States had lost this superiority, but that any attempts to regain it, despite increases in the defense budget, were becoming increasingly unrealistic. This was a tacit recognition of the greater momentum of the Soviet military buildup by Soviet commentators themselves. Yet they couched this recognition in language designed to give the impression that the United States was solely responsible for the arms race.

3. *It is impossible to speak of waging a limited nuclear war, since any use of nuclear weapons, no matter on how limited a scale it might be begun, carries the danger of a massive retaliatory blow by the other side.*

The continuity of the Soviet declaratory deterrence strategy is clearly demonstrated in this theme, since it was used previously against the LNO strategy as proposed by Schlesinger, as well as against the "limited war" concept first espoused back in the mid-1950s. It is the standard Soviet threat of uncontrolled escalation to strategic nuclear war, which Soviet commentators have repeatedly used in their efforts to persuade U.S. observers and analysts that the U.S. nuclear arsenal cannot be used even in a limited fashion to pursue political goals (such as the enhancement of deterrence against expansionary uses of Soviet military power), without an unacceptable risk of escalation. Slobodenko argued this line in typical fashion in *International Affairs*:

> Arguments that a nuclear war under the present-day conditions can be controlled and waged according to rules imposed on the enemy are utterly false. It is much easier to decide on the non-use of nuclear weapons than to confine their use within certain limits. The use of nuclear weapons even on a small scale can cause a chain reaction and turn what would seem to be a limited nuclear conflict into a nuclear conflagration.[9]

This was a highly presumptuous statement by Slobodenko, since he knew full well that the use of any kind of military power was governed by the political objectives being sought. The nature of these political objectives imposes its own limits on the level of military force employed, whether it be conventional or nuclear. The only objective that would call for the use of all-out nuclear war would be a decisive struggle in which the winner imposed a "Carthaginian peace" on the loser; i.e., effectively destroyed the opponent as a political entity. And if this were the case, then there would be no process of "escalation" to such levels, since one nation (presumably the aggressor) would be trying to gain the advantage of surprise.

Even though Soviet analysts had long since recognized the fact that the United States had retreated in the level of military force it was willing to actively commit according to the tenets of realistic deterrence (see chapter 8), Soviet commentators nevertheless continued in their efforts to portray the United States in as aggressive a light as possible while inhibiting U.S. willingness to use its strategic arsenal for deterrence purposes. In doing so, they made use of American statements that supported their own declaratory deterrence themes. A prime example of this was in an article by L. Semeyko in a September 1980 issue of *New Times*:

> The inevitability of escalation is not denied even by H. Brown, who has admitted that implementation of the new strategy could lead to an all-out nuclear war. In his message to the NATO countries' defense ministers about the directive he signed, he once again stated with regard to nuclear war: " . . . We have no illusions about the difficulties of limiting its escalation and consequences." That would seem to be a realistic assessment. So why then is there a need for the suicidal concept? Why try to reconcile "limited" and "prolonged" nuclear strikes? After all, even Clausewitz said: Any attempt to limit the use of force in war is ridiculous. But since the collapse of the strategy of "massive retaliation" the United States has been persistently seeking the possibility of the "rational" use of nuclear weapons.[10]

The actual Soviet view of the countervailing strategy as enunciated in PD 59, however, showed that the Soviets were well aware of the intent behind the latest U.S. strategic doctrine, as well as of its shortcomings. An examination of these themes is quite useful in determining what kind of strategic doctrine and accompanying posture can best deter the Soviets.

The Real Soviet View

1. *The countervailing strategy represents a new U.S. attempt to adopt a nuclear warfighting doctrine, thus abandoning its pure retaliatory stance.*

As has been demonstrated by previous chapters, this theme of Soviet perception is entirely consistent with past Soviet perceptions of previous U.S. doctrinal concepts, beginning with massive retaliation in the 1950s. From the Soviet vantage point, a nuclear warfighting doctrine is the only truly rational doctrine for a state to adopt; they therefore expected the United States also to accept the logic of this proposition and move towards a nuclear warfighting strategy itself. Any public U.S. declarations of deterrence strategies that lack the elements of a warfighting strategy with the objective of victory, or at least a "favorable war outcome," cannot really be trusted, according to Soviet thinking.[11]

In their statements along this line, Soviet analysts concentrated on the renewed emphasis on counterforce and the notion of limited nuclear war in asserting that the United States was again in pursuit of a strategy that would restore the political utility of its strategic arsenal. Slobodenko made this point well in his article in *International Affairs*:

> The new nuclear strategy proceeds from the possibility of waging a "limited" nuclear war and provides for the first nuclear strike at a limited number of the most important military objectives and control centres of the Soviet Union, leaving the forces of "assured destruction" in the reserve, which would prevent

the conflict from growing into an all-out war. In point of fact, this is nothing else but a modified version of the previous "target selection" and "counterforce capability" concepts. American political observer J. Anderson noted in *The Washington Post* in an article entitled "Not-So-New Nuclear Strategy": "In fact, Carter's directive is only the latest refinement of a policy that has been on the books for six years." Yet there is something new to it. Thus, it is planned to wage a "protracted but limited nuclear war." This means that there are provisions for a few selective strikes instead of one, which should follow in sequence. The possibility for using nuclear weapons in local wars is also an important innovation.[12]

Actually, Slobodenko was in error in his belief that there was anything new or innovative even in the notion of a "protracted but limited nuclear war"; the idea can be traced to one of the rungs described by Herman Kahn in his book *On Escalation: Metaphors and Scenarios*, in which he describes a limited counterforce war.[13] The logic of the American strategy, tenuous though it was from the Soviet standpoint, was explained concisely by commentator Lemeyko during a Moscow radio broadcast of "International Observer's Roundtable":

And the substance of the new nuclear strategy is that Washington now intends to deal a nuclear blow primarily not at cities but at military targets. In the opinion of the American strategists, this makes it possible, without beginning a universal atomic war, supposedly to inflict a limited preventive [!] strike at particular installations and regions. And here Washington hypocritically asserts that such a strategy must promote the maintenance of peace, since the other side, fearing partial retaliation, will behave more circumspectly and tractably.[14]

L. Semeyko, in a September 1980 issue of *New Times*, not only pointed out the emphasis on counterforce and limited nuclear war, but also emphasized that the new strategy was "a gamble not on preventing nuclear war, as is proclaimed, but on unleashing and actively waging it."[15] But the Soviets were well aware of the slowness with which the United States was moving to implement the tenets of the countervailing strategy. The explanation for this U.S. difficulty was, predictably enough, the continued growth of the Soviet Union's strategic nuclear might, which was restraining the United States from such "adventuristic" plans:

What occasioned this turnabout in Washington's nuclear strategy? If you consider Directive 59 as a whole, it is a U.S. attempt to get out of the "nuclear impasse" which developed back in the sixties thanks to the creation of the socialist community's mighty defense potential. All this time the strengthening of the USSR's nuclear missile might has curbed U.S. aggressive aspirations. This might is curbing them all the more now that strategic equilibrium exists between the USSR and the United States. Washington is now hoping to secure strategic superiority primarily through the qualitative development of its nuclear forces. At the same time it is not forgetting the quantitative aspect of the matter either.

> Hence the new nuclear strategy, which is essentially based on the strategy of "superior countermeasures" announced by the Pentagon 18 months ago.[16]

The most disturbing part about the above passage was Semeyko's reference to the Soviet nuclear missile forces' being the main reason for the restraining of U.S. "aggressive aspirations," and not any U.S. desire for peaceful relations or for arms control or disarmament. Given such a perception, there still existed no incentive for the Soviets to engage in anything resembling serious arms-control negotiations other than its potential as a propaganda exercise.

2. *The United States is far more vulnerable to nuclear destruction at any level of nuclear war than the Soviet Union, no matter how limited U.S. strategy might try to make it.*

This theme of Soviet perception was one the Soviets had undoubtedly held in private for a long time, since the lack of U.S. defense against a nuclear attack of any kind had been quite apparent since the mid-1960s. The reason that the Soviets did not make mention of it before this time was that the United States still possessed nuclear superiority until 1969, and then parity until the late 1970s, when the Soviet Union attained a level of marginal strategic superiority. Now that the United States was recognizing its own vulnerability on defense and growing inferiority in strategic offensive forces, Soviet commentators were making the most of their opportunity to remind the United States of this disparity. In doing so, they made frequent use of U.S. calculations concerning the likely number of people in the United States that would be killed as a result of a nuclear war:

> These documents [Presidential Directives 53 and 58] show that the President and his advisers by no means expect that after an American preventive nuclear attack the Soviet Union will sit idle-handed. They understand that the answer will be appropriate, that the retribution will be inevitable and that the adventurist actions of official Washington will be detrimental to the population of the United States. . . . Other calculations were cited in one of the documents prepared by a number of American governmental departments in 1978. 140 million will die in case of a nuclear conflict—this is more than half of the population of the United States.

> Naturally, the question arises: have the architects of the American policy taken into account these calculations while drawing up directive 59? There is every indication that Carter, Brzezinski and co. are little worried about this. The main thing for them is to survive. And for the purpose it is planned beforehand to "harden shelters for the key persons," to establish a kind of bunker for them.[17]

By pointedly mentioning the disparity in the relative abilities of the United States and the Soviet Union to survive and recover from a nuclear exchange, the Soviets were trying to get the most propaganda value out of it as possible, in the process hoping to restrain the United States from taking any effective action in the event of confrontation with the Soviet Union. In the following passage from an article by doctor of historical sciences V. Zhurkin in the September 1980 issue of *Literaturnaya Gazeta*, the author combines this perception of U.S. vulnerability with elements of declaratory deterrence in an effort to prove that the United States could not safely make use of even so-called limited nuclear strikes, which were less than all-out war:

> By threatening to use (still more by using) nuclear warheads against "selected" enemy military targets, Washington would above all jeopardize its own country. After all, confronted by such a truly apocalyptic decision, the other side would make one assumption: that Washington was prepared and was about to follow the path of nuclear escalation to the end. In those conditions the only possible decision for the other side is to respond not according to the "rules" proposed by Washington, but by is own choice. The authors of Presidential Directive 18 conscientiously calculated what a modern nuclear war would mean to the United States: The loss of about 140 million Americans, that is, nearly three-fifths of the population, and about 75 percent of the country's economic potential. When he was just a professor, Henry Kissinger called such an outcome, in brief, "the end of history."[18]

By making such statements regarding the likely level of U.S. fatalities, the Soviets were making one point unmistakably clear: the United States is too vulnerable to nuclear attack or retaliation by the Soviet Union to rationally threaten the Soviets with even a highly selective nuclear attack. Therefore, the so-called nuclear warfighting strategy enunciated in PD 59 cannot be considered credible.

3. *The Soviets continued to mirror image their own concepts of nuclear warfighting with the objective of victory onto U.S. strategy, asserting that the actions of the United States made the concept of victory denial too irrational to be truly indicative of U.S. intent.*

While mirror imaging has been a constant of the Soviets' perception from 1954 on, it played an especially important role in their determination of how believable U.S. doctrine really was.

It is important here, however, to make the distinction between Soviet projection of their own intentions onto U.S. doctrine and projection of their own actions in carrying out such a doctrine. Soviet analysts clearly saw a disparity between U.S. words and apparent intentions as opposed to U.S. efforts to match military capability to declared doctrine. Soviet analysts such as L. Semeyko traced the current alleged U.S. emphasis on victory in a nuclear war back to the signing of Memorandum 242 by then president Nixon on January 17, 1974, which was the initial statement of the Schlesinger Doctrine.

Schlesinger, it will be recalled, tried to move U.S. strategic doctrine away from the purely retaliatory doctrine of mutual assured destruction by linking U.S. actions in a nuclear confrontation to postwar political objectives. This was the notion of early war termination, which was later to evolve into the idea of victory denial. In the following passage from his article, Semeyko clearly shows the projection of Soviet doctrinal intentions onto those of the United States:

> In approving plans for waging "limited" nuclear war as it was understood at that time, the memorandum set the objective of "achieving the speediest end to the war on terms acceptable to the United States and its allies." (Let us observe that this formula later migrated into the statements of Defense Secretary H. Brown). But what is meant by "acceptable terms" for ending military actions? There is scarcely any need to guess. This expression has always meant the achievement of particular political war aims, in other words definite success in the war. With regard to a generalized nuclear war, Memorandum 242 contains an even clearer form of words: " . . . to secure for the United States and its allies the most advantageous possible outcome from a war."

> Hence it was hardly just, even in the mid-seventies, to accuse American military doctrine of excessive "modesty" or exaggerated emphasis on "deterrence." If the U.S. military and political leadership had been completely denying the idea of possible victory in a nuclear war, the various concepts for fighting it would not, it would seem, have been elaborated in such detail in the seventies. And this is not to mention Presidential Directive 59, adopted in the summer of 1980, with its much more clearly expressed gamble on winning a nuclear clash.[19]

Semeyko had made this assertion even more emphatically in the September 1980 issue of *New Times*, in which he maintained that the change in the types of targets to be attacked in the event of war from population centers to primarily military targets was definitive proof that the United States desired to attain victory in a nuclear war:

> Political and military control centers have now been included in the list of vulnerable targets. That is not merely an arithmetical increase in the number of targets (an increase of about 50 percent, according to some American data), but a clear intention of winning a nuclear war, a possibility ostensibly denied by America's leaders themselves in view of the catastrophic consequences of such a war. It is hard to reach any other conclusion since the destruction of the whole complex of strategically important targets is, according to the Pentagon's calculations, capable of paralyzing the enemy and forcing him to capitulate, and not merely of producing an "impression" on him by means of individual selective strikes.[20]

The question that undoubtedly arose in the minds of Soviet analysts, though, was, how credible could the U.S. countervailing strategy actually be, since the weapons systems needed for its implementation would take years to deploy? The answer was given quite clearly by G. Trofimenko, a longtime follower of U.S. strategic doctrinal developments since the late 1960s, in the December 1980 issue of *SShA: Ekonomika, politika, ideologia*:

> No matter how hard the American civilian and military leaders try to frighten the Soviet Union with their "well orchestrated" strategy of counterforce superiority, the U.S. does not possess this kind of superiority because the majority of the systems on which Directive 59 relies will begin to be deployed only in the second half of the 1980s. . . . Naturally [the USSR] will not change its strategy simply because someone in Washington has tried to perpetrate another bluff by publicizing yet another directive—particularly in view of the fact that U.S. political and military leaders already have published an excessive amount of various types of "strategic" doctrines, memoranda and directives.[21]

A more straightforward statement of the bottom line Soviet evaluation of the U.S. countervailing strategy one could not find. Barely three months after its enunciation, the Soviets were calling the U.S. bluff by declaring, in effect, that the latest development in U.S. strategic doctrine was little more than another ill-disguised sham. And true to Trofimenko's words, the use of Soviet military power to support "national-liberation movements," along with the acquisition of increased sealift, airlift, and logistics capabilities to support such military power projection, continued to increase through the end of 1981.[22]

Conclusions

Although U.S. doctrine paid a great deal of lip service to the idea of waging a nuclear war with the objective of some sort of acceptable outcome, or victory denial, U.S. actions subsequent to the declaration of PD-59 showed that the United States did not really have its heart in the matter.[23] The Soviets were quick to pick up on this, noting that the United States was making no serious moves towards reducing the vulnerability of its own population to nuclear attack, and hence were undeterred by the new declaration, although for declaratory deterrence purposes they denounced any perceived U.S. intent to adopt a nuclear warfighting strategy as "adventuristic." Soviet employment of its military power continued the pattern of gradual but constant increase in scale, while Soviet military programs showed increasing efforts to augment even further the Soviet ability for rapid power projection to such areas as Africa and the Middle East.

It is eminently clear from our analysis of the Soviet reaction to the U.S. countervailing strategy that mere changes in declared U.S. strategic doctrine do little or nothing to enhance the credibility of U.S. deterrence against Soviet-sponsored aggression, particularly against the more subtle form of aggression, employing proxy forces of Soviet minor allies, while the Soviets themselves provide mainly logistical, sealift, and airlift support. The SALT talks, and the virtual U.S. abandonment of them, have had no discernible effect on the pace of Soviet military programs, which may serve as an indication of how little seriousness the Soviets give to such talks as ends in themselves. Indeed, given the Soviet perception that their increased strategic power not only had forced the United States to make more accommodating changes in its strategic doctrine but had compelled the United States to seek arms-control negotiations in the first place, it is not surprising to find that SALT has had so little effect in the way of producing the strategic stability it has sought. As other authors have pointed out, the Soviets have no word for stability in the sense that the United States understands it, nor has it appeared anywhere in their literature.[24]

What then, are the overall implications of the evolution of the Soviet perception and reaction to U.S. strategic doctrine? And what must the United States do, both in the near and long term, to buttress its rapidly deteriorating strategic posture? These will be the central themes of our final chapter.

Notes

1. See Leon Gouré, "The U.S. 'Countervailing Strategy' in Soviet Perception," *Strategic Review*, Fall 1981, p. 59.
2. N. Chervov, "The Threat of the 'Nuclear Directive': What the So-Called New Strategy of the White House Entails," Interview by APN Commentator Vasiliy Morozov, 20 August 1980, trans. FBIS, *USSR Daily Report*, 25 August 1980, p. AA1.
3. Kobysh, "On the 'New U.S. Nuclear Strategy,'" *Izvestiya*, 23 August 1980, p. 5, trans. FBIS, *USSR Daily Report*, 28 August 1980, p. AA2.
4. A. Slobodenko, "The Strategy of Nuclear Adventurism," *International Affairs*, January 1981, p. 26.
5. Ibid.
6. A.G. Arbatov, "Strategic Parity and the Policy of the Carter Administration," trans. in *Soviet Press Selected Translations*, No. 81*2, February 1981, p. 53.
7. Ibid., p. 55.
8. Kobysh, "Nuclear Strategy," p. AA5.
9. Slobodenko, "Nuclear Adventurism," pp. 30-31.
10. L. Semeyko, "Directives 59: Development or Leap?" *Novoye Vremya*, No. 38, 19 September 1980, pp. 5-7, trans. FBIS, *USSR Daily Report*, 30 September 1980, p. AA2. See also N. Ponomarev, "In Militarist Intoxication," *Krasnaya Zvezda*, 6 September 1980, p. 3, trans. FBIS, *USSR Daily Report*, 10 September 1980, p. A2.
11. See also Gouré, "Countervailing Strategy," p. 55.
12. Slobodenko, "Nuclear Adventurism," p. 30.
13. The reader is advised to refer to all of Herman Kahn's discussion of the 44 rungs of the "escalation ladder," including the rung involving limited counterforce war, to gain a better appreciation of the kind of logic used by U.S. planners in formulating PD 59. See H. Kahn, *On Escalation: Metaphors and Scenarios* (New York: Praeger, 1965), pp. 37-195.

14. V. Lemeyko, "International Observers Roundtable." Interview by V. Katin, APN political observer, 24 August 1980, trans. FBIS, *USSR Daily Report*, 25 August 1980, p. CC6.
15. Semeyko, "Directives 59," p. AA3.
16. Ibid.
17. V. Goncharov, "Directives 53, 58, 59," *Tass*, 12 August 1980, trans. FBIS, *USSR Daily Report*, 13 August 1980, pp. AA2-AA3. See also Gouré, "Countervailing Strategy," p. 60.
18. V. Zhurkin, "In pursuit of the Impossible Goal: The 'New U.S. Nuclear Strategy,'" *Literaturnaya Gazeta*, 17 September 1980, p. 14, trans. FBIS, *USSR Daily Report*, 22 September 1980, p. AA1. See also G. Trofimenko, "Who Threatens Whom? Discussions with Soviet Generals and Experts of the Military Sciences," Interview by Ferenc Varnai on 23 September 1980, trans. FBIS, *USSR Daily Report*, 26 September 1980, p. AA3.
19. L. Semeyko, "Strategic Illusions," *Novoye Vremya*, No. 50, 12 December 1980, pp. 12-15, trans. FBIS, *USSR Daily Report*, 31 December 1980, p. AA4. See also Chervov, "Nuclear Directive," p. AA1.
20. Semeyko, "Directives 59," p. AA2.
21. G.A. Trofimenko, "Washington's Strategic Fluctuations," *SShA: Ekonomika, Politika, Ideologia*, No. 12, December 1980, p. 58; Gouré, "Countervailing Strategy," p. 60.
22. For the latest detailed compilation of Soviet power projection efforts into the Third World, see James Bussert, "Soviets Flex Rapid Deployment Force," *Defense Electronics*, Vol. 14, No. 1, January 1982, pp. 90-96.
23. Gouré, "Countervailing Strategy," pp. 60-61.
24. J. Dziak, *Soviet Perceptions of Military Power: The Interaction of Theory and Practice* (New York: Crane, Russak, 1981; published in cooperation with the National Strategy Information Center), foreword, p. ix.

PART V

TOWARD A NEW
STRATEGIC DOCTRINE

10.
The Soviet View: What Is to Be Done?

The Soviet Mindset and Its Implications

In the course of this study's examination of the length and breadth of the Soviet perception and reaction to the development of U.S. strategic doctrine since 1954, three basic themes of Soviet perception have emerged as the most salient and significant. These three interact with each other, as might be expected, in the current Soviet view of U.S. strategic doctrine.

The first major theme of Soviet perception is that Soviet analysts have consistently tended to project their own strategic concepts of nuclear warfighting with the objective of meaningful victory onto the intentions of U.S. strategic planners. U.S. statements regarding deterrence and the essential unwinnability of nuclear war were dismissed as propaganda by Soviet analysts, who evaluated U.S. doctrine and associated capabilities in terms of their nuclear warfighting potential rather than by the U.S. criterion of deterrence. This should not be surprising, since the Soviets have their own firmly held beliefs about what is truly rational in strategic planning. From their standpoint, a nuclear warfighting doctrine based on the capacity for nuclear war survival, war waging, war winning (it was hoped), and subsequent recovery was and is the only really logical doctrine in accordance with the "laws of war," as defined by the Soviets, for a state to adopt.[1] This being the case, if one assumes that Soviet analysts saw the United States as equally rational (albeit "aggressive" and "adventuristic"), it is only natural that Soviet analysts should have expected U.S. planners to attempt to adopt and implement a nuclear warfighting doctrine similar to their own. Just as a number of U.S. analysts have made the error of mirror-imaging U.S. strategic thought onto Soviet planners and decision makers, so too have Soviet analysts committed the same ethnocentric error. As we have seen in the course of this book, however, and as Leon Gouré has pointed out in a recent article in *Strategic Review*,[2] the consequences of Soviet mirror-imaging have been much different for Soviet doctrine and military programs than has been the case for the United States. This has been particularly true with respect to arms control. For while Soviet analysts and commentators have compartmentalized their discussions of arms control and strategic doctrine as separate considerations, the former merely being a tool of the latter to restrain U.S. strategic growth, U.S. arms-control advocates have pursued SALT and other disarmament talks as ends in themselves, confidently believing that the Soviets also shared their convictions about the political nonutility of nuclear weapons. No U.S. advocate of arms control has *ever* given the Soviet perspective concerning U.S. doctrine and programs any serious consideration or felt that it really mattered much. The few attempts made have merely been ethnocentric projections of the author's imagination onto what he believed to be the Soviet mindset. They would make amusing reading if their consequences for U.S. planning were not so serious.[3]

Examples of Soviet mirror-imaging can be found throughout the entire period of their pronouncements on U.S. strategic doctrine. The earliest and most consistently found example was the Soviet reaction to U.S. discussions of the possible adoption of a preemptive strategy in the late 1950s. The Soviet themselves privately had accepted the concept of a preemptive strategy as early as May 1955,[4] although they only alluded to such a strategy in their public pronouncements. The Soviets were, however, concerned over the possibility that the United States might also adopt a preemptive strategy, since this would have virtually negated the effectiveness of their own warfighting strategy. This same concern was reflected in later Soviet reactions to counterforce, Schlesinger's LNO strategy, and the U.S. countervailing strategy, since from the Soviet standpoint all of these were attempted moves toward a nuclear warfighting orientation in U.S. doctrine.

Another element of Soviet mirror-imaging was the projection of the objective of victory in a nuclear war as a primary consideration in U.S. strategic doctrine. This was a logical continuation of the Soviets' own warfighting mindset. After all, if a state were going to adopt a warfighting strategy, then it only made sense for some sort of conditions for defining victory to be established. In a nuclear war, the Soviets conceived of victory in the following terms:

1. Though damaged, the Soviet Union continues to function politically, economically, and militarily after the initial exchange.
2. Prosecution of the war continues until all enemy forces are destroyed or defeated.
3. Europe is occupied.
4. The Soviet Union recovers in a reasonable time and Soviet-directed socialism prevails in the world.[5]

The Soviets saw a particularly significant step in this direction in the LNO strategy, in which Schlesinger linked deterrence to postwar political objectives. To the Soviets, this was a great leap away from the pure deterrence objective of war avoidance with its subsequent objective of early war termination should deterrence fail. (This was later to evolve into the notion of victory denial in the U.S. countervailing strategy.)

However, this Soviet predilection for mirror-imaging came into conflict with the second major theme of Soviet perception, which emerged near the end of the massive retaliation period. This was that the Soviets increasingly began to admit, both in public as well as in private analyses, the likelihood and the necessity of having to wage limited wars with the use of conventional and/or nuclear weapons.[6] This was not in harmony with the Soviet projection of their warfighting strategy onto U.S. planning. If the Soviets had really believed that the United States was moving toward a preemptive strike strategy, then Soviet readiness levels would have reflected a high degree of anticipation of such a strike. Yet it was not until recent years that Soviet strategic forces were brought up to a level that would have made launch on warning or launch under attack in response to an attempted U.S. first strike possible.[7] Further indications of the lack of a high state of Soviet readiness were repeated calls for efforts to raise the readiness of the armed forces to a high degree, thus implying that such a condition did not in fact exist.[8]

Rather, the buildup of Soviet nuclear and conventional forces across the board shortly after the accession of the Brezhnev-Kosygin regime to power in 1964 demonstrated that the Soviets were in fact striving for a flexible capability similar to that postulated by the United States in its flexible response doctrine. The shift by the United States during the 1960s and early 1970s toward the pure deterrence posture of mutual assured destruction, with its associated objective of war avoidance, helped convince the Soviets that the United States was being increasingly restrained in its range of potential responses to Soviet actions by its fear of uncontrolled escalation to total war. The two major exceptions to this trend, in the Soviet view, were the escalation concept as espoused by Herman Kahn and the LNO strategy as enunciated by Schlesinger. Although the former was never really a part of U.S. strategic doctrine and the latter was never officially adopted, both concepts were highly disturbing to Soviet analysts in terms of their implications for the credibility of Soviet declaratory deterrence. Part of the deterrent value of the Soviet strategic posture was its implied threat that any local conflict that involved the Soviet Union might escalate uncontrollably into a total nuclear war. Both the escalation concept and the LNO strategy, as well as the limited nuclear war options of the subsequent countervailing strategy, strongly implied that the United States might ignore the Soviet threat of uncontrolled escalation and would thus be free to employ the use of force at whatever level it chose. Other than these exceptions, the Soviet perception of the probability of limited war's occurring became increasingly pronounced.

There was a discrepancy, therefore, between the first two themes of Soviet perception. Since the Soviet projection of its own strategic concepts onto U.S. doctrine was quite apparent, there had to be some means of reconciling this to the fact that the United States, however much it ostensibly desired to adopt a nuclear warfighting strategy, was nevertheless moving in the opposite direction, to a deterrence strategy geared to the waging of more limited conflicts and the notion of MAD. This discrepancy was resolved by the third major theme of Soviet perception, which concluded that the evolution of U.S. strategic doctrine was the result of a *forced* response to the growth of Soviet strategic power. Soviet analysts had previously credited the development of the Soviet ICBM as having been a significant factor in the U.S. shift from massive retaliation to flexible response. They attributed similar status to the attainment of strategic parity with the United States in 1969, which they saw figuring prominently in the U.S. abandonment of flexible response in favor of realistic deterrence, as well as in the U.S. willingness to engage in the Strategic Arms Limitation Talks.[9] Whether the Soviets arrived at this conclusion by reasoned analysis or simply used it as a convenient rationalization for the buildup of Soviet military power is a moot point. The fact remains that this conclusion provided a self-sustaining impetus for the buildup of Soviet military power with no clear definable upper limit. It also implied no obvious penalty for too much military buildup.

The correlation of these perceptions with the use of military power in support of Soviet foreign policy objectives is quite high (see Appendix B). During the massive retaliation period, when the United States possessed a demonstrable strategic superiority over the Soviet Union, Soviet use of its military power consisted of little else other than threatening to use it or engaging in military maneuvers near the area in dispute. The one major exception to this, of course, was suppression of the Hungarian Revolution, which can be explained by the fact that it occurred in an area under Soviet influence, so that the Soviets felt obliged to use force to control what they considered a vital interest—the suppression of so-called counterrevolutions.

During the flexible response period, however, a noticeable change in the character of Soviet military behavior took place. In addition to the general pattern of threats and maneuvers, the Soviets began to provide logistical support on an ever increasing scale to its clients in the Third World. This pattern was most noticeable during the latter half of the 1960s. There were two major aberrations from this pattern during the flexible response period. The first was the occurrence of the Cuban missile crisis, in which Khrushchev prematurely attempted to challenge U.S. strategic superiority by installing intermediate-range ballistic missiles in Cuba. The other was the Soviet intervention in Czechoslovakia in 1968. Like the earlier intervention in Hungary, this could be rationalized as a Soviet-perceived protection of vital interests, as proclaimed in the subsequently declared Brezhnev Doctrine, which reserved the Soviet right to protect socialist regimes from the threat of counterrevolution.

The level of Soviet military activity increased even more significantly in scale during the realistic deterrence period. Aside from continued major supply efforts to Vietnam and the Middle East, the Soviets supported Cuban proxy forces in armed interventions in Angola, Ethiopia, and Yemen, as well as sending Soviet "advisers" to Mozambique, Syria, Libya, and Algeria. The Soviets recently escalated one step further by their armed intervention in Afghanistan in 1979, in that it marked the heretofore unprecedented use of Soviet troops outside of its generally recognized East European sphere of influence. Apart from this use of Soviet military power, the trend during this period has been a greater Soviet willingness to use its logistical airlift and sealift capability in support of its proxies in "national-liberation movements" not contiguous to Soviet territory.

The overall trend since 1954 can therefore be summarized as a fairly constant, if very gradual, increase in scale of the use of Soviet military power in support of its foreign policy objectives. This matches up very closely with the Soviet perception of an increasingly restrained United States because of its forced accommodation to an unfavorably altered strategic balance.

What are the implications, therefore, of the Soviet mindset regarding U.S. strategic doctrinal development for U.S. decision making? First of all, it should by now be painfully clear that a Soviet perception that provides a self-sustaining motivation for the buildup of its conventional and strategic power does not give the Soviets any serious incentive to engage in arms control or disarmament negotiations with the United States or the West in general. Indeed, since the Soviets have seen favorable changes for them in U.S. strategic doctrine as having resulted mainly from increases in Soviet strategic power, in addition to the fact that they believe this increased power also to have been responsible for compelling the United States to seek arms-control negotiations with them, there is practically no reason why the Soviets should cease their buildup, regardless of any unilateral action the United States might take. And if there is any remaining doubt that the Soviet military buildup is not based on the simpleminded notion of "action-reaction,"[10] the mere fact that the Soviets have been conducting antisatellite experiments in low earth orbit, an area in which the United States has not made the initial effort, should be enough to dispel those doubts.[11]

Secondly, the United States should not be primarily concerned with the "bolt from the blue" first counterforce strike on its land-based ICBM force. The low state of readiness of Soviet strategic forces, coupled with the Soviet recognition of more limited conflict being possible would make such an attack highly unlikely, particularly since the Soviets assume that they will have ample strategic warning during any crisis situation. Furthermore, the main rationale behind the Soviet strategic posture is not necessarily what some might believe it to be, that is, preparation for an all-out nuclear war with the United States, although this is not discounted as a contingency. Rather, the

Soviet strategic posture of balanced strategic offensive and defensive capabilities is designed to restrain as much as possible the U.S. threat to use its military power in response to Soviet-sponsored "national-liberation movements" in areas vital to Western and U.S. interests and security. This means that the Soviet leadership is really quite sincere when it says that it wishes to avoid themonuclear war with the United States. After all, Hitler did not want a war with the West either—at least not until he was ready for it. He would have preferred to achieve the domination of Europe purely by diplomatic means, since it had been so successful up until September 1939. In the same way, it should be understood clearly that the stated Soviet desire to avoid thermonuclear war with the United States does not mean that the Soviets do not have political objectives harmful to our national security and well-being, nor does it mean that they are unprepared for the contingency of strategic nuclear war should their foreign policy meet with serious reverses that threaten the long-term success of their socialist revolution in the world. For a state that has predicated the success of its foreign policy upon the expansion and ultimate triumph of its revolutionary ideology throughout the world to be compelled to accept a status quo would be the equivalent of admitting defeat. Should the Soviets ever be confronted with such a situation, the temptation to use their military power to force the issue might become well-nigh irresistible, and the subsequent risk of general war alarmingly great.

Our Fundamental Error in Grand Strategy

Given the foregoing, how must the U.S. leadership, as well as its strategic planners, respond to the challenge posed by the Soviet Union? In considering the U.S. response, one might do well to meditate about an area which has not really been in vogue in U.S. thinking during the postwar era: the realm of grand strategy.

Grand strategy, simply defined, is that ultimate long-range objective toward whose achievement all the energies, resources, and planning of a given nation are ultimately directed. We are, of course, stating an ideal; it is exceedingly rare that a nation is actually able to carry out its grand strategy with such singleminded sense of purpose and organization, although some nations have done so more effectively than others. The Soviet Union has a grand strategy as embodied in the tenets of Marxism-Leninism; it is the establishment of *bezopasnost'*, of "total safety," for Soviet-directed socialism. Such a total kind of security implies a corresponding lack of security for those nations whose social systems are perceived by the Soviets as unalterably opposed to the establishment of this kind of Soviet *bezopasnost'*, the United States being chief of sinners in this regard.

The United States, on the other hand, has often been assumed by both

Soviet and U.S. analysts to be subscribing to the grand strategy of containment as expounded by George Kennan in the July 1947 issue of *Foreign Affairs*.[12] This is not true. Although the United States has paid much lip service to the so-called grand strategy of containment, its unstated grand strategic objective has been quite different, as has been indirectly reflected in successive strategic doctrines since massive retaliation (which had assumed that the United States would be relatively invulnerable to nuclear retaliation from the Soviet Union). This grand strategic objective has been nothing other than the avoidance of nuclear war involving an actual nuclear attack on U.S. territory.

An implied objective of every nation's grand strategy is the preservation of the security and well-being of the nation-state against all foreign threats. On the surface, it would seem that the avoidance of nuclear war is synonymous with this implied objective. It in fact is not synonymous, but contradictory to it. It is entirely possible for the United States to become so progressively isolated by the growing establishment of Soviet *bezopasnost'* , even while succeeding in the avoidance of nuclear war involving an attack on U.S. territory, that its security and well-being would not be preserved, but sacrificed. Conversely, it is possible for a nation to have the preservation of its national security and well-being as its implied grand strategic objective while subordinating the avoidance of nuclear war as only one means of attaining that objective. The other means related to the threat of nuclear war would be the attainment of the capability to block or nullify the effects of an attempted nuclear attack against one's territory. In making the avoidance of nuclear war its implied grand strategic objective, the United States has unwittingly committed the cardinal sin of grand strategy: the confusion of the means with the higher objective. On the tactical level, such an error leads merely to the loss of an individual battle: on the operational level, it leads to the loss of a campaign; on the strategic level, it often leads to the loss of war; but on the grand strategic level, it can lead to the loss of the nation itself.

The arguments of those who are in favor of such things as arms control or disarmament center around the notion that a nuclear war cannot be survived, cannot therefore be won, and should thus be avoided at all costs. Their supporting arguments revolve around the current superiority of the means of nuclear attack over the means of defeating such an attack or negating its effectiveness. This is a classic example of the error of allowing the available means to dictate overall strategy, instead of formulating strategy in accordance with a properly understood grand strategic objective with the aim of acquiring the eventual means to implement the strategy fully. The Soviet Union took the latter course. It first adopted a preemptive strike concept as the best means it then had available for negating as much as possible a U.S. nuclear attack's effectiveness. It then adopted civil defense as another major means, along with extensive antiaircraft defenses and a limited antiballistic missile defense around its main center of government. Its current research and development efforts in the areas of lasers and charged particle beams are merely further steps in the ongoing Soviet effort to attain the objective of eventually having the capability to defeat an attempted nuclear attack against its territory or to negate its effectiveness as much as possible.[13]

The U.S. notion of the "unwinnability" of nuclear war has been dictated by the observation that the *present* means of nuclear attack are superior to those available for defense against it. To say, however, that the attainment of the capability for defeating a nuclear attack and thus rendering it ineffective is technologically impossible is highly presumptuous, to say the least. It is reminiscent of those who claimed at the turn of this century that man would never fly. In a consideration of what course U.S. strategy ought to take, some reflection on the new realities of the U.S. geopolitical position ought to be taken into account as well.

The Geopolitical Reality and Its Demands for U.S. Strategy

This discussion of geopolitics is of a more abstract and theoretical nature than similar discussions by other recent authors,[14] but its ultimate relevance to U.S. grand strategy and strategic doctrine will readily be seen. It was Mackinder who postulated the notion that control of the "world island" of the continents of Europe, Asia, and Africa was tantamount to world domination. Since many of the world's natural resources are still concentrated in this world island, particularly in Africa, this makes the prevention of domination of the world island by a hostile power a paramount concern of the United States. This was also a consideration in Mahan's advocacy of global sea power for the United States as an essential element of its national security.

For all of the history of the United States until the acquisition of an intercontinental nuclear delivery capability by the Soviet Union, the United States was able to rely on the expanses of the two oceans surrounding it as a buffer against foreign powers. So long as powers friendly to the United States controlled the seas surrounding it, the United States could, without fear of interference, mobilize its resources in order to deal with any foreign threat. This was what enabled the United States to be the decisive influence on the outcome of both world wars in this century. Once the Soviet Union, with the development of its ICBM, had acquired the capability to breach the oceans, however, the basis of U.S. security, its control of the world's oceans, was effectively neutralized. No longer could the United States mobilize its national strength without fear of interference; it now stood as naked to attack and devastation as any landlocked European country.

Great Britain was able to preserve its security during the nineteenth and twentieth centuries by pursuing a "balance of power" policy with respect to the continent of Europe, allying against any power or combination of powers that threatened to dominate the continent. The United States is in an analogous geopolitical position, although on a much larger scale. The United States is to the world island of Europe, Asia, and Africa what Great Britain was to the continent of Europe during the nineteenth and early twentieth centuries; it is the insular power that bases its security and well-being on the prevention of any hostile power or combination of powers from dominating the world island.[15]

The advent of space travel has done far more than merely open up new vistas for man's exploration; it has also, however regrettable this is, opened up a new arena for man's conflicts. Although present technology has not yet been perfected, it is entirely possible, indeed inevitable, that man will devise and deploy space-based defenses capable of defeating a nuclear attack however it is launched, whether by bombers, submarine-launched or land-launched ballistic missiles, or even cruise missiles.[16] Given such potential for the nation that succeeds in firmly establishing such space-based defenses, the implication for the United States is clear; extraterrestrial space is simply the geopolitical extension of the seas into the vertical dimension. It is just as real an avenue of attack for an enemy's missiles and spacecraft as an undefended shoreline is for an enemy's naval fleets and amphibious landing craft. Therefore, the geopolitical demands imposed by the strategic potential of space-based defenses require that the United States not merely ''share'' extraterrestrial space with the Soviet Union, but that it have the capacity to dominate it utterly, without challenge or question. Such a requirement is merely the logical modern extension of Mahan's earlier advocacy of sea power with the objective of global sea control as the means of insuring U.S. security. With such dominance of space, and with the acquisition of space-based defenses against intercontinental nuclear attack, the position of the U.S. would then return to what it has traditionally been; it would once again become the insular geopolitical ''balancer''—relatively secure against physical attack, and able to use its military power, economic resources, and political influence in conjunction with its allies to prevent the domination of the world island by any hostile power or coalition of powers. Having the ability to defeat any attempts at nuclear attack against its territory, the United States, and the world as well, would be freed from the inherent insanity of mutual assured destruction, and the United States would be in the best position of its entire history to preserve the rights of nations to seek freedom and self-determination against the depredations of would-be imperial powers, no matter what their nationality or ideology might be.

To Fulfill the Mirror Image: A Foundation for U.S. Grand Strategy

In considering the mindset of our principal adversary at this moment in history, one gets the distinct impression that the Soviets most fear a mirror image of their own strategic doctrine. The evidence presented in this book shows this to be true, and it is true in more ways than one. Deterrence, after all, ultimately exists only in the mind of the national leader at the moment of decision. The formulation of a new strategic doctrine for the United States, as discussed previously, first requires the establishment of the proper grand strategic objective. This grand strategic objective determines the inherent nature of the strategic doctrine that is meant to achieve it. This strategic doctrine will, in turn, determine the basic direction and emphasis of military programs that are to implement it.

The overriding grand strategic objective of the United States is both the preservation of the American nation-state against the full range of foreign threats and the establishment of an international environment that best promotes the freedom and prosperity of the greatest number of people. Its geopolitical manifestation is the prevention of the domination of the world island of Europe, Asia, and Africa by any power or combination of powers hostile to American ideological principles or economic interests.

Since the main threat to the security and well-being of the United States is the possibility of nuclear war with the Soviet Union, there are two means of negating this threat. One means is the avoidance of nuclear war altogether and the pursuit of arms control and disarmament negotiations with the Soviet Union. The other means is the attainment of the capability to defeat a nuclear attack by the strategic nuclear forces of the Soviet Union and the reduction of the effectiveness of any such attack as much as possible. Although the former is desirable as the more peaceful means of attaining U.S. grand strategic objectives, the latter is recommended more as the one to be vigorously pursued, because it does not rely upon the assumption of pacifistic intent on the part of the Soviet Union.

U.S. strategic doctrine, therefore, ought to be directed toward acquisition of the means for nuclear war *survival*, as distinguished from the ability to wage a nuclear war solely in the offensive sense. If the people and the industrial base of the United States can be reliably safeguarded from a nuclear attack, the subsequent ability of the United States to mobilize its industrial and military might fully and bring it to bear successfully against the adversary is virtually guaranteed. Before the onset of war, the Soviet Union should be made fully aware that the United States will do everything within its capacity to prevent the successful carrying out of any attempted Soviet nuclear attack, no matter whether it be for reasons of preemption or otherwise.

The attainment of the capacity for nuclear war survival can be accomplished by the creation of a three-tiered strategic defense described as follows:

1. *Civil defense*. This is the lowest of the three tiers and the most basic element of strategic defense. It is the least technologically sophisticated and the most easily implemented, and it consumes the least in terms of national re-

sources. It is the defense of last resort against nuclear attack if, for some reason, the upper two tiers should not be able to block the entire nuclear attack of the opponent. Its implementation would involve an extensive evacuation plan for all major cities in order to disperse the population to outlying areas less likely to be attacked, the construction of both blast shelters and fallout shelters for the population in areas that contain industries vital to the war effort and to the welfare of the population in general, the stockpiling of wartime reserves of food and medical supplies in the event that agricultural production were disrupted, and a comprehensive educational program for both the schools and the general public on realistic defensive measures to be taken in the event of a crisis.

2. *Antiaircraft and antiballistic missile defense*. This intermediate tier of strategic defense is more technologically sophisticated, requires more effort and resources to implement, but has the principal advantage of blocking an opponent's nuclear attack at a greater distance from our territory. Its implementation would consist of the construction of a moderate number of surface-to-air missiles (SAMs) and fighter interceptor aircraft to defeat the relatively small number of Soviet intercontinental bombers that are expected, in addition to the construction of additional radars to detect them reliably.

The antiballistic missile component of this tier could realistically be implemented in the near future (within one or two years) by simply building and redeploying the Safeguard and Sprint ABM systems to the currently permitted maximum of one site with 100 ABMs at that site. In addition, the necessary radars for these ABMs could be built and deployed at other future sites, along with a number of undeployed "spare" ABMs, to act as a hedge against the possibility of an attempted rapid deployment of an ABM system by the Soviets or simply to bolster U.S. strategic defenses should the current ABM limitation be scrapped or a severe crisis occur.

3. *Space-based defense*. This is the most technologically sophisticated of the three tiers, admittedly the most expensive, and yet potentially the most effective and decisive tier of the proposed three-tiered defense. It is capable of blocking an opponent's nuclear attack at a sufficiently great distance from our territory to pose the least likelihood of damaging effects from fallout. The implementation of these systems requires that a crash research and development effort be made in order to reduce the lead time for their deployment. Principal weapons under consideration for use in such a defense are high-energy lasers and particle beam weapons deployed in a series of satellites commanding the approaches of extraterrestrial space to our country from the Soviet Union.[17]

If one attempted to construct this proposed three-tiered defense all at once, the cost would be staggering. There are two main ways to alleviate this problem. The first way is to immediately scrap all projected additional offensive strategic improvements and programs until the three-tiered defense can be made operational. It is survival that this doctrine is trying to achieve, not the further expansion of an already considerable offensive strategic force. Qualitative improvements can be made with some benefit, and certain weapons systems such as the cruise missile can prolong the useful life of our bomber force, but otherwise such offensive strategic force improvements do little to carry out the objectives of U.S. grand strategy.

The other main method of reducing the economic burden involved in the construction of the three-tiered defense lies in the nature of the defense itself. The first two tiers, civil defense and the antiaircraft/ABM, would obviously be built first, whereas the third tier is primarily still in the research and development phase. As the civil defense tier nears completion, funds for it can be pared back to the minimum level needed for its maintenance while the second tier is undergoing construction. As the third tier, space-based defense, becomes ready for deployment, funds for the first two tiers can be reduced to maintenance levels while the third tier receives the main emphasis. As the final tier becomes operational and is improved upon, some aspects of the first two tiers can be reduced or even eliminated, thus freeing resources for other purposes.

The construction of an effective three-tiered defense, therefore, is the means by which the United States would eventually achieve its strategic objective of nuclear war survival and thus attain its grand strategic objective as well. It would nullify the military effectiveness of nuclear weapons to the greatest extent possible, and hence negate their political utility as a coercive instrument. The fulfillment of U.S. grand strategic objectives, however, has one other crucial component, which has not been touched upon but which provides a positive goal the United States can strive to achieve; the component is what we commonly call ideology.

A strategy based on mere survival or the maintenance of the status quo has never been wholly effective against a revolutionary ideology that promises, however erroneously, a better life for the downtrodden and oppressed. A revolutionary ideology can be defeated on its own terms only by a counter-revolutionary ideology, pursued with equal if not greater vigor, that promises the same thing. It is all the more effective if it can provide proof that it can deliver what it promises. We as Americans have for too long ignored the roots of our own ideology—one that stresses the ultimate value and worth of the individual, both to the God who made him as well as to the society in which that individual lives. It is an effective counterpoint to Marxist-Leninist ideology, which downgrades the worth of the individual in favor of the eventual creation of a perfect socialist "utopia," the process of which has already cost the lives and freedom of far too many more people than such a utopia could ever be worth, even if one assumes that the flawed moral nature of men could ever permit its attainment in the first place. There is far too much good that the United States could do for the needs of the world at large, given the vision and the determination to do so, to permit its needless destruction at the hands of a false savior of mankind that conceals its insatiable imperial ambitions beneath a cloak of benignity. The U.S. experiment has not yet run its final course; let us therefore take those steps we know must be taken to preserve our nation and the values it has stood for, so that the course of U.S. history may not end in the smoldering ruin or the emasculated shell of a defeated nation, but in the final triumph of its Judeo-Christian and democratic ideals.

Notes

1. See *Marxism-Leninism on War and the Army*, trans. U.S. Air Force (Washington, D.C.: U.S. Government Printing Office, 1972), pp. 310-323, for the discussion of the laws governing armed struggle as perceived by the Soviets.
2. L. Gouré, "The U.S. 'Countervailing Strategy' in Soviet Perception," *Strategic Review*, Fall 1981, pp. 51-52.
3. The most glaring example of such ethnocentric "pseudoanalysis" can be found in F.M. Kaplan's *Dubious Specter: A Skeptical Look at the Soviet Nuclear Threat* (Washington, D.C.: Institute for Policy Studies, 1980), pp. 55-58. Kaplan only cites one Soviet source in what amounts to a four-page chapter purporting to deal with the so-called Soviet view. Good scholarship demands more than such superficial, shallow treatment, and skepticism more than mere presumptuousness.
4. "World-wide Historic Victory of the Soviet People," *Voennaia Mysl'*, No. 5, May 1955, pp. 12-13, trans. J.R. Thomas (Santa Monica, Calif.: RAND, T-110, 1959), p. 25.
5. J. Dziak, *Soviet Perceptions of Military Power: The Interaction of Theory and Practice* (New York: National Strategy Information Center, 1981), p. 28.
6. For the most recent analysis of this question, see J.D. Douglass and A.M. Hoeber, *Conventional War and Escalation: The Soviet View* (New York: National Strategy Information Center, 1981).
7. J. Collins, *American and Soviet Military Trends since the Cuban Missile Crisis* (Washington, D.C.: The Center for Strategic and International Studies, 1978), pp. 84-85. Even at the time the above book was printed, Soviet readiness posture was still quite relaxed in comparison to that of the United States.
8. An example of this Soviet call for attaining a high state of readiness can be found in an editorial: "The Tasks of Soviet Military Science in Light of the Decisions of the 24th CPSU Congress," *Voennaia Mysl'*, No. 8, August 1971, trans. FBIS, FPD No. 0011/74, February 28, 1974, p. 6. See also V.D. Sokolovskiy and M. Cherednichenko, "Military Strategy and Its Problems," *Voennaia Mysl'*, No. 10, October 1968, trans. FBIS, FPD No. 0084/69, September 4, 1969, p. 37.
9. The same admission is made on the American side, although implied and at much greater length, in J. Newhouse, *Cold Dawn: The Story of SALT* (New York: Holt, Rinehart, & Winston, 1973), pp. 66-102.
10. "Action-reaction" is a concept often used by arms control theorists to describe what they believe is the driving mechanism of the arms race. Presumably, if one side builds a weapons system, the other will do the same out of a desire not to be outdone. A similar analogy, equally simplistic, is Paul Warnke's characterization of the U.S.-Soviet strategic relationship as akin to "apes on a treadmill." Both metaphors assume identical strategic outlooks on the part of both the United States and the Soviet Union, a myth long since disproven, though still employed. See

also Newhouse, *Cold Dawn: The Story of SALT*, pp. 66-102, for an example of the use of this metaphor in practice.

11. G.E. Wasson, ed., "Soviet Arms Buildup Threatens Parity With the West," *Defense Electronics*, Vol. 14, No. 1, January 1982, p. 62. See also E. Rajah, "Does Soviet Air Power Endanger World Peace?" *Defense Electronics*, Vol. 14, No. 1, January 1982, p. 102.

12. See X (George Kennan), "The Sources of Soviet Conduct," *Foreign Affairs*, Vol. 25, No. 4, July 1947, pp. 566-582.

13. For a discussion of the strategic potential of these weapons, see G.H. Stine, *Confrontation in Space* (Englewood Cliffs, N.J.: Prentice Hall, 1981), pp. 99-120.

14. Recent discussions of "geopolitics" and the influence of nuclear weapons as a consideration in geopolitical strategy are C. Gray, *The Geopolitics of the Nuclear Era: Heartland, Rimlands, and the Technological Revolution* (New York: Crane, Russak & Co., 1979), and T.P. Rona, *Our Changing Geopolitical Premises* (New York: National Strategy Information Center, 1982).

15. Kissinger used a similar analogy in *Nuclear Weapons and Foreign Policy* (Garden City, N.Y.: Doubleday & Co., 1958), though he subsequently argued that it was no longer valid. It is explained briefly in S.R. Graubard, *Kissinger: Portrait of a Mind* (New York: W.W. Norton & Co., 1973), pp. 65-66.

16. See Stine, *Confrontation In Space*, pp. 99-109.

17. Ibid., pp. 99-120.

Appendix A

The following is a composite table constructed from various sources of the aggregate numerical levels of U.S. and Soviet ICBMs, SLBMs, and strategic bombers.

Comparison of U.S.-U.S.S.R. ICBM/SLBM/Bomber Deployments
1960-1979

United States				Soviet Union		
Year	ICBMs	SLBMs	Bombers[1]	Year	ICBMs	SLBMs[2]	Bombers[3]
1960	18	32	1,845	1960	35	0	140
1961	63	96	1,700	1961	50	0	140
1962	294	144	1,705	1962	75	0	140
1963	424	224	1,218	1963	100	0	140
1964	834	416	1,092	1964	200	0	140
1965	854	496	882	1965	270	0	140
1966	904	592	644	1966	300	0	140
1967	1,054	656	588	1967	460	0	140
1968	1,054	656	560	1968	800	80	140
1968	1,054	656	560	1969	1,028	196	140
1970	1,054	656	550	1970	1,299	304	140
1971	1,054	656	505	1971	1,513	448	140
1972	1,054	656	455	1972	1,527	500	140
1973	1,054	656	422	1973	1,527	628	140
1974	1,054	656	437	1974	1,575	720	140
1975	1,054	656	432	1975	1,618	784	135
1976	1,054	656	432	1976	1,527	845	135
1977	1,054	656	432	1977	1,477	909	135
1978	1,054	656	382[4]	1978	1,400	1,015	135
1979	1,054	656	382	1979	1,398	1,028	156[5]

1. Early figures include medium bombers stationed in Western Europe.
2. Excludes Golf- and Hotel-class SLBM-carrying subs, whose missiles had a range of roughly 500 miles. Only Polaris-type SLBMs included.
3. The number of Soviet Bear and Bison heavy bombers has remained at less than 200 since their deployment in 1955.
4. Includes 66 FB-111 medium bombers.
5. Includes Backfire bomber.

Sources: Bonds, *The US War Machine*, 1978; Bonds, *The Soviet War Machine*, 1976; Brown, General George S., *Military Posture for FY 1978*, 1977; Luttwak, Edward, *The Strategic Balance 1972*; Luttwak, Edward, *The US-USSR Nuclear Weapons Balance, 1974; Statistical Abstract of the United States*, 1961-1968; *The Military Balance, 1979-1980*.

Appendix B

Chronology of Major Events Involving the Use of Soviet Military Power, 1954-1982

MASSIVE RETALIATION

1955 Formation of Warsaw Pact

1956 Soviet suppression of Hungarian Revolution

Threat of military force used in Polish crisis

Soviets threaten Great Britain and France with nuclear weapons during Suez crisis

1957 Development of Soviet ICBM

Military response threatened by Soviets in the event of Turkish attack on Syria

1958 Soviets announce military maneuvers in Transcaucasus and Bulgaria in response to U.S. intervention in Lebanon

Threat of retaliation made after Quemoy-Matsu crisis against possible U.S. attack on China

Khrushchev demands that Berlin be made free city within six months of November 1958

1959-61 Demands on Berlin repeated—no other action taken

1957-62 Khrushchev engages in "strategic bluffing" involving Soviet ICBM capability and deployment

FLEXIBLE RESPONSE

1962 Khrushchev attempts to install Soviet IRBMs in Cuba—United States responds with naval quarantine of Cuba, thus forcing Soviet retreat

1965-75 Soviets supply North Vietnam by sea and rail—military advisers also sent

1967-72 Soviet military advisers present in Egypt*

Massive resupply effort of Egyptian forces mounted by Soviets after Arab defeat in 1967 Arab-Israeli War

1967-68 Soviet supply effort to Yemen

1968 Soviet intervention in Czechoslovakia

REALISTIC DETERRENCE

1973 Soviets engage in threatening military maneuvers during Yom Kippur War—later resupply Egyptian forces

1972-79 Buildup of Soviet military power in Cuba through shipment of nuclear-capable MiG-23 warplanes, development of possible nuclear submarine base, and installation of Soviet combat brigade

1975-76 Cuban "proxy army" transported and supplied by Soviets in intervention in Angolan civil war

1977-78 Cuban forces intervene with Soviet support in Ethiopia-Somalia conflict

1978 Soviets supply arms to Vietnam prior to Vietnamese invasion of Kampuchea

1979 Soviet military advisers and Cuban forces train and support South Yemeni forces in invasion of North Yemen

1979-82 Soviet troops invade Afghanistan and set up puppet government in unprecedented use of Soviet forces outside Eastern Europe

1981-82   Soviets employ military maneuvers in Polish crisis

*Following Sadat's order for Soviet advisers to leave, Soviets began slow withdrawal of advisers, which was not completed until shortly after Soviet invasion of Afghanistan.

Sources: Wolfe, Thomas W., *Soviet Power and Europe, 1945-1970*, 1970
          U.S. News and World Report, January 14, 1980
          Defense Electronics, January 1982.

SELECTED BIBLIOGRAPHY

Non-Soviet Sources

Alexander, Arthur J. *Decision-Making in Soviet Procurement*, Adelphi Papers Nos. 147, 148 (Winter 1978-79).

Aliano, Richard A. *American Defense Policy from Eisenhower to Kennedy: The Politics of Changing Military Requirements*. Athens: Ohio University Press, 1975.

Bonds, Ray, ed. *The Soviet War Machine*. New York: Chartwell, 1976.

————. *The US War Machine*. New York: Crown, 1978.

Bottome, Edgar M. *The Missile Gap*. Cranbury, N.J.: Associated University Presses, 1971.

Brodie, Bernard. *Strategy in the Missile Age*. Princeton, N.J.: Princeton University Press, 1959.

Brown, Anthony Cave, ed. *Dropshot: The United States Plan for War with the Soviet Union in 1957*. New York: Dial Press/James Wade, 1978.

Brown, Harold. *Department of Defense Annual Report: Fiscal Year 1979*. Washington D.C.: U.S. Government Printing Office, 1978.

————. *Department of Defense Annual Report: Fiscal Year 1980*. Washington, D.C.: U.S. Government Printing Office, 1979.

Buzzard, Anthony W. "Massive Retaliation and Graduated Deterrence." *World Politics* 8 (January 1956): 228-237.

Collins, John M. *American and Soviet Military Trends since the Cuban Missile Crisis*. Washington, D.C.: Center for Strategic and International Studies, 1978.

Dallin, Alexander. *Red Star on Military Affairs, 1945-1952*. Santa Monica, Calif.: RAND, RM-1637, February 10, 1956.

Deane, Michael J. *Political Control of the Soviet Armed Forces*. New York: Crane, Russak, 1977.

————. *The Soviet Concept of the "Correlation of Forces."* Arlington, Va.: Stanford Research Institute, Strategic Studies Center, 1976.

Dinerstein, Herbert S. *Soviet Strategic Ideas, January 1960*. Santa Monica, Calif.: RAND, RM-2532, February 19, 1960.

————. *On the Question of the Pre-emptive Blow by General of the Army V. Kurasov (Red Star, April 27, 1958)*. Santa Monica, Calif.: RAND, T-87, May 12, 1958.

————. *War and the Soviet Union: Nuclear Weapons and the Revolution in Soviet Military and Political Thinking*. New York: Praeger, 1959.

Directory of Soviet Officials, Volume I: National Organizations. Washington, D.C.: National Foreign Assessment Center, CR 78-14025, 1978.

Dulles, John Foster. "Challenge and Response in U.S. Policy." *Foreign Affairs* 36 (October 1957): 25-43.

Endicott, John E., and Stafford, Roy W., Jr. *American Defense Policy*. New York: Johns Hopkins University Press, 1977.

Ermarth, Fritiz W. "Contrasts in American and Soviet Strategic Thought." *International Security* 3 (Fall 1978): 138-153.

Fallows, James. "Muscle-Bound Superpower: The State of America's Defense." *The Atlantic* 9 (September 1979): 59-78.

Foreign Broadcast Information Service, 1959-81.

Frank, Lewis Allen. *Soviet Nuclear Planning: A Point of View on SALT*. Washington, D.C.: American Enterprise Institute for Public Policy Research, 1977.

Garthoff, Raymond L. *Soviet Strategy in the Nuclear Age*. New York: Praeger, 1958.

————. *The Soviet Image of Future War*. Washington, D.C.: Public Affairs, 1959.

————. *Soviet Military Policy: A Historical Analysis*. London: Faber & Faber, 1966.

Gibert, Stephen P. *Soviet Images of America*. New York: Crane, Russak, 1978.

Gouré, Leon. *Civil Defense in the Soviet Union*. Berkeley and Los Angeles, Calif.: University of California Press, 1962.

————. *Soviet Limited War Doctrine*. Santa Monica, Calif.: RAND, P-2744, May 1963.

————. *War Survival in Soviet Strategy*. Coral Gables, Fla.: Center for Advanced International Studies, 1976.

————. *Soviet Commentary on the Doctrine of Limited Nuclear Wars*. Santa Monica, Calif.: RAND, T-82, March 5, 1958.

————. *Some Soviet Views on Air Strategy*. Santa Monica, Calif.: RAND, T-84, April 3, 1958.

————, Kohler, Foy D., and Harvey, Mose L. *The Role of Nuclear Forces in Current Soviet Strategy*. Coral Gables, Fla.: Center for Advanced International Studies, 1975.

Hoag, Malcolm W. *On Local War Doctrine*. Santa Monica, Calif.: RAND, P-2433, August 1961.

Horelick, Arnold. *Some Soviet Views on the Nature of a Future War and the Factors Determining Its Course and Outcome*. Santa Monica, Calif.: RAND, T-97, September 15, 1958.

————, and Rush, Myron. *Strategic Power and Soviet Foreign Policy*. Chicago: University of Chicago Press, 1966.

Husband, William B. "Soviet Perceptions of US 'Positions of Strength' Policy in the 1970s." *World Politics* 31 (July 1979): 495-517.

Kahn, Herman. *On Escalation: Metaphors and Scenarios*. New York: Praeger, 1965.

————. *On Thermonuclear War*. Princeton, N.J.: Princeton University Press, 1961.

Kennan, George. "The Sources of Soviet Conduct." *Foreign Affairs* 25 (July 1947): 566-582.

Kintner, William R., and Scott, Harriet Fast. *The Nuclear Revolution in Soviet Military Affairs*. Norman: University of Oklahoma Press, 1968.

Kissinger, Henry A. *Nuclear Weapons and Foreign Policy*. Garden City, N.Y.: Doubleday, 1958.

Kohler, Foy D., Harvey, Mose L., Gouré, Leon, and Soll, Richard. *Soviet Strategy for the Seventies: From Cold War to Peaceful Coexistence*. Coral Gables, Fla.: Center for Advanced International Studies, 1973.

Kolkowicz, Roman. *Soviet Strategic Debate: An Important Recent Addendum*. Santa Monica, Calif.: RAND, P-2936, July 1964.

———. *The Red "Hawks" on the Rationality of Nuclear War*. Santa Monica, Calif.: RAND, RM-4899-PR, March 1966.

———. "Strategic Parity and Beyond." *World Politics* 23 (April 1971): 431-451.

Lambeth, Benjamin. *The Political Potential of Equivalence: The View from Moscow and Europe*. Santa Monica, Calif.: RAND, P-6167, August 1978.

Luttwak, Edward. *The Strategic Balance 1972*. Washington, D.C. Center for Strategic and International Studies, 1972.

———. *The U.S.-U.S.S.R. Nuclear Weapons Balance*. Washington D.C.: Center for Strategic and International Studies, 1974.

Morgan, Patrick M. *Theories and Approaches to International Politics*. Palo Alto, Calif.: Page-Ficklin, 1975.

Newhouse, John. *Cold Dawn: The Story of SALT*. New York: Holt, Rinehart & Winston, 1973.

Peeters, Paul. *Massive Retaliation: The Policy and Its Critics*. Chicago: Foundation for Foreign Affairs, 1959.

Quanbeck, Alton H., and Blechman, Barry M. *Strategic Forces: Issues for the Mid-Seventies*. Washington, D.C.: Brookings, 1973.

Scott, Harriet Fast. *Soviet Military Doctrine: Its Continuity, 1960-1970*. Menlo Park, Calif.: Stanford Research Institute, Strategic Studies Center, 1971.

———, and Scott, William F. *The Armed Forces of the USSR*. Boulder, Colo.: Westview, 1979.

Scott, William F. "Soviet Military Doctrine and Strategy: Realities and Misunderstanding." *Strategic Review* 3 (Spring 1975): 57-66.

Snyder, Jack L. *The Soviet Strategic Culture: Implications for Limited Nuclear Operations*. Santa Monica, Calif.: RAND, R-2154-AF, September 1977.

Sokolovskiy, V.D., ed. *Soviet Military Strategy*. Trans. and annotated Herbert S. Dinerstein, Leon Gouré, and Thomas W. Wolfe. Santa Monica, Calif.: RAND, R-416-PR, April 1963.

———. *Soviet Military Strategy*. Trans. and ed. Harriet Fast Scott. New York: Crane, Russak, 1975.

Taylor, Maxwell D. "Security Will Not Wait." *Foreign Affairs* 39 (January 1961): 174-184.

Thomas, John R. *World-Wide Historic Victory of the Soviet People*. Santa Monica, Calif.: RAND, T-110, January 29, 1959.

Ulam, Adam B. *Expansion and Coexistence: The History of Soviet Foreign Policy, 1917-67*. New York: Praeger, 1968.

U.S. News and World Report, January 14, 1980.

Wohlstetter, Albert. "The Delicate Balance of Terror." *Foreign Affairs* 37 (January 1959).

Wolfe, Thomas W. *Soviet Power and Europe, 1945-1970*. Baltimore: Johns Hopkins, 1970.

————. *The Soviet Voice in the East-West Strategic Dialogue*. Santa Monica, Calif.: RAND, P-2851, January 1964.

————. *Soviet Strategic Thought in Transition*. Santa Monica, Calif.: RAND, P-2906, May 1964.

————. *Communist Outlook on War*. Santa Monica, Calif.: RAND, P-3640, August 1967.

————. *Soviet Policy in the Setting of a Changing Power Balance*. Santa Monica, Calif.: RAND, P-4055, March 1969.

————. *The Global Strategic Perspective from Moscow*. Santa Monica, Calif.: RAND, P-4978, March 1973.

————. *Some Recent Signs of Reaction against Prevailing Soviet Emphasis on Missiles*. Santa Monica, Calif.: RAND, P-2929, June 1964.

Wright, Quincy. "International Conflict and the United Nations." *World Politics* 10 (October 1957): 24-48.

Zimmerman, William. *Soviet Persepctives on International Relations, 1956-1967*. Princeton: Princeton University Press, 1969.

Translations of Soviet Primary Sources

The following is a listing of Soviet books from the Officer's Library series translated by the U.S. Air Force, along with JPRS and FBIS translations of *SShA: Economika, Politika, Ideologia* and *Voennaia Mysl'*, respectively. JPRS translations of any Soviet books are also listed. Periodicals and books will be referred to by English translations of titles.

Arbatov, G.A. "American Foreign Policy at the Threshold of the 1970's." *USA: Economics, Politics, Ideology* No. 1 (January 1970). Trans. JPRS No. 49934, February 26, 1970: 13-26.

Davydov, Yu. *The Nixon Doctrine*. Moscow: Izdatelstvo Nauka, 1972. Trans. JPRS No. 58317, February 26, 1973.

Dzhelaukhov, Kh. "The Evolution of US Military Doctrine." *Voennaia Mysl'* No 9 (September 1967). Trans. FBIS, FPD No. 0132/68, September 5, 1968: 93-98.

Editorial. "On Guard for Peace and the Building of Socialism." *Voennaia Mysl'* No. 12 (December 1971). Trans. FBIS, FPD No. 0003/74, January 17, 1974: 1-19.

————. "The Party of Lenin: The Fighting Vanguard," *Voennaia Mysl'* No. 3 (March 1971). Trans. FBIS, FPD No. 0020/74, March 29, 1974: 1-14.

————. "The Tasks of Soviet Military Science in Light of the Decisions of the 24th CPSU Congress." *Voennaia Mysl'* No. 8 (August 1971). Trans. FBIS, FPD No. 0011/74, February 28, 1974.

Ivanov, S. "Soviet Military Doctrine and Strategy." *Voennaia Mysl'* No. 5 (May 1969). Trans. FBIS, FPD No. 0116/69, December 18, 1969: 40-51.

Kalachev, N. "Attack without the Employment of Nuclear Weapons." *Voennaia Mysl'* No. 2 (February 1973). Trans. FBIS, FPD No. 0045/73, November 20, 1973: 93-101.

Kruchinin, V. "Contemporary Strategic Theory on the Goals and Missions of Armed Conflict." *Voennaia Mysl'* No. 10 (October 1963). Trans. FBIS, FPD No. 965, July 20, 1966: 13-25.

Krylov, N. "The Nuclear-Missile Shield of the Soviet State." *Voennaia Mysl'* No. 11 (November 1967). Trans. FBIS, FPD No. 0157/68, November 18, 1968: 13-21.

Kvitnitskiy, A., and Nepodayev, Ym. "The Theory of the Escalation of War." *Voennaia Mysl'* No. 9 (September 1965). Trans. FBIS, FPD No. 952, March 2, 1966: 14-27.

Larionov, V.V. "The Transformation of the 'Strategic Sufficiency' Concept." *SShA: Ekonomika, Politika, Ideologia* No. 11 (November 1971). Trans. JPRS No. 54676, December 10, 1971: 33-44.

Lomov, N.A., ed. *Scientific-Technical Progress and the Revolution in Military Affairs.* Moscow: Voennoe Izdatelstvo, 1973. Trans. and published U.S. Air Force. Washington, D.C.: U.S. Government Printing Office, 1973.

Lukonin, S., and Migotlat'yev, A. "The 24th CPSU Congress on Current Problems in the Building of Communism and the Strengthening of the Defensive Might of the USSR." *Voennaia Mysl'* No. 5 (May 1971). Trans. FBIS, FPD No. 0016/74, March 18, 1974: 1-24.

Mal'yanchikov, S. "On the Nature of Armed Struggle in Local Wars." *Voennaia Mysl'* No. 11 (November 1965). Trans. FBIS, FPD No. 953, March 8, 1966: 12-24.

Marxism-Leninism on War and Army. Moscow: Progress, 1972. Trans. and published U.S. Air Force. Washington, D.C.: U.S. Government Printing Office, 1972.

Milovidov, A.S., and Kozlov, V.G., eds. *The Philosophical Heritage of V.I. Lenin and Problems of Contemporary War.* Moscow: Voennoe Izdatelstvo, 1972. Trans. and published U.S. Air Force. Washington, D.C.: U.S. Government Printing Office, 1972.

Mil'shtein, M., and Semeyko, L.S. "The Problem of the Inadmissibility of a Nuclear Conflict (On New Approaches in the United States)." *SShA: Ekonomika, Politika, Ideologia* No. 11 (November 1974). Trans. JPRS No. 63625, December 10, 1974: 1-12.

Perifilov, V. "Limited Warfare in U.S. Foreign Policy." *Voennaia Mysl'* No. 4 (April 1971). Trans. FBIS, FPD No. 0019/74, March 25, 1974: 105-120.

Petrovskiy, V.F. "The Evolution of the 'National Security' Doctrine." *SShA: Ekonomika, Politika, Ideologia* No. 11 (November 1978). Trans. FBIS, *USSR Daily Report Annex*, November 17, 1978: 2-13.

Samorukov, B. "Combat Operations Involving Conventional Means of Destruction." *Voennaia Mysl'* No. 8 (August 1967). Trans. FBIS, FPD No. 0125/68, August 26, 1968: 29-41.

Selected Soviet Military Writings, 1970-1975. Trans. and published U.S. Air Force. Washington D.C.: U.S. Government Printing Office, 1977.

Semenov, G., and Prokhorov, V. "Scientific-Technical Progress and Some Questions of Strategy." *Voennaia Mysl'* No. 2 (February 1969). Trans. FBIS, FPD No. 0060/69, June 18, 1969: 23-32.

Sevast'yanov, K., Vasendin, N., and V'yunenko, N. "Comments on the Article 'Augmenting Strategic Efforts in Modern Armed Conflict.'" *Voennaia Mysl'* No. 9 (September 1964). Trans. FBIS, FPD No. 896, March 2, 1965: 34-43.

Sokolovskiy, V.D., and Cherednichenko, M. "Military Strategy and Its Problems." *Voennaia Mysl'* No. 10 (October 1968). Trans. FBIS, FPD No. 0084/69, September 4, 1969: 32-43.

Stepanov, K., and Rybkin, Ye. "The Nature and Types of Wars of the Modern Era." *Voennaia Mysl'* No. 2 (February 1968). Trans. FBIS, FPD No. 0042/69, April 25, 1969: 68-80.

Tolstikov, O. "Civil Defense in Nuclear-Rocket War." *Voennaia Mysl'* No. 1 (January 1964). Trans. FBIS, FPD No. 939, August 4, 1965: 28-37.

Trofimenko, G.A. *SShA: Ekonomika, Politika, Ideologia* No. 12 (December 1971). Trans. JPRS No. 54971, January 19, 1972: 1-15.

————. "Some Aspects of U.S. Military and Political Strategy." *SShA: Ekonomika, Politika, Ideologia* No. 10 (October 1970). Trans. JPRS No. 51895, December 1, 1970: 14-31.

Vasendin, N., and Kuznetsov, N. "Modern Warfare and Surprise Attack." *Voennaia Mysl'* No. 6 (June 1968). Trans. FBIS, FPD No. 0005/69, January 16, 1969: 42-48.

Yermakov, S. "Counterinsurgency Plans in the System of Military Plans of Imperialism." *Voennaia Mysl'* No. 5 (May 1968). Trans. FBIS, FPD No. 0013/69, February 4, 1969: 60-68.

Primary Soviet Sources

The following primary Soviet sources are grouped by periodicals, with the articles from each periodical listed alphabetically by author. The full name of the periodical will be cited, except for *Mirovaia Ekonomika i Mezhdunarodnaye Otnosheniia* and *Kommunist Vooruzhennykh Sil*, which will be cited as *MEMO* and *KVS*, respectively. The periodicals *Soviet Military Review, International Affairs*, and *New Times*, having been translated into English by the Soviets themselves, will be listed by their English titles. The list of Soviet books used will be given at the end of the bibliography.

International Affairs

Andreyev, O., and Lvov, L. "The Arms Drive Strategy Cannot Win." *International Affairs* No. 11 (November 1960): 62-67.

Baryshev, A. "New US Doctrines, Same Old Aims." *International Affairs* No. 12 (December 1969): 12-16.

Baturin, M. "Peace and the Status Quo." *International Affairs* No. 1 (January 1958): 71-76.

Dadyants, G. "Cold War: Past and Present." *International Affairs* No. 6 (June 1960): 5-10.

Fyodorov, L. "International Relations and the Battle of Ideologies." *International Affairs* No. 3 (March 1960): 7-16.

Gerasimov, G. "The First Strike Theory." *International Affairs* No. 3 (March 1965): 39-45.

———. "Pentagonia, 1966." *International Affairs* No. 5 (May 1966): 24-30.

Glagolev, I., and Larionov, V. "Soviet Defence Might and Peaceful Coexistence." *International Affairs* No. 11 (November 1963): 27-33.

Gromov, L., and Strigachov, V. "The Arms Race: Dangers and Consequences." *International Affairs* No. 12 (December 1960): 14-18.

Gromyko, Anat., and Kokoshin, A. "US Foreign Policy Strategy for the 1970s." *International Affairs* No. 10 (October 1973): 67-73.

Kamenev, V. "The Big Lie About 'Small' Atomic Wars." *International Affairs* No. 9 (September 1956): 61-70.

Konenenko, A. "U.S. Military Doctrines." *International Affairs* No. 9 (September 1956): 61-70.

———. "Present-day U.S. Military Thinking and the Arms Drive." *International Affairs* No. 3 (March 1958): 31-35.

Konovalov, Y. "The Tentacles of 'Bases Strategy.'" *International Affairs* No. 7 (July 1963): 52-47.

Kortunov, V. "Arms Race Policy Historically Doomed." *International Affairs* No. 10 (October 1976): 3-13.

Korionov, V. "The Crisis of the 'Positions of Strength' Policy." *International Affairs* No. 3 (March 1958): 31-35.

Kuzmin, V. "The Guam Doctrine: Old Objectives, New Techniques." *International Affairs* No. 12 (December 1971): 32-37.

Larionov, V. "The Doctrine of 'Flexible' Aggression." *International Affairs* No. 7 (July 1963): 46-51.

Matveyev, V. "Washington's 'New' Doctrines." *International Affairs* No. 4 (April 1971): 25-31.

Melnikov, Y. "U.S. Foreign Policy: A Threat to Peace." *International Affairs* No. 1 (January 1967): 64-70.

Migolatyev, A. "The Military-Industrial Complex and the Arms Race." *International Affairs* No. 11 (November 1975): 63-71.

Mil'shtein, M. "A Dangerous Anachronism." *International Affairs* No. 2 (February 1960): 26-30.

Oleshchuk, Y. "'Small Wars' and the Aggression in Viet-Nam." *International Affairs* No. 5 (May 1966): 35-39.

Pechorkin, V. "The Theory and Practice of Counter-Guerrilla Warfare." *International Affairs* No. 10 (October 1963): 26-31.

———. "About 'Acceptable' War." *International Affairs* No. 3 (March 1963): 20-25.

———. "Crisis of Imperialism's Military Doctrines." *International Affairs* No. 7 (July 1962): 32-37.

Proektor, D. "Military Détente: Primary Task." *International Affairs* No. 6 (June 1976): 35-43.

Prokopyev, N. "Problems of War and Peace in Our Age." *International Affairs* No. 12 (December 1967): 57-62.

Rubinstein, M. "U.S. Bases: An Instrument in the Struggle for World Domination." *International Affairs* No. 3 (March 1955): 71-82.

Sosnovsky, L. "Strategy of U.S. Neocolonial Wars." *International Affairs* No. 10 (October 1971): 34-38.

Talensky, N. "Atomic and Conventional Arms." *International Affairs* No. 1 (January 1955): 23-29.

———. "The Military Aspect of Co-existance." *International Affairs* No. 7 (July 1960): 64-66.

———. "On the Character of Modern Warfare." *International Affairs* No. 10 (October 1960): 23-27.

———. "The Late War: Some Reflections." *International Affairs* No. 5 (May 1965): 12-18.

———. "'Preventive War': Nuclear Suicide." *International Affairs* No. 9 (September 1962): 10-16.

———. "The 'Absolute Weapon' and the Problem of Security." *International Affairs* No. 4 (April 1962): 22-27.

———. "Prevention of a Surprise Attack." *International Affairs* No. 8 (August 1958): 53-55.

———. "Military Strategy and Foreign Policy." *International Affairs* No. 3 (March 1958): 26-30.

Teplinsky, B. "The Strategic Concepts of U.S. Aggressive Policy." *International Affairs* No. 12 (December 1960): 36-41.

———. "Some Aspects of US Global Strategy." *International Affairs* No. 5 (May 1970): 70-75.

———. "U.S. 'Grand Strategy.'" *International Affairs* No. 2 (February 1964): 24-29.

———. "U.S. Military Programme." *International Affairs* No. 8 (August 1967): 46-51.

———. "Military Bases and American Strategic Doctrine." *International Affairs* No. 9 (September 1959): 79-85.

Trofimenko, G. "Anti-Communism and Imperialism's Foreign Policy." *International Affairs* No. 1 (January 1971): 49-54.

———. "From Confrontation to Coexistence." *International Affairs* No. 10 (October 1975): 33-41.

Vasilyev, V. "The U.S.A. Thwarts Solution of Surprise Attack Problem." *International Affairs* No. 2 (February 1959): 56-60.

Vronsky, B. "An 'Agonizing Reappraisal' of Dulles Legacy." *International Affairs* No. 4 (April 1960): 50-56.

Yeremenko, A. "The Strategic and Political Value of Military Bases." *International Affairs* No. 11 (November 1960): 57-61.

Yermashov, I. "The Crisis of American 'Atomic Age Strategy.'" *International Affairs* No. 1 (January 1960): 48-56.

———. "The Doctrine of 'Acceptable War': Illusions and Reality." *International Affairs* No. 11 (November 1960): 15-21.

Yudin, Y. "A Chain of Miscalculations." *International Affairs* No. 7 (July 1957), 34-45.

Zhilin, P., and Rybkin, Y. "Militarism and Contemporary International Relations." *International Affairs* No. 10 (October 1973): 23-29.

Kommunist Vooruzhennykh Sil

Bochkarev, K. "On the Character and Types of Wars of the Contemporary Epoch." *KVS* No. 11 (June 1965): 8-17.

Fedulayev, Ye. "Strategy of Reckless Adventurism." *KVS* No. 16 (August 1962): 83-87.

Glazov, V. "Concerning Some Peculiarities of Conducting Military Operations in a Nuclear War." *KVS* No. 3 (February 1964): 41-46.

Khvatkov, G. "Problems of War and Peace and the Revolutionary Process." *KVS* No. 1 (January 1970): 28-35.

Kondratkov, T. "Limited War: Instrument of Imperialist Aggression." *KVS* No. 8 (April 1969): 24-31.

Konstantinov, S. "The Military Doctrines of American Imperialiam." *KVS* No. 23 (December 1962): 78-85.

Korzun, L. "Strategy of Aggression." *KVS* No. 3 (February 1967): 90-92.

Levin, V. "The Europe of Our Days and NATO." *KVS* No. 19 (October 1975): 77-82.

Lipkin, R., and Tsema, V. "The Nuclear Forces of American Imperialism." *KVS* No. 20 (October 1970): 82-85.

Lomov, N. "On Soviet Military Doctrine." *KVS* No. 10 (May 1962): 11-21.

———. "The Influence of Soviet Military Doctrine on the Development of Military Art." *KVS* NO. 21 (November 1965): 15-24.

Malyanchikov, S. "The Character and Peculiarities of a Nuclear-Rocket War." *KVS* No. 21 (November 1965): 70-74.

Migolat'yev, A. "The Aggressive Essence of the Military-Political Strategy of American Imperialism." *KVS* No. 10 (May 1971): 78-84.

Palevich, D., and Poznyak, I. "The Peculiarities and Character of a World Nuclear-Rocket War." *KVS* No. 20 (October 1964): 77-82.

Ponomarev, N. "Crisis of Bourgeois Theories of War and Peace." *KVS* No. 16 (August 1964): 9-17.

———. "The Changing Relationship of Forces in the World and the Crisis of the Military Doctrines of Imperialism." *KVS* No. 14 (July 1971): 13-20.

———. "Adventurism of Military-Political Concepts of Imperialism." *KVS* No. 1 (January 1966): 42-48.

Rybkin, E. "On the Essence of a World Nuclear-Rocket War." *KVS* No. 17 (September 1965): 50-56.

Sablukov, A. "Imperialist Aggressors: The Bitterest Enemies of Peace, Democracy, and Socialism." *KVS* No. 9 (May 1965): 75-83.

Shmuratov, V. "Doctrines of Aggression and Piracy." *KVS* No. 15 (August 1965): 75-80.

Volkov, N. "Imperialism: Enemy of the Peoples and of Social Progress." *KVS* No. 13 (July 1975): 68-76.

Yesikov, G. "The Most Burning Problem of the Present." *KVS* No. 7 (April 1962): 60-68.

Mirovaia Ekonomika i Mezhdunarodnaye Otnosheniia

Bogdanov, O. "Nuclear Weapons and the Problem of World Security." *MEMO* No. 8 (August 1958): 3-15.

Bykov, O. "Concerning Some Features of the Foreign Policy Strategy of the USA." *MEMO* No. 4 (April 1971): 53-64.

Chernov, I., and Yudin, Iu. "The Insolvent Policy of Military Blocs (Concerning the Tenth Anniversary of the North Atlantic Alliance)." *MEMO* No. 4 (April 1959): 68-80.

Dikin, L. "Problems of USA Military Policy and Strategy in the Reports of the Rockefeller and Gaither Committees." *MEMO* No. 7 (July 1958): 94-101.

Inozemtsev, N. "'Atomic Diplomacy' of the USA: Plans and Activities." *MEMO* No. 3 (March 1958): 29-43.

Konenenko, A. "'Local Wars' in the Policy and Strategy of the USA." *MEMO* No. 10 (October 1958): 16-25.

Larionov, V. "The Development of the Armed Means and Strategic Concepts of the USA." *MEMO* No. 6 (June 1966): 74-81.

Mil'shtein, M. "Concerning Certain Military-Strategic Concepts of American Imperialism." *MEMO* No. 8 (August 1962): 85-95.

———. "American Military Doctrine: Continuity and Modifications." *MEMO* No. 8 (August 1971): 30-41.

———, and Slobodenko, A. "The Aggressive and Adventuristic Character of the Strategic Concepts of the USA." *MEMO* No. 3. (March 1957): 76-89.

———. "Problems of the Correlation of Policy and War in Contemporary Imperialist Ideology." *MEMO* No. 9 (September 1958): 58-73.

New Times

Dashichev, Vyacheslav. "Theory and Practice of 'Little Wars.'" *New Times* No. 37 (October 1957): 7-10.

Fyodorov, Mikhail. "New Message, Old Doctrines." *New Times* No. 10 (March 1971): 8-9

Glazov, V. "The New 'Local War' Conceptions." *New Times* No. 48 (November 1964): 6-8.

Golikov, F.I. "Who Is Advocating 'Preventive' War and Why." *New Times* No. 17 (April 1958): 5-6.

Iordansky, V. "Atomic Blackmail: A Futile Weapon." *New Times* No. 19 (May 1955): 12-15.

Isayev, F. "The 'Small Atomic Weapons' Myth." *New Times* No. 13 (March 1955): 7-10.

———. "Fallacies of the Policy of Strength." *New Times* No. 10 (March 1955): 4-9.

Krementsov, M. "The U.S. Atomic Business." *New Times* No. 22 (May 1954): 7-10.

———, and Starko, G. "Military Bases in Foreign Territories." *New Times* No. 21 (May 1955): 18-21.

Mil'shtein, M. "Bases and Security." *New Times* No. 6 (February 1958): 6-7.

———, and Slobodenko, A. "'Limited War': Weapons of Unlimited Aggression." *New Times* No. 40 (October 1958): 13-15.

Rovinsky, L. "The Rocket and Peace." *New Times* No. 37 (September 1957): 14-16.

Rubinstein, M. "The Atom Business: Calculations and Miscalculations." *New Times* No. 25 (June 1954): 16-20.

Simonyan, R. "'Realistic Deterrence': The Real Implications." *New Times* No. 10 (March 1977): 18-20.

―――. "The Pentagon's Nuclear Strategy." *New Times* No. 35 (September 1977): 22-24.

Starko, G. "Crisis of America's 'Peripheral Strategy.'" *New Times* No. 33 (August 1960): 19-22.

Teplinsky, B. "Polaris and U.S. Strategy." *New Times* No. 8 (February 1963): 6-9.

Zorin, Valentin. "The Three McNamara Doctrines." *New Times* No. 3 (January 1963): 12-14.

Soviet Military Review

Arbatov, G. "Strength-Policy Impasses." *Soviet Military Review* No. 1 (January 1975): 46-48.

Glazov, V. "Strategic Concept of the Aggressors (Substance and Content of the Theory of Escalation)." *Soviet Military Review* No. 4 (April 1967): 47-50.

―――. "The Evolution of U.S. Military Doctrine." *Soviet Military Review* No. 11 (November 1965): 56-57.

Khomenko, E. "Wars: Their Character and Type." *Soviet Military Review* No. 9 (September 1965): 7-9.

Kondratkov, T. "What is a 'Limited War'?" *Soviet Military Review* No. 8 (August 1973): 48-49.

Kulikov, N. "On Just and Unjust Wars." *Soviet Military Review* No. 3 (March 1977): 8-10.

Matsulenko, V. "The 'Small War' Theory at the Service of the Imperialists." *Soviet Military Review* No. 4 (April 1966): 53-55.

Mochalov, V. "What Lies Behind the Theory of 'Limited' Wars?" *Soviet Military Review* No. 8 (August 1969): 54-56.

―――. "Concerning the 'Theory of Limited Wars.'" *Soviet Military Review* No. 2 (February 1965): 40-42.

Redko, Y. "Anti-Guerrilla Doctrines." *Soviet Military Review* No. 3 (March 1965): 54-55.

Sergeyev, P., and Trusenkov, V. "Evolution of the US Military Doctrine." *Soviet Military Review* No. 11 (November 1976: 52-54.

Simonyan, R. "Doctrine of the American Aggressors." *Soviet Military Review* No. 1 (January 1969): 50-52.

Sokolovskiy, V.D. "On the Soviet Military Doctrine." *Soviet Military Review* No. 4 (April 1965): 6-9.

Zavyalov, V. "Flexible Response Strategy: Theory and Practice." *Soviet Military Review* No. 5 (May 1965): 36-38.

Voenno-Istoricheskii Zhurnal

Nikitin, N. "The Evolution of the Military Doctrines and Strategic Concepts of the

USA after the Second World War." *Voenno-Istoricheskii Zhurnal* No. 4 (April 1977): 64-69.

Potapov, I. "The Evolution of the Strategic Concepts of Imperialism in the Postwar Period." *Voenno-Istoricheskii Zhurnal* No. 5 (May 1971): 42-50.

Shavrov, I. "Local Wars and Their Place in the Global Strategy of Imperialism." (Part I) *Voenno-Istoricheskii Zhurnal* No. 3 (March 1975): 57-66.

Shavrov, I. "Local Wars and Their Place in the Global Strategy of Imperialism." (Part II) *Voenno-Istoricheskii Zhurnal* No. 4 (April 1975): 90-97.

Voennyi Vestnik

Garin V. "Atomic Weapons of the Army of the USA (According to Material in the Foreign Press)." *Voennyi Vestnik* No. 11 (November 1954): 77-81.

Karpovich, B. "The Ideological Preparation of the American Soldier for Atomic War." *Voennyi Vestnik* No. 6 (June 1955): 78-84.

Pukhovskii, N. "The Creative Character of Soviet Military Science." *Voennyi Vestnik* No. 1 (January 1954): 17-24.

Soviet Books and Monographs

Dmitriyev, Boris. *Pentagon i Vneshniaia Politika SShA (The Pentagon and U.S. Foreign Policy)*. Moscow: Izdatelstvo Instituta Mezhdunarodnikh Otnoshenii, 1961.

Grechko, A.A. *The Armed Forces of the Soviet Union*. Moscow: Progress, 1977.

Konenenko, A. *Atomnoe Oruzhie v Voennykh Planakh SShA (Atomic Weapons in the Military Plans of the U.S.A.)*. Moscow: Voennoe Izdatelstvo, 1957.

Kulakov, V.M. *Ideologia Agressii (Ideology of Aggression)*. Moscow: Voennoe Izdatelstvo, 1970.

Mil'shtein M.A., and Slobodenko, A.K. *O Burzhuaznoi Voennoi Nauke (On Bourgeois Military Science)*. Moscow: Voennoe Izdatelstvo, 1961.

Sokolovskii, V.D. *Voennaia Strategia (Military Strategy)*. 1st ed. Moscow: Voennoe Izdatelstvo. 1962.

———. *Voennaia Strategia* (Military Strategy). 2nd ed. Moscow: Voennoe Izdatelstvo, 1963.

———. *Voennaia Strategia* (Military Strategy). 3rd ed. Moscow: Voennoe Izdatelstvo, 1968.

Trofimenko, G.A. *Strategia Globalnoi Voiny (Strategy of Global War)*. Moscow: Izdatelstvo "Mezhdunarodniye Otnosheniia," 1968.

———. *SShA: Politika, Voina, Ideologia (U.S.A.: Politics, War, Ideology)*. Moscow: Izdatelstvo "Mysl'," 1976.

Name Index